PARK TO PARKS

Susan Barton
Lord Mayor of Leicester
2023-24.

PARK TO PARKS

The story of New Parks, Western Park, Braunstone Frith and Kirby Frith

SUSAN BARTON

DB PUBLISHING

First published 2021 by DB Publishing, an imprint of JMD Media Ltd,
Nottingham, United Kingdom.

ISBN 9781780916194

Printed in the UK

CONTENTS

ABOUT THE AUTHOR

Susan Barton is an historian and author, born and living in West Leicester. She has a PhD from De Montfort University where she is an honorary visiting research fellow. This is her eighth book on historical themes, ranging from winter sports, travel and tourism, Leicestershire's knitted textile industry and sport. Su has been a lecturer, teacher and is now a councillor on Leicester City Council, supporting local communities. She enjoys dance and hiking, too.

FOREWORD

Park to Parks was chosen as a title because I felt it conveyed the idea of the transformation of the landscape over centuries: 'park' in the medieval sense, as exemplified by Leicester Forest and the Frith, to the enclosures that created what became the agricultural district of New Park, the carving out of a 'park' in the modern sense as a place of recreation, and the 20th-century housing estates which include the word Park in their names.

Although it is a local history this is also part of a wider history as national events and economic and social changes shaped the area's development. It has been a challenge knowing when to stop writing as new discoveries seem to be coming to light on a daily basis, pieces of this four-dimensional jigsaw puzzle in time and space. Therefore, *Park to Parks* represents a stage in the historical research journey.

Lockdown through the Covid pandemic of 2020 and 2021 made access to many primary sources impossible but, luckily, I already had notes or copies of many original documents or was able to make use of some of the National Archive's online digitised resources. Using local newspaper archives allowed me to populate the landscape story with real men and women who shared the space in other eras, most of whom are otherwise forgotten.

For those wishing to explore New Parks, Western Park, Braunstone Frith and Kirby Frith further, modern technology such as Google Street View and Google Earth can be used to virtually visit the area even by those outside Leicester.

Thank you for reading. I hope you find something interesting in the book.

Susan Barton

ACKNOWLEDGEMENTS

Many grateful thanks to the following people who have supported and helped with this project, especially those members of the community who shared their precious documents and photographs with me.

Paul Ambrose
Grahame Appleby
Carl and Wendy Bebbington
Su Bird
Tony Booth
Anne and Nick Butler
Stefan Cabaniuk
Philip Dodd
Paul C. Dunn
Lucy Eddowes
Robert and Chris Freeman
Cathy Harrell
Sarah Hughes
Robin Jenkins
Beverley Lambie
David Lyne
Paul Mason
Tom Murtha
Milan Popovich
Stephen Swabey

Records Office of Leicester, Leicestershire and Rutland
Imperial War Office, London

INTRODUCTION

Park to Parks explores the story of the centuries-long transformation of the hunting park of Leicester Forest, via its enclosure to create the New Park in 1526, its pastoral past, the creation of a public park and the development of the 20th-century communities of New Parks, Western Park, Braunstone Frith and Kirby Frith.

Archaeological discoveries indicate an ancient past but the recorded history begins when the area was the section of Leicester Forest nearest to the town, run in medieval times under Forest Law as a deer park for royal and aristocratic hunting parties but where common people had rights to gather wood and graze animals. Henry VIII realised more income could be derived if the land was enclosed and rented out for pasture and other agricultural use.

The rest of the area, the Frith, was enclosed about 80 years later, further restricting access to Leicester dwellers and neighbouring villagers and eliciting protests. From this time, we see the rise of medium-sized country estates, often rented out to tenant farmers or farmed by their owners. With industrial Leicester on the doorstep, the interaction between town and rural dwellers led to conflict with the urban poor, for whom the countryside was a source of food to supplement their diet, either through unauthorised gathering of fruit, nuts and other produce, or by poaching to obtain meat. For farmers and their labourers, the countryside represented business and an income, and for landowners a source of prestige. Some newly enriched local businessmen transformed themselves into country gentlemen.

As farming profits fell and Leicester's population grew, building land became valuable, landowners sold their estates and farms to be developed for urban activities, such as leisure in the form of Western Park and golf courses, an airport, industry, but most of all for housing.

The 20th century saw the emergence of new neighbourhoods: Western Park Garden Suburb, then the 1930s housing developments of mainly semi-detached homes, New Parks Estate, Braunstone Frith and Kirby Frith. These communities needed facilities for socialising, worship, leisure and education, and each developed its own sense of identity.

Since 2015, these communities have been reunified for the first time since the days of Leicester Forest, into the administrative division of Leicester City Council called Western Ward.

While *Park to Parks* is concerned with an area to the west of Leicester, it is representative of other suburban areas of Britain that grew up on the borders of industrial cities in the 20th century.

New Parks

How grandly beautiful the autumnal hues!
Here elms dark green, light green, and golden green,
And yellowing poplars mark the calm serene;
There, oak and thick pine darker shades diffuse:
And aspens white and willows grey infuse
Their gentler tints, and where hills intervene,
Kissing the heavens that stoop to bless the scene
How softly blend their ever varying blues!
A-near the ash droops with its berries red,
And scarlet hips the golden wild-briars grace,
And blood-black hollyhocks uplift their head,
And roses crimsoning all the season long;
While paling orange dyes the hawthorn's lace,
Where the red-breast is turning all to song!

A sonnet by Joseph Dare, *New Parks*, 13 October 1854.

1
A CORNER OF LEICESTER FOREST

An ancient landscape

Looking around the New Parks, Braunstone Frith, Kirby Frith and Western Park areas of Leicester, seeing the extensive built-up estates of 20th-century housing, it's hard to imagine that until very recently, in historical terms, this was open countryside and not the distinct communities of the present day. Even so, this was not an empty or purely natural landscape before the 20th-century planners and developers moved in. Since ancient times people have made it their home or gone back and forth along the tracks, footpaths and roads leading to and from what was, or was to become, Leicester.

Archaeology and artefacts found in the area show that the roots of the community go way back into deep history, long before there were any written records. The oldest discoveries were some prehistoric flints, perhaps from as long ago as 10000BCE. In 1873 a flint scraper was found on Shoulder of Mutton Hill, about 18 inches below ground, and later, in 1982, 16 pieces of worked flint, including two more scrapers, were discovered there. These flint tools, probably from the late Neolithic (the last part of the Stone Age) or early Bronze Age, provide evidence that people were going about their daily tasks, in this space, thousands of years ago.[1]The scrapers, possibly used for cleaning animal hides or for woodwork, were found on what is now Western Park, on Shoulder of Mutton Hill, near Hinckley Road and the railway line. These flint tools and a shard of pottery, thought to be from the late Bronze Age, about 1200BCE to 500BCE, show that people have been living or working in the area over a very long time. Other flint tools have been unearthed near Glenfield Road, between Brampton Avenue and Westfield Road.[2] Nearby on the site of the former Western Park Open Air School, an arrowhead from the Neolithic or Bronze Age was found. The site of a possible round house has been recorded not far away on Gooding Avenue in Braunstone Estate.[3]

Other crop marks, or scars left on the surface of the ground, where Sunningdale Road is now, were recorded before the area was developed as an industrial estate, an

1 Historic Environment Record for Leicester (HER)
2 HER
3 HER

indication that this may have been the site of huts or barrows, although it is likely it was a medieval rabbit warren.[4] Crop marks are not always self-explanatory or easy to interpret. Other Neolithic or Bronze Age artefacts found in the area include part of a polished flint adze or axe, unearthed in a garden on Birds Nest Avenue and another one discovered on Glazebrook Road. The Glazebrook Road axe is thought to have been made in Camborne in Cornwall, showing that, even in those ancient times, people travelled or traded goods over long distances.[5]

In the late Iron Age, before the Roman conquest, many tribes of Celts lived in Britain. The place that became Leicester was in the region ruled by the Corieltauvi tribe. This group's territory stretched from present-day Leicestershire, through the Nottinghamshire and Lincolnshire area. No doubt the Corieltauvi, who were living in the area before the Romans arrived in Britain, would have made use of the hills to the west of the settlement for hunting, collecting wood and for living and farming. Evidence for this is the large Iron Age site at Glenfield Park, just outside the city border. This was discovered during excavations in 2013 and 2014 by the University of Leicester Archaeology Service (ULAS), ahead of the construction of the Optimus Point warehouse and distribution centre off Ratby Lane. These excavations revealed an extensive site, demonstrating long-term settlement there through the Iron Age and into the Roman period. The site contains the remains of roundhouses, with living areas, craft or food preparation space and associated pits. There were many domestic finds, including pottery, quern stones, burnt bones, metal objects and debris from metal working, dating from between 400 and 300BCE. An exciting discovery was of an enclosure where eight complete or near-complete cauldrons were found, buried in the base a ditch. Three other cauldrons were found elsewhere in the settlement. The metalwork finds on the site are of international importance and include a sword and scabbard from the later third or second centuryBCE.[6] Although the excavation site is just outside Leicester's modern boundaries, the area of the settlement may have extended into what later became Kirby Frith and the Western Park golf course.

Leicester was one of the Corieltauvi tribe's main bases or perhaps their capital until the Roman's conquest after about 44CE when the invaders took over lands already occupied by Celtic tribes. The name of the Corieltauvi was incorporated by the Romans, along with the Latinised version of the Brittonic word *rath* or ramparts, when they gave their own name to the town, Ratae Corieltauvorium.

The Romans were active around the western area of Leicester, as well as in the centre of the town where there are more obvious remains like the Jewry Wall, now the tallest section of non-military Roman masonry standing in Britain. There was a Roman settlement or farmstead in the corner of Western Park, at Shoulder of Mutton

---

4 HER

5 HER

6 https://www2.le.ac.uk/services/ulas/discoveries/projects/iron-age/glenfield-cauldrons

Hill, around the area of the off-road cycle track up to the railway line. Finds there include a moratorium (a flat dish with a lip like a jug), a beaker base, the rim of a jar, bowls and other items.[7] Close to where these items were found, by the 20th-century park keeper's house, later the Eco House, a Roman pottery kiln was identified in the 1990s. The chamber and stoke hole of the kiln were once thought to have been part of a granite wall but turned out to have probably been the kiln's flue-arch.[8] Items found show that grey ware pots, including jars and lids were made there.

Other finds around the locality are an early Roman bracelet and medal dug up at a house on Aikman Avenue, grey ware pottery pieces discovered on land between Brampton Avenue and Westfield Road, a silver coin from the time of the reign of the emperor Trajan, who ruled between 98CE and 117CE, unearthed on Westfield Road and a similar one found in a garden on Hinckley Road.[9] A Roman or perhaps Iron Age quern, used for grinding corn into flour, was found buried in the grounds of New Parks Junior School.

A sandstone quarry, probably one of the places where the Romans got the material to make the bricks to create the buildings of Ratae Corieltauvorium, was situated off the modern Glenfield Road, between Westfield Road and Brampton Avenue, the area occupied by the former St Andrew's Tennis Club and on the other side of Glenfield Road near Sandhurst Road. Quarrying for sandstone took place at other sites around the Leicester side of the neighbourhood, in the area that was known as Dane Hills. Quarrying continued after the Roman period: the ashlar stones in Leicester Castle appear to have originated in the Dane Hills area. There may also have been a quarry in Western Park itself, near the site known as the Gullies where the old field name Brick Kiln Close gives a clue as to what some of the material dug out was used for. Other quarrying locations were on the site of the former EcoHouse car park, situated in what was once known as Stone Pit Close. Bricks used in the construction of the Glenfield tunnel and Midland Railway bridges were made from locally extracted materials in the mid-19th century which practically exhausted the supply. However, quarrying continued into the more recent past in some places such as behind the Convent on Glenfield Road.

An important Roman road linked the town of Ratae Corieltauvorium with a fort at Manduessedum, now called Mancetter near Atherstone, where it connected with Watling Street, the present-day A5. Travellers would leave the town of Ratae Corieltauvorium across the river by what were later called the West Bridge and Bow Bridge, then probably followed the line of what is now King Richard's Road. Some

---

7 Edward Tura, *A Roman Occupation Site,* Western Park, Glenfield and Western Park District Archaeological and Historical Group, 1983, p.4

8 Richard Clark: *Archaeology in Leicestershire and Rutland 1999*, www.le.ac.uk (accessed 14 February 2016)

9 HER

remains of this road may remain buried under the houses and gardens of Westfield Road, Meadway, Westhill Road and Letchworth Road, where some residents claim to recall inhabitants having unearthed sections of what may have been a Roman road. Cobbles believed to be from a Roman road have been discovered, indicating its possible route.

This road appears to continue through Western Park, passing the old farm house, now Western Park House, up the hill across the sports pitches, through Alexton Spinney on the Park Rise side of the Park. It then seems to cross New Parks Way, continuing across Frolesworth Road and up Allexton Gardens, where remains of it have been identified, before crossing the former Western Park Golf Course at Kirby Frith, and onwards across Kirby Muxloe Golf Course, where RAF aerial photographs taken in 1948 show markings on the ground as evidence of the route of a road. The line of the road has been traced by archaeologists from that point to Mancetter.[10] There may be a second road dating from Roman times buried within Western Park. Cobbles of the type used in Roman road-building have been discovered in nearby gardens that don't seem to be on the projected route of the Mancetter road. This may have been an industrial road connecting the quarry workings with the town for building purposes. Much of Roman Leicester was built with bricks and sandstone from around Western Park.

In Anglo-Saxon times, Legreceastre (Leicester) was a principal city of the kingdom of Mercia, where Angles from the East of England, Saxons from Warwickshire and Celts from the hills of Charnwood came together to meet and trade. From 658CE, when Christianity first came to Leicester, these disparate cultural groups became united in a common religion. Leicester continued to be an important place with its own cathedral until 870, a status lost thanks to the pagan Vikings who attacked the town in 868. From 877 the Norsemen began to settle permanently. Leicestershire was adjacent to the boundary of the Danelaw that followed the line of the Roman Road, Watling Street. The Danelaw was the area ruled by the Danes, created in 886 following a treaty with King Alfred. As one of the five Boroughs of the Danelaw, Leicester retained some prominence.

Travellers, traders and soldiers would have continued to traverse the future Western Park and New Parks along the ancient and Roman tracks and roadways. The Anglo-Saxon ruler of Mercia, Aethelflaed, retook the town in 918, when the Danes there surrendered without a fight. Uniquely for a woman of the time, King Alfred's daughter Aethelflaed ruled in her own right and not as the wife of a king, although she was the widow of Aethelred. Known as the Lady of Mercia, she died shortly afterwards in her castle at Tamworth so no doubt she and her followers crossed through the area along the Roman road on the way to join Watling Street that leads to Tamworth. Aethelflaed's

10 A.D. McWhirr: *The Roman Road from Leicester to Mancettter*. Transactions of Leicester Archaeological Society, Vol. 42, 1966–67, pp.1–5

brother Edward, King of Wessex, gained control of the whole of Mercia but Leicester was back under the rule of Danes, led by Olaf Guthfrithsson, for two years from 940 to 942 when it was recovered by Edmund, the successor to his brother Aethelstan.[11] Olaf had met with Edmund in 939 at Leicester, where they agreed on the division of England between them. In 1013 the Danes under Sweyn, King of Denmark, again ruled the Five Boroughs of Leicester, Derby, Lincoln, Nottingham and Stamford. In 1016 Leicester was sacked by Edmund Ironside during wars against the Danes who finally left in 1041, although some of them would have settled down and remained.[12]

During the years of Danish rule, the area that now includes New Parks and Western Park formed part of a much larger area of unclaimed land or 'waste' which provided hunting grounds, supplied food, wood for fires and building, and other construction materials. In the *Domesday Book* of 1086's description of the Leicester Forest area, it says that in addition to houses, mills and lands there was a wood called Hereswode, a Danish word meaning wood of the army or people, a name which dated to the Danish occupation. The name Hereswode may refer to the rights of local peasants and Leicester dwellers who were allowed to gather wood and other supplies in the Forest. Dane Hills, the name given to the area between what is now Western Park and Fosse Road, could be a reference either to the Danish occupation or Danu, a pagan deity or, most likely, just means dunes or hills. There is little recorded evidence about this pre-Norman period of Leicestershire history as, frustratingly, no charters are known to have survived from the Anglo-Saxon period.

Medieval management of the Forest

By the time of the Norman Conquest in 1066, an area 14 miles long and just four miles wide, containing about 5,000 acres, had been defined as Leicester Forest and delineated with clear boundaries. Ownership of Leicester Forest was granted by King William I to one of his Norman-born supporters, Hugh de Grantesmenil, together with the lordship of Leicester Castle.

For most people, the word forest conjures up an image of an area of wooded land with lots of trees but the original medieval meaning defined a forest as a place preserved and protected for royal or aristocratic hunting. It did not necessarily have to contain woodland but could be moorland or other types of landscape, for example Cannock Chase or Exmoor. In Latin the word *foris,* from which the word is derived, means outside, in the case of forests, outside the normal common law of the land, a place where Forest Law applied.

11 Paul Courtney: *Saxon and Medieval Leicester: The Making of an Urban Landscape*, Transactions. Leicestershire Archaeological and Historical Society (LAHS), 72, 1998, pp 110–145, p.114

12 James Thompson, *History of Leicester, from the time of the Romans to the end of the Seventeenth Century,* Leicester, 1849, p.18

Stone marking the freebord, the boundary of the Frith in Western Park.

Forest Law was designed to protect vert and venison, that is the animals that could be hunted as game and the greenery (vert) that sustained them. This system was introduced by the Normans in the 11th century and was at its height in the late 12th and early 13th century. Under Forest Law, hunting was reserved for the king or nobility and those they invited. This was enforced with strict punishments for common people who dared to defy the law and encroach on to areas where previously, as in the days of the Hereswode, they had been allowed to take all they needed.

The part of Leicester Forest nearest to the town was called the Frith, described as scrub on the edge of the forest or poorly stocked woodland.[13] An early meaning of the word frith is 'peace' and in Forest Law the term was applied to districts where wild animals were immune from random hunting. Only the king, and those upon whom he chose to confer this right, were allowed to hunt certain game animals such as deer. The deer had special protection during the breeding season.[14]

In the case of Leicester Frith it seems that the 'peace' applied not just to the beasts but to Leicester dwellers who had liberty of access, unlike the rest of the Forest which was strictly managed and access was reserved or completely private.[15] This was a continuation of the rights passed down from the days when it was the Hereswode. Local people could gather wood in the Frith for fires, building and repairs. The poorer people of the town were allowed to 'fetch on their backs' out of the forest 'broken,

13 Anthony Squires, *Leicester Forest, its woodlands and parks in Medieval Leicestershire, Recent Research on the Medieval Archaeology of Leicestershire*, Leicestershire Fieldworkers, Monograph No. 3, 2015, pp.161–194, p.164

14 Levi Fox and Percy Russell: *Leicester Forest*, Edgar Backus, Leicester, 1948, p.31; Squires, p.173

15 Fox and Russell, p 31

The Gullies, Western Park.

dead and rotten wood'.[16] On their return to Leicester they would pay a fee, known as Bridge Tax, at the West Bridge or North Gate entrances to the town. Townsfolk also had common rights to graze cattle and for pannage, that is turning out pigs in autumn to feed, particularly on acorns, beech mast and other kinds of nuts. What is thought to be the remains of a boundary wall or freebord, sometimes spelt freeboard), indicating the border of the Frith or deer park within the pale of the forest, can be seen in Western Park but, like the possible Roman roads and 16th-century drains, this needs further archaeological investigation.

This boundary continued along the bank of trees and bushes in the park, now known as the Gullies. On the Leicester side of the boundary the land lay within the parish of St Mary de Castro, and along its length at regular intervals were small cast-iron markers with St Mary's written on them. Many of these were taken up during World War Two, to be melted down for the war effort. The last of these markers survived until it was removed by an unknown person in the early 21st century. The land in St Mary's parish on the town side, which included the area known as Dane Hills, once formed part of the West Field, one of three great open fields surrounding Leicester, which already existed around the manor of Bromkinsthorpe before the Domesday survey completed in 1086. Bromkinsthorpe, sometimes written as Bruntestonetorp, was a small settlement around the Braunstone Gate area, just outside the residential area of the town of Leicester. Bromkinsthorpe freeholders claimed ancient common rights in Leicester Forest, which belonged to 'their lands, pastures or cottages' as did the burgesses or freemen of Leicester, until these rights were removed at the time

16 Charles J. Billson, *The Open Fields of Leicester,* Transactions, LAHS, 1926, pages 1-34, p.9

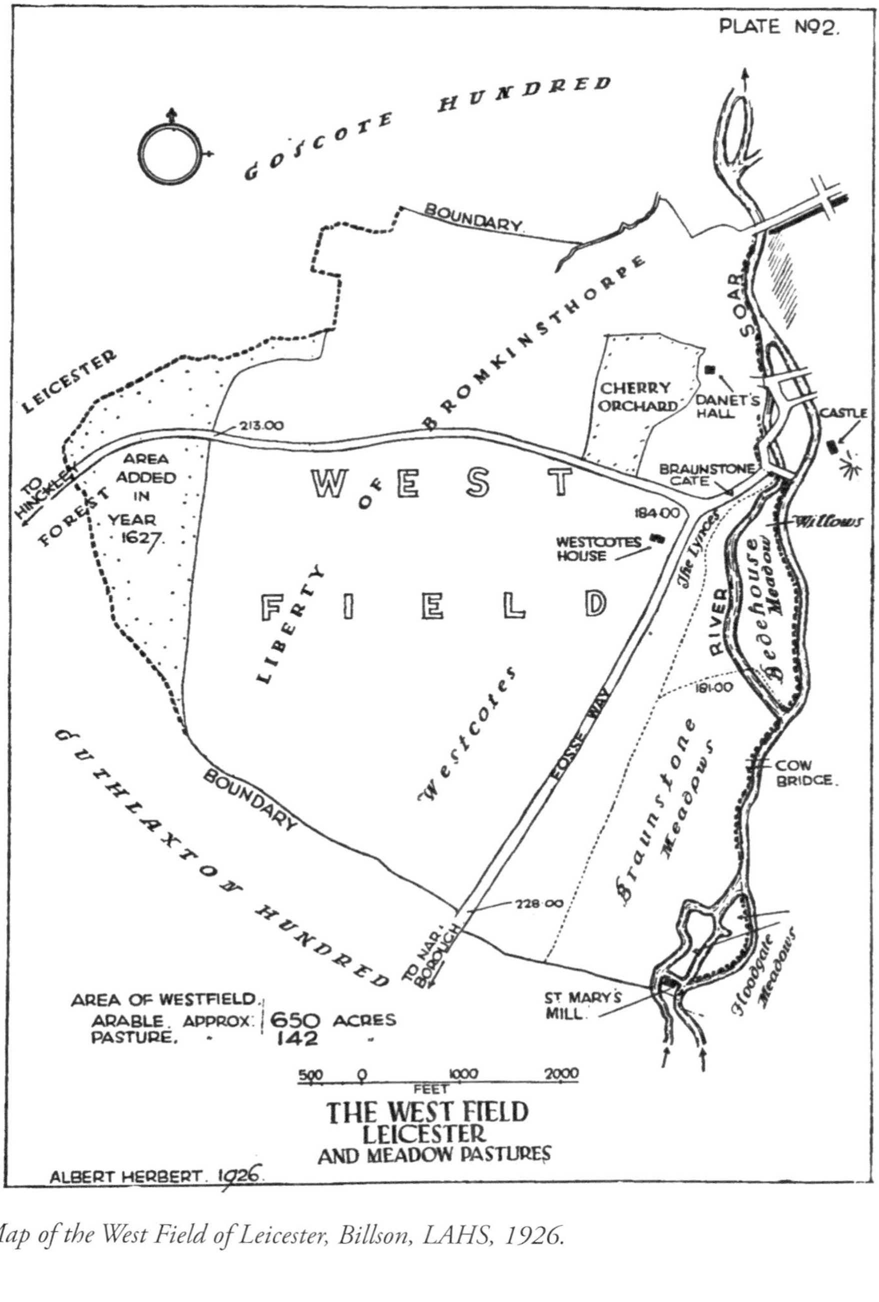

Map of the West Field of Leicester, Billson, LAHS, 1926.

of the 1627 enclosures.[17] Bromkinsthorpe was divided between Dannet's Hall and Westcotes and the West Field enclosed. No definite date has been discovered for this, but it appears to have happened quite early in the history of enclosure, probably

17 Billson, p.9

before the 16th century. There are some visible remains in Western Park of what may have been the ridge and furrow of the strips of land cultivated in the medieval West Field, although there do not appear to be any remains of the headlands, that is the banks of earth indicating where ploughs turned round at the end of a strip. This might be worthy of further investigation by archaeologists and historians.

The land was drained by a brook or small river called the Dove, or 'dark' water, which now flows between Western Park Road and the park. It gave its name to Doveland Wood and the Doveland Gate entrance into the forest situated on Shoulder of Mutton Hill from where Doveland Lane led to Leicester, the route of the present Hinckley Road. The name is still recalled in Dovelands School.

A problem when researching the medieval period locally is the scarcity of records, including from Swanimote Court Rolls before 1599, that recorded how the area was managed.[18] Despite the lack of these important records, there are some references to features that give an idea of what the area may have looked like. What is now known as Meynell's Gorse was once called the King's Wood, described as so full of wild animals belonging to the Duke of Lancaster that it made no value of the pasture of Wheatcroft, which lay on the other side of Braunstone Lane.[19]

In the 13th century, along with the Earldom of Leicester, Leicester Forest was inherited by Simon de Montfort. In turn, de Montfort gave Doveland Wood, in an area that was under the control of the Bromkinsthorpe manor, to Leicester Abbey in 1240.[20] This wood was situated in what was later part of the Winstanley estate, near to the modern-day Gooding Avenue.[21] Other sources date de Montfort's gift of Doveland Wood to 1255, when it was described as a 'plot of woodland in open country called Doveland with its gate as it is presently enclosed'.[22]

After de Montfort was killed in 1265 at the Battle of Evesham, Leicester Forest was granted to Edmund Crouchback (1245–1296), the second surviving son of King Henry III and Eleanor of Provence. He was called Crouchback not because of some physical characteristic but because he took part in the Ninth Crusade in 1271, Crouch meaning cross. As a crusader knight, Edmund wore a cross on his surcoat covering his armour. From 1267 Edmund took the title Earl of Leicester. He also became Earl of Lancaster in 1276, linking the two titles. In 1268 the king made Edmund the Constable of Leicester Castle, a royal possession. When his brother became King Edward I, he confirmed Edmund's possessions in Parliament in the Great Charter of Leicester in 1284. As Earl of Leicester and of Lancaster he held the rights to vert and venison in Leicester Forest. Edmund may not initially have spent a lot of time

18 Squires, p.165 and 169
19 Squires, p.174; Fox and Russell, p.71
20 Squires, p.172
21 Squires, p.179
22 Squires, p.179

in Leicester, or in his forest, as his favourite home was at Grosmont Castle. Edmund had two sons, Thomas and Henry, the 2nd and 3rd Earls of Lancaster and Leicester.

Thomas, the eldest of Edmund Crouchback's sons, was one of the most powerful barons under Edward II. As well as inheriting Leicester Forest, he was de facto governor of England between 1314 and 1318. However, Thomas played a leading role in the rebellion against the King in 1321 but was defeated at the Battle of Boroughbridge in March 1322. He was taken prisoner, convicted of treason and sentenced to death. In retribution, Leicester paid a heavy price for Thomas's actions. The town was left devastated by King Edward and its lands lay uncultivated. Even fodder and hay for the animals was destroyed. As the Earl had been attainted his lands, including Leicester Castle and the Forest, as well as fishing rights in the Soar, his mills and even the ovens in Leicester, were forfeited to the Crown. To facilitate this, an audit of all the Earl's possessions was commissioned in 1322, carried out locally by Roger de Belegrave and Roger Anneys who was receiver of the revenues of the Forest of Leicester.

Anneys' accounts for the auditors show various income and outgoings for the forest. These include payments of £2 15s 2d for cattle agisted, taken in to reserved parts of the forest for two weeks in September. Agistment means taking in and feeding cattle or other animals on pasture land for payment, originally it meant specifically the income from pasture in the King's forests. Fern in the reserved parts was sold for 4s 6d and nuts for two shillings. The sale of 32 oak trees, felled to make a fence around the forest, brought in £1 0s 9d. The sale of their bark raised an additional 4s 2d. The new fence may have replaced an earlier one as old fencing around the forest was sold for 8s 6d while some old stakes were sold for 14s 8d. As well as this, 545 perches of old hedge was sold for £4 12s 6 1/2d.[23]

Anneys' accounts show some of the other activities that took place in the forest in the early 1320s. The Prior of Ware held an interest in the land as a tithe on the sale of oaks, nuts and ferns and the agistment of the cattle had to be paid to him. Old hedges near to the roads to Groby and Glenfield, surrounding the future New Parks area, had to be replaced with a mixture of new and old timber. The two foresters and fencers engaged in this work of repairing and mending holes in the fence were supplied with 13 quarts and one and a half bushels of maslin, a mixture of rye and a little wheat for making bread, as part of their allowances as well as their wages of half a mark (6s 8d) a year. Within the forest were lodges where the foresters lived and which served as administrative offices for doing business, storage places and assembly points where hunting parties could meet.

Anneys records that 4s 7d was paid as wages to a man repairing the houses at the lodge (*apud la Luge*) in the forest, together with two quarters of lime for pointing the houses. This lodge may have been the lodge in the Frith, the moated site known as the

23 Levi Fox, *Minister's Accounts of the Honor of Leicester (1322–1324)*

Bird's Nest, still identifiable in New Parks.[24] As the name Bird's Nest does not appear in the written record until later in the 14th century, this could have been an earlier building on the same site or a different one elsewhere.

The third Earl of Leicester's younger son, Henry of Grosmont (1310–1361), the brother of the executed Thomas, soon had the titles restored to him in 1323. Henry who took part in the siege of Calais in 1347, was honoured as a founder Knight of the Garter and given the title Duke of Lancaster in 1351, only the second man to have held this new noble title of Duke in England. The first was Edward, the Black Prince, created Duke of Cornwall in 1337. Leicester Forest, linked to the owners of Leicester Castle, was an important area for hunting.

Leicester was undoubtedly one of Duke Henry's favourite homes. The many presents given to him by the Borough of Leicester, show that he often stayed in the castle.[25] His longest period of residence seems to have been in the first half of 1356, while he was settling the final details for the Trinity Hospital in the Newarke, before he set off for Normandy with Edward III, for the wars in France. Henry of Grosmont does not seem to have lived for very long at any of his other castles. Demonstrating the importance of Leicester Forest to the ducal household, there was a house for the chief forester near to the castle, as reported, 'The popularity of Leicester Forest as a hunting place doubtless accounted for much of the duke's partiality to Leicester castle. Here he could hunt the fallow deer with his pack of greyhounds, to say nothing of the smoking and digging out of foxes.'[26]

Duke Henry of Grosmont died in Leicester where he was buried in 1361. The royal family, including King Edward III and the Black Prince, attended the funeral. Henry had no son but two daughters. The eldest, Matilda, inherited the titles but died so they passed to her younger sister, Blanche. Blanche married Edward III's son John of Gaunt, or Ghent, who inherited the wealth of Duke Henry. The title of 1st Duke of Lancaster of the second creation was revived and bestowed on him by the king in 1362. John of Gaunt, regent to his nephew, the boy king Richard II, claimed the title King of Castile through his marriage to his second wife Constance of Castile. Important in the later history of England and of Leicester, both the Houses of Lancaster and of York were descendants of John of Gaunt.

Throughout the 14th century, hunting in the Forest was especially important. Duke Henry had a new hunting lodge erected in the Frith at a site known as the Briddesnest by 1352. This lodge was pre-eminent as a centre of sporting activity. It was also an

24 Squires, p.174
25 M. Bateson: *Records of the Borough of Leicester*, II, xx, 60, 67–68, 76–7.
26 Kenneth Allan Fowler, *Henry of Grosmont, First Duke of Lancaster, 1310–1362*, Thesis presented for the degree of PhD in the University of Leeds, 1961, p.844; Fox and Russell, p.44

administrative centre for the Forest.[27] The Dukes of Lancaster often held court at Leicester Castle and entertained royal visitors. During these visits the Forest often witnessed the colourful scenes and pageantry of hunting parties when the Dukes were entertaining distinguished guests such as King Edward III and his successor Richard II. In 1390, for example, John of Gaunt entertained King Richard II, the queen, the royal dukes of York and Gloucester, the Archbishop of York, and other leading nobility in a hunting party in Leicester Forest. This is described by Henry of Knighton, a canon of Leicester Abbey who died around 1396. Knighton wrote that this was 'an occasion surpassing in splendour anything that had been seen before. Huge crowds assembled to watch the display of pageantry and courtly pride of this gorgeous cavalcade'. The procession would have passed through the Western Park area, perhaps along a track that would eventually become Hinckley Road or along the old Roman road to Mancetter.

The Birds Nest Lodge was mentioned by name in documents in 1362, when reference to the purchase of locks for the gates of the Frith and the doors of Bird's Nest (Briddesnest) appears in the accounts for 1361–62 of Richard Gilbert, receiver of Heathley.[28] This is probably the same place that was repaired in 1322, mentioned by Anneys or the lodge in the Frith referred to in 1351 when it was built or repaired for Henry of Grosmont.[29] Bird's Nest Lodge was again rebuilt with a moat in 1378. At this time it was occupied by William de Rothwell, one of the foresters of the Frith, and so was sometimes referred to as Rothewellelogge, or Rothwell's Lodge.

The names of the men working on the rebuilding of 1378 are recorded as Robert Hod, Adam Irysh, William Redford and Robert Ireland. To repair the roof they used 1,500 Swithland slates. The pool referred to in the following extract was the moat:

And 12s. 8d. for the wages of Robert Hod, Adam Irysh, William Redford and Robert Ireland making the head of the pool in the Fryth, for 9 1/2 days, each at 4d. a day. And 4s. 7 1/2d. for 1,500 slates purchased at Swithland, including carriage to the lodge in the Frith, at 3s. 1d. per 1,000.

And 20s. for the wages of John of London holing and repairing the said slates and old tiles, for four days at 5d. at day. And 2s. 1d. for 260 stonlaths purchased from Richard of Braunston, at 10d. per 100. And 6d. paid to the same Richard for 2,000 slate pins. And 20s. paid to Henry of Klyipeston for 960 stonails for the said house called the Lodge in the Frith. and 3s. 4d. for the wages of Philip the Slater and Thomas the Slater with two servants, each with his servants for two days, at 10d. per day.

Total: 26s. 6 1/2d.[30]

27 'Fowler' Thesis, p.845
28 HER
29 'Fowler' Thesis, p.845
30 Fox and Russell, p.33

Site of Bird's Nest Lodge, taken in 2021.

One of the 'parkers' who managed the area around this time, in 1381, was Henry Ballard.[31]

A drawbridge was added to the Bird's Nest and the moat scoured in 1526, around the time of the first enclosure of Leicester Forest, showing the site was fortified. There were fish ponds nearby. This structure has been described as a lodge of Leicester Forest, the centre of the Leicester Frith Deer park. It would have had a resident keeper and as a hunting lodge would have been a place where huntsmen could rest and change horses after an exhausting chase. In 1560 it was described as having seven bays in the south side, eight on the west, three on the east and nine on the north, so it was quite a large structure. There was a hall with three bays, stairs and two bays over the porter's ward. It had a total of seven chimneys. This survey was commissioned for the Duchy of Lancaster by Francis Cave, George Vyncent and John Harware and carried out by William Durrante, William Woodland, Richard Symson, Robert Butler and others, in anticipation of its sale, possibly due to the attainder and confiscation of lands following the execution of Henry Grey, Duke of Somerset, because of his involvement in the Wyatt Rebellion of 1554.[32]

Writing in the late 19th century, Agnes Fielding Johnson described the site, then in the lands of Bird's Nest Farm, as:

> 'An extensive spinney in the tall trees of which the rooks for centuries have had their habitation. Around it lies a clearly defined moat, and on the island thus formed are to be seen the remains of the foundations of a building which tradition has named "John of Gaunt's Summer House", and which imagination readily peoples with forms and fancies incidental to the seasons of leisure in the life of the last of our princely Earls.'[33]

By 1950, however, what remained of these earthworks on the site of Bird's Nest Lodge was covered over when the New Parks Estate was built. The site, off Battersbee

31 Squires, p.174
32 Fox and Russell, Appendix II
33 Mrs T. Fielding Johnson, *Glimpses of Ancient Leicester,* Leicester, 1891

Road, is now scheduled by Historic England under the Ancient Monument and Archaeological Areas Act of 1979 which gives it special protection.

The Norman lords introduced rabbits to Leicester Forest and large warrens were created in which the animals could live and breed before being killed for food and their coney fur. As early as 1349 the list of keepers of Leicester Forest included one man 'as in warren'. There were several warrens in the area. One called Braunstone Warren was recorded in the accounts of Kirby Muxloe Castle in 1480. In 1605 there was a Galliard's Warren, situated at a place called Frith Lane Gate with a warrener called Thomas Galliard. The warren had spread over into a surrounding area. The soft sandstone made an ideal habitat for rabbits, easy for them to dig and make burrows in. The possible remains of a medieval rabbit warren have been identified in the area of what became the industrial estate near Sunningdale Road.

When John of Gaunt's son, Henry of Bolingbroke, became king as Henry IV, after usurping Richard II in 1399, the Leicester Forest lands passed with him into the ownership and control of the Crown, making it a Royal Forest. However, it had been administered under Forest Law since 1266 when Edmund, Earl of Leicester was given power to manage it as if it were already a royal forest.[34] According to John Nichols in his *History and Antiquities of Leicestershire* published between 1795 and 1815, citing William Lord Cobham, 'Frith Park, otherwise called the new Park of Byrdesnest' was given by Lancastrian King Henry VI to his new wife, Margaret of Anjou, in his marriage settlement in 1445.[35] Queen Margaret also received the honour of Leicester and several manors in or around the Forest.[36]

Another royal occasion, of a traumatic kind, took place in 1485 when King Richard III, accompanied by his army and followers, estimated at between 8,000 and 10,000 men, rode through the area on the morning of Sunday, 21 August, marching westwards after crossing the Bow Bridge on his way out of Leicester, to meet his adversary Henry Tudor at Bosworth Field.[37] Richard's forces were said to consist chiefly of foot regiments, marching five in rank, his Majesty 'gorgeously dressed, upon a large white courser, richly caparisoned, attended by his body guards'.[38] This scene of excitement, as King Richard confidently rode out to secure his kingdom in a cavalcade of men wearing livery and armour, horses, grooms and wagons carrying supplies, ordnance and fodder, created an amazing spectacle for the people of Leicester and along the route, who would have turned out to cheer the army on its way.

---

34 Squires, p.172

35 Squires, p.174, *Nichols' History of Leicestershire*, 2 January1783

36 Star Chamber Proceedings, p.134

37 Philippa Langley and Michael Jones: *The Search for Richard III, The King's Grave*, John Murray, London, 2013, p.184; David Baldwin: *Richard III*, Amberley Publishing, Stroud, 2013, p.209

38 William Hutton: The Battle of Bosworth Field, 1788, quoted in Western Park sales brochure, ROLLR 8D62/Box76/9

The route Richard and his army took would surely have been along the old Roman road towards Mancetter, crossing what is now Western Park.[39] Henry Tudor and his army of between 2,000 and 5,000 men had marched up Watling Street which crossed this road and they were resting near to the junction at Merevale Abbey.[40] After his defeat by Henry, Richard's body, 'stripped of its armour and clothing, trussed up with the hands tied together and flung naked over a horse' and humiliatingly stabbed in the buttocks, was carried back to Leicester by the same route a few days later. [41] The local inhabitants would perhaps have been shocked when the news of Richard's death reached the town but many would have turned out along the road to greet the new King Henry VII, with his grizzly trophy, dejected prisoners and jubilant army as they entered Leicester, heralding the beginning of the new Tudor dynasty.

Feuding in the Forest

The Frith was bordered by the lands controlled by two of the most powerful men in the country during the Wars of the Roses. These were the Hastings family of Ashby de la Zouch and Kirby Muxloe, loyal Yorkists whose head was a close companion of Edward, son of the Duke of York, who deposed Henry VI and became king as Edward IV. William Hastings was granted the stewardship of part of Leicester Forest deer park by Edward IV who now controlled the possessions of the Duchy of Lancaster. This allowed Hastings to gain power and wealth. Hastings proceeded to create his own emparked area at Kirby Frith after he was granted a licence to do so by the king in 1474.[42] Sir William Hastings became one of the most important courtiers and lord chamberlain to Edward. The other powerful faction was the Grey family of Groby and Bradgate, who fought for the Lancastrian cause until Elizabeth Woodville, the widow of Sir John Grey who was killed at the second battle of St Albans in 1461, married the Yorkist king Edward IV without the approval of Hastings whose advice had not been sought. The Grey interest in the area dated back to 1264.

Elizabeth Woodville's two sons from her first marriage, Thomas and Richard Grey, were now stepsons of the king and as such secured many advantages for themselves. The eldest, Thomas, born in 1455, became Marquis of Dorset and his younger brother was knighted as Sir Richard Grey in 1475. This aggrandisement of the Greys led to resentment between these families; the Hastingses no doubt felt pushed out as they saw rewards they had anticipated for themselves go to the Greys. There seems to have been some temporary reconciliation between the two magnates as between 1480 and 1483, while Edward IV was still king, men from the Greys' lands of Groby and Ratby were

39 Glen Foard, Glen and Anna Curry: *Bosworth 1485: A Battlefield Rediscovered*, Oxbow Books. Oxford, 2013, pp.93–94

40 Baldwin, p.209

41 Langley and Jones, p.207

42 Squires, p.186

allowed to work on the building of nearby Kirby Muxloe Castle for Hastings. It has been suggested that the collaboration between Hastings and Grey on the building of Kirby Muxloe Castle may have been seen as evidence that the two may also have been in political collaboration at some point.[43] Edward IV's former mistress Elizabeth (Jane) Shore became mistress to both Thomas Grey and Hastings and was accused of acting as a go-between in a conspiracy against Richard. Any truce seems to have broken down during the events following King Edward's death.

Animosity between the two families and their factions helped to allow Richard III to become king. Hastings had helped Richard gain control of both the boy king Edward V and his brother Richard, Duke of York, by persuading their mother Elizabeth to allow the younger boy to leave sanctuary and join his older brother in the Tower of London. Apparently loyal to Richard, facilitating the execution of Richard Grey and other opponents of the Protector, it was a shock when Richard suddenly turned on Hastings and had him executed too.

After being attainted by Richard in 1484 which lost him his lands and titles, Thomas Grey escaped to France where he became a supporter of Henry Tudor until his mother seemed to change her attitude towards Richard and a marriage between his half-sister Elizabeth of York and the usurper appeared to be on the cards. Grey then deserted Henry but was intercepted and detained in Paris as a hostage and played no part in the Battle of Bosworth. When Henry became king and married Elizabeth of York, Thomas Grey became the king's brother-in-law. He returned to England and was reinstated as Marquis of Dorset. King Henry VII, never fully trusted him and ensured he never become a powerful figure at court.

The rivalry between the Grey and Hastings families continued into the next generations with frequent outbreaks of intimidation and violence in and around Leicester and the Frith. At this time, the nobility retained their own private armies, dressed in their master's liveries. It was said that anyone suspected of being a supporter of Hastings or of Grey was likely to be attacked by supporters of the other side when they were on the streets of Leicester. When the widowed Queen Margaret of Scotland came to stay with her brother Henry VIII in London in 1516, both Grey, Hastings and Hastings' step-father Sir Richard Sacheveral who held lands at Braunstone, blatantly exceeded their quota of liveried bodyguards who caused trouble whenever they met around London, to the anger of Cardinal Wolsey.[44]

Evidence given at the Court of Star Chamber in 1516, which tells us about life in the Frith, relates another incident of animosity and mutual disrespect between the

---

43 David A. Ramsay: *The Surnames, Occupations and Early working practices within the Bradgate area of Leicestershire, 1296–1890*, 2003, p.11

44 *Star Chamber Proceedings, Part of the Evidence in a 16th Century Suit relating to Leicester and the Forest of Leicester, with an introduction and Notes by S.H. Skillington,* Leicestershire Archaeological Society, p.137

two factions. The Frith was common land where people in adjacent communities could let their livestock free to graze. Each autumn there was a 'dryft' in which the animals were rounded up and penned in the 'Pynfold' (pinfold) in Leicester Frith. The animals were then returned to their owners to be kept close to home or indoors during the winter. The Marquis of Dorset's brothers, Leonard and John Grey, were supervising this process when Sacheverell's chaplain, a priest called Richard Frampton, along with two other men armed with swords and bucklers (shields), Robert Carter and Charnelles, came to get their master's beasts from the pinfold. Lord Leonard Grey said that Frampton would have to swear on oath that the animals, a mare and foal, belonged to Sacheverell, as was the usual custom of the forest. Other servants of Sacheverell went into the pinfold to get the horses but refused to swear that they belonged to their master, so Grey would not let them take the animals, saying, 'Go to your master Mr Sacheverell, and let him come himself or send one of you or any other of his servants that will swear they be his beast and no man's else and they will be delivered.'[45] Other tenants and commoners who followed the rules were annoyed and said, 'Why shall you not swear as well as you have made us to swear for our cattle in times past?'[46]

Another of Sacheverell's servants came for his master's cattle but again he would not take the oath to confirm ownership. Later in the afternoon, between 12 and 16 of Sacheverell's servants appeared with bows and arrows. Some of them shot them up and down by the pinfold, coming within six yards of Lord Leonard 'and did no reverence to him'. They hung around for an hour or two, drank some ale, and then left without actually harming anyone.[47]

The trouble between the families continued and perhaps escalated over the next few years, culminating in a fight between hundreds of men in 1524, details of which, from the Marquis of Dorset's side, survive in recorded depositions given before the court of the Star Chamber in September 1525. George Hastings, Earl of Huntingdon, was the grandson of the executed Sir William and son of his heir, Sir Edward Hastings, and Lady Mary Hungerford. When Sir Edward died, Lady Hungerford married Sir Richard Sacheveral in 1509 and lived in a house in the Newarke in Leicester. One day in 1524 the Marquis of Dorset's servants were in Leicester when those of Lady Hungerford found out. Being seriously outnumbered they hid in a pub 'at the sign of the George'. When the mayor and other civic dignitaries came to sort out the situation the men said, 'We beseech you that we may go peacefully home to my lord marquis's place to Byrdesnest up the King's high street of Leicester, for we bear malice to no man. 'The Marquis of Dorset seems to have occupied the lodge in the Frith known as the Bird's Nest at this time, probably because of his interest in Leicester

45 Star Chamber Proceedings, p.137
46 Star Chamber Proceedings, p.150
47 Star Chamber Proceedings, p.138

Forest, the 'Chase', because he held the adjacent manor of Glenfield. John Rede, one of the Leicester leaders, advised the men to leave town by a back road but they refused, saying it would shame their master if they were to sneak off. One of the marquis's men, Anthony, went to get his horse from another pub on the high street 'at the sign of the Rose' but was spotted by Sir Richard Sacheverall's servants who were waiting around the High Cross. They gave chase with their swords and bucklers at the ready. Anthony escaped to the Rose, got his horse and made off down the back lane, over a hedge and ditch. Other evidence given to the court said that Sacheveral had 200 to 300 armed men in Leicester, the castle and the Newarke, ready to beat home the Marquis of Dorset (Thomas Grey) if he came to Leicester for the assizes. Cardinal Wolsey ordered both Hastings and Grey to put up bonds of £1,000 for their good behaviour. Soon after, the Marquis was sent off to Wales as Lord Master of Princess Mary's Council.

Other reports were given to the court of parties of Grey's men meeting groups of Sacheverall's on the road to the forest carrying swords and drawn bows with 'nokked' arrows ready to shoot. On 8 September 1525, Thomas Dunham, a 19–year-old servant of Lord John Grey, told the Star Chamber that he had been sent somewhere by Lord Leonard but met Mr Sacheverell, accompanied by seven score (7x20, ie 140) of horses or thereabouts on the road near Kirby Muxloe. Dunham had no option but to ride along with them until they all stopped and 'bode styll'. Dunham tried to continue but was stopped by Sacheverell's servant, Mr Wygley, who told him to come back to Mr Sacheverell. Dunham said he would not. 'By God's blood, knave, thou shalt not choose,' replied Wygley.

Dunham rode away but was caught up by George Villers of Hoby, galloping on a horse with a crossbow bent and an arrow in it. Villers placed himself in front of Dunham and said, 'Stand, knave, how far wilt thou go?' To which Dunham replied, 'I have been about my master's business. I trust ye will not stop me in the highway.' Villers responded, aiming his crossbow with an arrow at the ready at Dunham's thigh, 'By God's blood, knave, thou shalt speak with Mr Sacheverell 'ere thou go.' So Dunham rode to Sacheverell and 'did off his cap to him'. Sacheverell only nodded at him. Then Wygley and Villers asked Dunham if he was a spy.While this was going on, Sir John Villers and Sir Richard Parker sent 30 men with bows towards the pinfold gate in Kirby, 16 of them riding up the hill towards the Leicester Forest gate where they got off their horses with their bows and arrows 'nokked', ready to shoot. Martin a Lee, Sir Thomas Chipman, a priest and John Grene, servant to Mr Sacheverell walked up and down in front of the fence or pale surrounding the Frith, with their arrows aimed. Dunham was asked why he was there. Dunham answered that he was assigned under Lord Leonard to walk as a keeper there. Sacheverell then arrived with his men. Dunham was told, 'Go, knave, as the deer are. For it is no walking for thee in the highway.' Dunham told them to go on their way through the forest. Martin a Lee and others threatened him with, 'Knave, and ever thou come in Leicester thou shalt have thy head broken.' This happened at the Doveland Gate, on the present day Hinckley Road, near the entrance to Braunstone Park, where Dunham said another man came at him with his sword out of its sheath and his buckler in his left hand but he did not hurt him, just gave him a fright.[48]

The altercation and intimidation described above may have been the same incident as that recounted by Fox and Russell in their 1948 book *Leicester Forest,* based on the Star Chamber papers of Henry VIII's time. In their version Thomas Denham (or Dunham) was one of Lord John Grey's keepers who was keeping an eye on Sir Richard Sacheverell (stepfather of Lord George Hastings) and his swarm of about 70 supporters who had been hunting. Sir John Villiers sent 30 men with bows to the pinfold gate near Kirby. Sixteen of them crossed the ford and were riding up Blood Hill (Ratby Lane) towards the Forest. They passed through the forest gate at the Kirby Frith corner and were in the reserved part of the Forest within the pale or boundary of the Frith near the highway. Here they dismounted with bows bent and arrows notched ready to shoot although they did not fire as they knew Denham was watching them. When Sacheveral arrived the whole party moved off 'along the broad lane with a good deal of ill temper, finally leaving the forest by Doveland gate, politely bowed out by Master Denham'.[49] In this version, perhaps evidence from another point of view, the incident seems to have been less aggressive and intimidating for Denham.

The hostility between the Grey and Hastings families continued through the rest of the 16th and 17th centuries. Both dynasties were of royal blood and were potential protestant successors to Queen Elizabeth I, the Greys through Lady Jane Grey and Henry VIII's sister Mary, and Hastings as a great grandson of Margaret Pole, daughter of Edward IV's attainted brother, George, Duke of Clarence. During the Civil War of 1642 to 1651 their descendants continued to be on opposite sides: Thomas, Lord Grey of Groby as MP for Leicester during the Long Parliament was Commander in Chief of the Parliamentary forces in the Midlands and was one of the regicides who signed the death warrant of King Charles I. Henry Hastings, Lord Loughborough was a Royalist army commander who supported Prince Rupert in the siege of Leicester.

The first enclosure and the birth of New Parks

The forest or chase remained mostly woodland and gorse but was administered for profit in a business-like manner until in 1526 part of it near Leicester was enclosed by Henry VIII. The king's commissioners sent to carry out a survey reported that 'it

48 Star Chamber Proceedings, p.1141
49 Fox and Russell, pp.61-62

was well replenished with deer', claiming to have seen a thousand of them. They also reported that there was little timber – lopping and cropping was likely to produce an income of £40 a year. If the trees were removed and the land given over to grazing, it could yield a high income, but the commissioners warned that this would hurt the town of Leicester and the villages around which would decay in a short time.[50]

King Henry had it divided into two unequal parts, the larger of which was subdivided into three areas and allocated to Glenfield, Kirby Muxloe and Braunstone. The smaller part was retained by Henry as a New Park. The King's New Park took in all the Frith on the town side with a new boundary running between the entrance to the forest at Doveland Gate and Groby Road. There is the possibility that some of the ground markings identified in Western Park could be the result of drainage works carried out at this time.

As the commissioners had warned, the people of Leicester lost some of their common rights in this area, for instance the Dean and Canons of the College of St Mary in the Newarke claimed their time-honoured common rights, which led to legal disputes over ownership between Leicester Corporation and the Duchy of Lancaster representing the King[51]. The land still belonged to the Crown through the Duchy but enclosure meant that the land in the newly created closes or fields of New Parks could be leased out to different people to be exploited, a source of additional income to Henry VIII who was always looking for extra money to fund wars and an increasingly opulent royal court.

One of Leicester's oldest charities is Wyggeston's Hospital, founded in 1513 with a legacy and endowment of land left by the town's richest man of the time, William Wyggeston, and his wife Agnes, to run an almshouse for the poor of Leicester. The almshouse was in the town next to St Martin's Church, now the site of St Martin's House. Henry Hastings, 3rd Earl of Huntingdon, donated some of his land in Leicester Forest to the Wyggeston's Hospital endowment in 1576.[52] This was the same year that Parliament ratified the revision of the statutes governing Wyggeston's that Queen Elizabeth I had allowed Huntingdon to introduce two years earlier.[53] Known as the Huntingdon Statutes, these regulated the running of the charity until 1849. This land may have been the area off Hinckley Road, that was sold for development in 1926 and 1934, and now contains part of Ainsdale Road and Hinckley Road.

During this time, Leicester Forest remained under Forest Law, governed by local men with rights of use at a meeting called the Swanimote Court, named after the swains or men who took part. No records from this court prior to 1599 have survived.

---

50 Squires, p.175
51 DMU Special Collections
52 Fox and Russell, p.69
53 James Thawley, *A Certain Hospital Forever: A recent history of Wyggeston's Hospital*, Leicester, 1996, p.3

A meeting of the Swanimote Court for Leicester Forest in 1599 during Elizabeth I's reign, nearly half century after the enclosure of the New Park, reiterated the regulations. All enclosed land within the forest should continue to be within the area of the forest covered by statute and no unlawful cattle, horses, other beasts and an agreed amount of sheep should be kept there. No swine or pigs were to go unringed. Braunstone residents were to keep to the area outside the forest gate in Doveland Lane.

The Swanimote Court proceedings also considered and pronounced on an important technological change: no firearms were to be permitted apart from those 'who mune [must] have it', which presumably meant those in authority or land owners.[54] No borderer (bordar, villein or peasant of the lowest rank who performed service in return for a cottage) could carry a crossbow, gun or tiller within the Forest with the intent to kill or disturb any of the Queen's game, enforced with fines of three shillings and four pence. The only people allowed to keep cattle in the Forest were those with common rights. A man in Glenfield, Richard Doodall, was specifically mentioned in the recorded proceedings and forbidden to keep any cattle in the Forest until he provided proof of his common right. Perhaps he had been caught making false claims to possession of such rights.

A survey of 1606 shows that New Parks, an area that included the present-day Western Park, at that time owned by Lord Cobham, had been cleared and drained. It was regularly grazed, providing grass for over a thousand sheep. The survey also mentions two lodges, one of which appears to be on the site of New Parks farmhouse. This was rebuilt and later, when the area was laid out as a public park at the end of the 19th century, known as the Pavilion. Near to the farm house there was a pool, well stocked with fish where an ancient dam, made of material quarried close by, held the water.[55]

This chapter has attempted to give an overview of the archaeology and medieval history of the area that formed part of Leicester Forest, managed under Forest Law as a park for aristocratic hunting but which was also a valuable economic resource for its timber and quarrying. Leicester Forest made a vital contribution to the subsistence of local people. Some of the history of this time is rather sketchy as there are few written records. There may be much for future archaeologists and historians to discover and provide answers to some of the uncertainties about the early history of the area. The next chapter will look at the enclosure of the forest and park to create not just a different landscape but a different way of life and class relationships in what became pastoral New Parks.

54 Proceedings of Swanimote Court, 1599
55 Fox and Russell, p.86

2

THE NEW PARKS: PASTORAL IDYLL?

The second enclosure and the clearing of the Frith

The Frith survived as forest or chase until the end of the Middle Ages and the coming of the Tudors, who now owned the land as they took over the former lands of the Duchy of Lancaster which were incorporated into the possessions of the monarchy. It remained mostly woodland and gorse but was leased out and administered for profit in a business-like manner, although by then it had probably lost many of its trees.

Henry VII was known for his parsimonious lifestyle but his son Henry VIII was notorious for his extravagance. As a consequence he was always looking for ways to bring in more funds to pay for his magnificent court, palaces and expensive wars with France and Scotland. As Leicester Castle was no longer regularly inhabited, the hunting parties came to an end. An area of land only used by townspeople and villagers to collect firewood and graze a few animals would not have generated much revenue. However, population growth increased the rents to be gained from agricultural land. In 1526 the area of Leicester Forest nearest to the town of Leicester was enclosed by order of Henry VIII. Fences or hedges were erected around parcels of land or pastures in the Frith and sold or rented out to tenants to raise money for the king.

The Dean and Canons of the College of St Mary in the Newarke, where De Montfort University is now, claimed compensation for the loss of their common rights in the unenclosed Frith on land which thereafter was leased out as pasture by the Duchy of Lancaster. In response to this claim, St Mary's was allocated some rights in Braunstone Frith as recompense for its lost common rights in the Forest. At the time it was first separated from Leicester Forest and divided into individual pastures, Braunstone Frith contained a single farm and was an extra parochial place in the Sparkenhoe Hundred.[56] King Henry's New Park took in all the Frith on the town side with a new boundary running between the Doveland Gate entrance to the Forest and Groby Road. At the time of its creation by enclosure in 1526, New Parks was estimated to be worth £70 7s 6d in rental income to the monarchy through

---

56 British History Online, Victoria County History

the Duchy of Lancaster.[57] This income was gained at the expense of the people of Leicester who lost their common rights, which caused hardship to those poorer inhabitants dependent on the Forest for fuel or foraging for food.

During the 16th century New Parks changed hands several times, reflecting the rise and fall of political fortunes during the instability of the reigns of the Tudors. Edward VI granted it to his step-mother Katherine Parr's brother, his 'beloved uncle' William Parr, Marquess of Northampton in 1550, along with other lands in the area. Parr didn't enjoy his new acquisition for long as after young King Edward died in 1553, he and his wife were involved in the conspiracy to make Lady Jane Grey queen. When this failed and Mary Tudor took the throne, Parr was accused of treason and arrested. He was sentenced to death on 18 August 1553 but was released later that year. However, he was attainted which meant his land and property were confiscated, taken into the control of the Crown, and Parr was stripped of all his titles. These titles were restored to him by Elizabeth I in 1559 shortly after she became queen.

The Bird's Nest Lodge, restored in 1526, around the time of enclosure seems to have been allowed to fall into disrepair but was still there in 1560 when it was owned by the Crown and valued at £25 13s 4d according to a survey carried out by a commission for the Duchy of Lancaster.[58] The keeper of the lodge in 1553 was, according to John Nicholls writing in the late 18th century, Sir John Harrington. If he was the same person who was a courtier and 1st Baron Harington of Exton in Rutland (1539/40–1613), he would only have been about 13 years old at the time. Soon after this, New Parks was granted by Queen Elizabeth to William Brooke, tenth Lord Cobham who held the area by 1571. During the reign of Mary I he had sided against her in the Wyatt Rebellion.

A powerful nobleman, Lord Cobham was a friend of William Cecil, whose son married his daughter. Cobham was Lord of the Cinque Ports with control of a number of seats in Parliament. As Cobham was William Parr's brother-in-law, some of the confiscated land returned to the family. During the time that New Parks was owned by the Lords Cobham it was cleared and drained, as evidenced by a survey of 1606, which mentioned two lodges. One of these, which had a well-stocked fish pond, may have become New Parks Farm. A living relic of this time, the wonderful old oak tree in Western Park, known as 'Old Major', dates from around 1597, when Elizabeth I was queen, only 70 years after the time of the 16th-century enclosure.[59]

57 Fox and Russell, p.134
58 Fox and Russell, p.124
59 Date calculated by Peter Canovan (Leicester City Council) using formula in 'Estimating the Age of Large and Veteran Trees in Britain', produced by the Forestry Commission, in 1998. This document is based on at least 40 years of records gathered by Alan Mitchell and John White. It also references Mitchell and Oliver Rackham, based on many years of Dendrochronology records gathered.

The 702 acres of pasture land provided grass to feed 1,000 sheep, whose wool was a major source of wealth in 16th century England and beyond. As well as the pasture, there were 112 acres of meadow, land on which grass for hay making was grown. This could be used for fodder in the winter. As well as the sheep there were cows for milking, and some other cattle and horses. There was also a small quarry of freestone but this was considered to have no value. New Parks's annual value was £400 but it was rented for just £260 a year.

When the 10th Lord Cobham, outlawed for debt, died in a duel in 1597, his son Henry inherited his title and lands. Just six years later, Henry, 11th Lord Cobham, was implicated in the treasonable Main Plot of 1603, against the new King James I whose accession he opposed. The plan was to install Lady Arabella Stuart on the throne through a coup d'etat. Cobham was attainted for his involvement, stripped of his titles and honours and imprisoned in the Tower until 1618. He died shortly after his release. His brother George was executed in 1603 for his own role in the separate Bye Plot which aimed to kidnap King James and force him to end the persecution of Catholics. As a result, New Parks was once again forfeited to the Crown.

Nichols claims that in 1620 Lord Cobham settled the Bird's Nest Lodge on his eldest son, George, although there was no Lord Cobham between 1603 and 1645.[60] Nichols, who gained much of his information through hearsay, seems to have been mistaken here. James I had granted a large part of the Cobham estates to the attainted Lord Cobham's wife, Frances Howard, daughter of the 1st Earl of Nottingham, for life in 1606. She lived until 1628. New Parks, though, had already been granted to Sir William Woodhouse of Norfolk, gentleman of the privy chamber with political connections to Sir John Grey and the Howard family who nominated him as Member of Parliament for Aldeburgh in 1604.[61] This was the same year Woodhouse obtained New Parks.

Woodhouse seems to have passed it on to Sir Thomas Knyvet (1545–1622), who foiled the Gunpowder Plot when he searched Parliament's cellars. Knyvet was also associated with the Howards through his niece's marriage and to Edward, George and Nathaniel Bacon, Woodhouse's cousins, although they or their heirs would not have been able to derive any income from rents from the land during widow Frances's lifetime. The Hastings family carried out a survey for King James I in 1606 which concluded that Leicester Forest was in a run-down state with only decayed trees. It was mostly grassland with a few old pollarded oaks, home to sheep, cattle, horses and rabbits escaped from nearby warrens. In 1614, John Sharman acquired some disputed property in the Frith, the use of which had previously been claimed by Leicester Corporation.[62]

---

60 British-history.ac.uk, accessed 20 February 2016

61 Sir William Woodhouse (c1570–1639): *The History of Parliament: the House of Commons 1604–1629*, ed. Andrew Thrush and John P Ferris, 2010

62 British History Online, Victoria County History

Old Major, oak tree, Western Park.

By 1624 the Crown recognised that there was no point in maintaining the area as a forest as there was little cover left for deer. It would be worth more as sheep pasture. Due to poor harvests, food prices were high. Many people relied on being able to make use of Leicester Forest for firewood, grazing and perhaps looking for naturally growing food. This was until the results of a survey of the Forest by Sir Miles Fleetwood on behalf of the government between December 1626 and March 1627. The intention was to disafforest Leicester Forest along with others elsewhere in England. What this meant was that any rights local people had to access or make use of the land under Forest Law were removed completely. People living in the area covered by the Forest, or in the town of Leicester, received compensation if they could prove they had a legal entitlement. Many ancient cottages were allotted two acres and newly erected ones only one acre.[63] At that time, a cottage did not refer to just a little house but a home, land around it and rights to use common land, an important part of the pre-industrial agrarian economy that allowed cotters and bordars to be almost self-sufficient and provide for themselves, even if they had little money. Those who

63 John Goodacre, *The Transformation of a Peasant Economy, Townspeople and villagers in the Lutterworth Area, 1500–1700*, Routledge, 2017, p.99

had moved in without any legal title, on 'assart' land they had cleared themselves, received nothing.

In February 1628 the Attorney General and court of the Exchequer confirmed the arrangements with the new King Charles I, just three years into his reign. King Charles agreed to let 1,598 acres to local wealthy landowners for a 'fine' or fee of £7,760, a huge amount, plus an annual rent, adding to the income of the Crown. These landlords rented this land to tenants who converted it to arable land. At the same time, traditional common rights in Leicester's West Field were eliminated. Obviously ordinary people, those who felt inadequately compensated and those who got nothing, were angry and upset about this as the poor people of Leicester had, from time immemorial been able 'to fetch on their backs broken, dead and rotten wood' from the forest. The changes had also interfered with bringing coal from the pits at Swannington to Leicester, in panniers carried on donkeys and mules, across the rough forest tracks.[64] In response there were riots and fences enclosing the land were dug up or levelled. Women took an active part in these 'digger' or 'leveller' riots and an observer of the Leicester Forest riots in 1627 noted that the protests were led by 'a certain number of ignorant women'.[65]

This wasn't the first time Leicester inhabitants had taken direct action in defence of their common rights. During the Midlands Enclosure Riots of 1607, led by 'Captain Pouch', alias John Reynolds of Desborough, riots in Northamptonshire spread to Cotesbach near Lutterworth. In Leicester there was a curfew in case the town residents tried to join in with the riots. As a warning of the consequences, a gibbet was erected in the town but protestors pulled it down. Perhaps it was this memory, combined with the worry that the poorest affected by the 1627–28 enclosures would be a burden on the poor rates, that caused Leicester Corporation to petition the King and his Privy Council. Challenges were made to the House of Lords, all to no avail. The petition to the Lords, in June 1628, claimed that families in 100 ancient cottages would receive compensation, but not those in newly built cottages. However, the government did drop legal proceedings against the rioters. The Crown allotted 20 acres to the burgesses of the town, in lieu of the loss of forest land and gave 40 acres to the borough of Leicester, the rents of which would be shared to help maintain the poor, who received grants for wood and coal. These grants, known as King Charles's Wood and Coal Money, were distributed by trustees annually just before Christmas, making paupers of people previously self-sufficient. The problem of poverty and hunger did not go away and despite improvements in agricultural methods and productivity there were food riots in the town in 1765 and in 1790.[66]

---

64 Mrs T. Fielding Johnson, *Glimpses of Ancient Leicester*, Leicester, 1891, p.204

65 John E. Martin, *Feudalism to Capitalism: Peasant and Landlord in English Agrarian Development*, 1983, MacMillan, Basingstoke. pp.180–215

66 Greaves, p.65

Nearly a century after John Sharman had taken over Braunstone Frith, William Inge, a descendant of Richard Inge of Leicestershire, who lived in Thorpe Constantine in Staffordshire, became the owner of Braunstone Frith in 1705. This land was farmed or leased out to successive generations of the Kirk or Kirke family, such as Richard Kirke who was there by December 1735, before John Kirke farmed it by 1794.[67] Sharman and Kirke are remembered today in Sharman Crescent and Kirk Walk in Braunstone Frith. In 1794, Braunstone Frith was described as consisting of a messuage, a dove house, two gardens, 150 acres of meadow and 100 acres of pasture.[68]

William Inge conveyed the Braunstone Frith farmhouse and its 230 acres to John Kirke for £7,594 in a 'lease and release' transaction in 1796. Inge was to receive £2,594 with the remaining £5,000 secured on the property with interest to be paid at £4 2s 0d a year by John Kirke, who became the owner.[69] However, Kirke died soon afterwards and Braunstone Frith passed to his nephew and heir, William Hooke.[70] In 1804 the lease of the farm of 230 acres was sold to John Pares of the Newarke for £7,000. William Phillips Inge received £6,100 15s 6d of this sum, presumably to pay off what was owing from the sale of the estate to Kirke with interest. The remainder of the £7,000 was divided unequally between the heirs of John Kirke. As part of the same transaction, Braunstone Frith was leased to John Pares of the Newarke on the remainder of 1,000–year lease, owned by Clement Winstanley.[71] The Winstanleys remained the owners until 1925 when it was sold to the council. At the time, the farmhouse was the only dwelling there. Braunstone Frith originally covered 232 acres and became a separate parish in 1857.[72]

New Parks agriculture

The name New Parks came into use from the time following the enclosures of the 16th century to create a new area of emparked land. The area though was mostly pastoral land, used mainly for grazing sheep, a major source of wealth for the emerging mercantile class, which included men like William Wyggeston of Leicester.

During the mid-18th century New Parks was in the hands of William Mitchell, who died in 1745. By 1781 it was owned by John Clarke, a sheep farmer who died in

67 Marriage Settlement, 19 December 1795, ROLLR 16D66/241; Bargain and Sale, 1794, ROLLR 16D66/242
68 Exemplification of Common Recovery, 1794, ROLLR 16D66/243
69 Lease and Release, 4–5 April 1796, ROLLR 16D66/244–245
70 Abstract of Title, 1796, ROLLR 16D66/258
71 ROLLR, Abstract of Title, 1804, 16D66/258
72 DMU Special Collections

Braunstone Frith Farm, 1971. (Records Office of Leicester, Leicestershire and Rutland)

1793, who had his farmhouse nearby.[73] The Bird's Nest Lodge building seems to have disappeared by 1790.[74]

When John Clarke died in 1793, he left his estate at New Parks for the benefit of his wife, Sarah, for life. After her passing, which didn't happen until 1826, their son John Clarke the younger had full control of his inheritance, with the condition that £5,000 was paid out of the estate to each of his two sisters, Ann and Elizabeth. The Clarke family were actively involved in the middle-class social life of Leicester. Ann Clarke gave five shillings a year to the Cheap Clothing Shop, presumably a charity to help clothe the poor of the town. The Eighth Annual Meeting of the society was held at the Female Asylum in the Newarke (spelt New-Works) in 1824, on the site of the De Montfort University's Hawthorne Building.

73 British-history.ac.uk, accessed 20 February 2016
74 J. Throsby, *Leicestershire Views*, ii. p.71

Old farm buildings, Western Park c.1900. (Records Office of Leicester, Leicestershire and Rutland)

For some reason, the younger John Clarke needed money and the year his mother died in 1826, he took out a mortgage of £33,000 to cover the value of the New Parks property as well as to cover the amount to be paid in legacies to his sisters. This may coincide with the rebuilding of the house, which Historic England describes as early 19th century, and may explain the reason for such a large loan. Another loan of £7,000 was taken out in 1837. Sarah and Ann were still being paid the income from their £5,000 legacies from the estate.[75] Altogether John borrowed £40,000 with interest from Revd James Ord (1759–1843) of Langton Hall, whose heiress wife had inherited property from a female cousin. New Parks remained with the Clarke family until 1843 when Revd Ord died and Clarke's bankruptcy forced its sale by public auction at the Three Cranes in Leicester, with a debt remaining to Revd Ord's son and heir James Pickering Ord.[76] There were no acceptable offers made in the auction but part of the estate was sold privately for £17,301 to John Mellor the elder (1780–1861), a hat manufacturer in business on Cheapside, an alderman and later mayor of Leicester. This added to the land nearby he had already purchased from Walter Ruding to benefit his son, John Mellor the younger (1809–1887), who became a barrister and Member of Parliament for Yarmouth and then Nottingham. Mellor now owned the fields called Johnson's Hill Close, Slater's Hill Close and Black Anna's Bower, pasture

75 Abstract of the Title of the Right Honourable Sir John Mellor to property forming part of the New Parks Estate in the County of Leicester, 1911

76 Langton Hall, Historic England https://historicengland.org.uk/listing/the-list/list-entry/1000961 accessed 18 August 2020

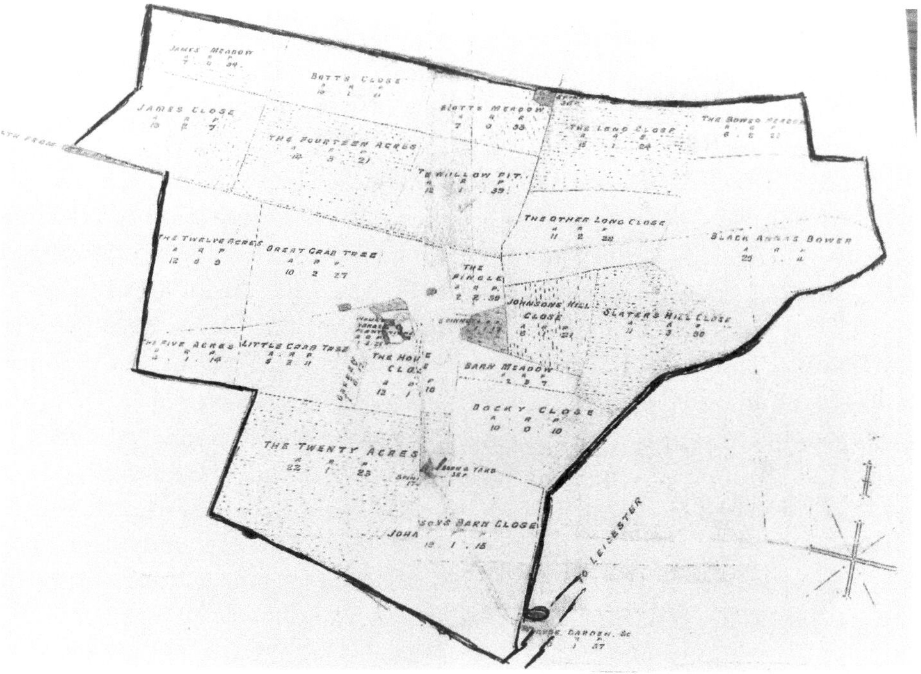

Composite field map from property deeds.

land of over 25 acres.[77] Other parts of the property were bought by Thomas Stokes and John Harris.

In the 19th century, wealthy industrialists and professional men were beginning to invest in land and property. By the mid-19th century many self-made industrialists, with recently acquired wealth, instead of reinvesting in their businesses and factories, were buying land. Land was important to them as high social status was the preserve of the aristocratic and gentry elites whose prestige was derived from their ownership of country estates which traditionally had given them power, income and influence. Those who had made fortunes through trade, industry and commerce were looked down on by the elite and not regarded as gentlemen as they worked for a living.

At the same time there was a persistent aspect of British culture that saw a rural, Arcadian society as the ideal. Successful industrialists, who had grown rich through their own entrepreneurial or technical skills, began to send their own sons to public schools where they could learn to become gentlemen.[78] They bought farms where they could live the life of gentlemen farmers, although this might be more of a secondary occupation, subsidised by their factories or professions. Leicester's businessmen were

77 Abstract of the Title of the Right Honourable Sir John Mellor to property forming part of the New Parks Estate in the County of Leicester, 1911

78 Martin Wiener: *English Culture and the Decline of the Industrial Spirit: 1850–1980*, Cambridge University Press, Cambridge, 1981

not immune from this trend; industrialists who had previously been content to live in or near their businesses now wanted to move out into the country. New Parks offered them the opportunity of a rural lifestyle, within a couple of miles of their main workplaces.

When Clarke sold his farm, the land was acquired by several owners; as well as John Mellor, the northern part was bought by Thomas Stokes, one of Leicester's leading hosiers, and another in 1863 by John Harris, also a hosier. Stokes was born in 1784 in Nottinghamshire. By 1841, when he was mayor of Leicester, Stokes was living on Welford Road with his wife, the former Mary Joyce of Blackfordby and their daughter, also called Mary. Politically he was a radical, a liberal who supported local banker Thomas Paget's election bid in 1835, and who described Paget as a man 'friendly to reform and economy'. Although he was a non-conformist in religion, he donated half an acre of land at Blackfordy near Ashby de La Zouch in Leicestershire as a site for a new church and for additional burials, perhaps to honour his wife. He also founded the village school in Dunton Bassett in 1849. Thomas Stokes agreed to purchase that part of the New Parks Estate, 240 acres, which had been occupied by Mr Worthington, one of Clarke's tenants, who had died.[79] According to his obituary of October 1867, Stokes signed for the estate in February 1845 and built New Parks House between then and 1846.

Thomas and Mary Stokes had one daughter, named after her mother, who in 1858 married a wealthy Scottish landowner, Hugh Henry Robertson Aikman, at St James Church in Westminster. When Thomas Stokes died in October 1867, they inherited the house and estate at New Parks. As well as New Parks House the Aikmans had a large estate in Lanarkshire and another house at 44 Portland Place in London. At Portland Place, in 1871, as well as the family there were 12 servants. Some of their six children were born at New Parks House, including their two eldest sons, Thomas Stokes George Henry Robertson Aikman in 1860 and Hugh Harry Robertson Aikman in 1866. Like their father, these sons had military careers. When his father died in January 1882, Thomas inherited his father's family estates and Ross House in Lanarkshire. Lieutenant-Colonel Thomas S.G.H. Robertson Aikman was keen on the sport of curling and in 1924, aged 64, won a gold medal at the first Olympic Games in Chamonix as the non-playing captain of the British team, all of whom were members of the Royal Caledonian Curling Club.

Major Hugh H. Robertson Aikman inherited his mother's family estate at New Parks when she died in January 1887. Hugh also owned a house and land at Dunton Bassett, where he made his home, and at Broughton Astley. Negotiations with Leicester Corporation began for the sale of the estate at New Parks in around

79 *Leicester Journal*, 8 March 1844

New Parks House. (Records Office of Leicester, Leicestershire and Rutland)

1924 and in 1933 the property was compulsorily purchased as land for building houses, what was to become the New Parks Estate.[80]

One of the other main land owners of the area now covering Western Park in the mid-19th century was John Mellor who died in 1861. The actual occupiers of the land were his tenants James Wykes, George White and Henry Billington. Mellor's heir was his son, Sir John Mellor, MP and judge, raised in Leicester but living in London, who became landowner following his father's death. At this time the area that became Western Park was still rural in character, the fields had picturesque names such as Slater's Hill Close, Johnson's Hill Close, Barn Meadow, Docky Close, Andrew's Close, Stone Pit Close and Black Anna's Bower Close, a name recalling the mythical creature or witch, Black Annis or Anna. According to a report of 1606, Black Anna's Bower was a 'cave digged out of the rock, where it was King Lear did hide himself'.[81]This close or field was important in the annual cycle of traditional holidays for the people of Leicester. According to historian Throsby, 'It had long been the custom on Easter Monday for the Mayor and his brethren, in their scarlet gowns, attended by their proper officers, in form, to go to a certain close, called Black Annis Bower Close, a parcel of land bordering upon Leicester Forest, to see the diversion of hunting.'[82] Supposedly a hare, the quarry was actually a dead cat covered in aniseed, which was

80 Negotiation and Compulsory Purchase, 1924–1933, ROLLR DE4674/2418
81 Fox and Russell, p.70
82 *Leicester Chronicle*, 2 April 1842

dragged from the field in Dane Hills, followed by townspeople before enjoying a fair. The mock-hunt of the dead cat ended in 1767 but the Dane Hill Fair continued on Easter Monday and Tuesday for around another century. The road leading to the fair, which passed Dannett's Hall, was lined with stalls and crowded with people in their best clothes. The fair was enjoyed especially by young working-class people who were amused with roundabouts and swings, and who treated themselves with nuts, gingerbread and confectionery sold from the stalls. The gingerbread stalls were said to be a favourite with the girls, while the boys were alleged to have preferred to damage fences and play pitch and toss or gambling games. The fields beyond that where the fair was held were also thronged with merrymakers.

To vary the entertainment, boys and girls would walk on to the Dane Hill Close, where they ran down the slopes, hand in hand. When they inevitably lost their footing, they all rolled together in a heap to the bottom of the hill. By 1853 the tree of Black Anna's Bower, hitherto the greatest attraction, had been removed but in 1851 there were still,

> 'Thousands of young people in the Bower and adjoining closes, amusing themselves and visiting the old tree which occupies the site of what is said to be have been the retreat of Black Anna, that mysterious female, whose solitary mode of life, weird influence and cruel practices are said to have made her in bygone times the terror of the people of Leicester.'[83]

A marionette theatre was added to the entertainment in 1853 and in 1857 a shooting gallery and photographic booth, a novelty at the time, were introduced.[84] The site of Black Anna's Bower is said to be to the rear of a house on the east side of Westfield Road.

The Dane Hill Fair shows the enduring relationship between the town dwellers, particularly the growing urban working-class and the adjacent rural area that became Western Park and New Parks. Newspaper reports of the Fair end in 1857 although a humbler incarnation with the name Old Dane Hills Fair was introduced by the nuns of St Catherine's Convent as a fundraising fete in the inter-war years.

Another local legend or folkloric memory could be the Lollards' Cave, the possible dwelling of itinerant Lollard preacher William Swynderby in the late 14th century. Swynderby was said by Henry of Knighton, to have lived in the lord's wood outside the town, 'in bosco domini duds'.[85] Although no location is given in older texts, this has become associated with the Western Park area. As Swynderby and the Lollards were looked on sympathetically by John of Gaunt, it could be that Leicester Forest, which he controlled, might have provided a safe haven for the heretics.

83 *Leicester Chronicle*, 26 April 1851
84 *Leicester Chronicle*, 2 April 1853; 18 April 1857
85 James Crompton, *Leicestershire Lollards*, LAHS Transactions, 44, 11–44, p.43

Quarrying in the area may have provided a cave in which Lollard followers could secretly meet. However, no reliable evidence of its existence has so far been found.

Shoulder of Mutton Hill

Perhaps the earliest mention of Shoulder of Mutton Hill was in a deed of Westcotes Manor dated 1704, which refers to a field next to Stone Pit Close.[86] Documentary and cartographic sources show an area of land called Shoulder of Mutton Close with evidence that quarrying of sandstone took place around the area throughout the centuries. A deed of 1831, when part of the New Parks Estate was sold by Walter Ruding of Westcotes to John Mellor, alderman and later mayor of Leicester, refers to newly erected buildings and a stone quarry in Shoulder of Mutton Close, occupied by a tenant, Robert Hargrave, and his subtenants. Fields included in the sale were Andrews Far Close, the East Part of Andrews Far Close and the West Part of Andrews Far Close, three pieces of land, subdivided from what had been two fields, occupied by Thomas Mitchell but previously rented to Thomas Martin. The adjacent field or close, containing a barn, was named Stone Pit Meadow, where Robert Metcalf had taken over as tenant from Joseph Gamble in 1828, on a ten-year lease that included the Stone Quarry in Shoulder of Mutton Close.[87] Included in the transaction was Ash Spinney, an area of 32 perches, rented to Thomas Martin. All this land was on the north side of the Leicester to Hinckley turnpike road. The *Leicester Journal*, in 1835, advertised white and grey sand, free from iron, for sale for the use of plasterers and builders at the Sandpit, Shoulder of Mutton Hill. Pasture land was also available to rent for livestock. An announcement in the same newspaper in 1845 describes a cottage to let on Hinckley Road, near the Sandpit. The dwelling had a good cellar, three rooms on the ground floor three upstairs and hard and soft water pumps. Five years later, it was available to let again and described as 'a cottage with small garden and shrubbery, pleasantly situated near the Hinckley Turnpike-road on the Shoulder-of-Mutton Hill' and the Shepherd's Cottage for sale or to let, with an acre and a half of land, or thereabouts, abutting on the Turnpike-road and upon the railway now in the course of construction'. Excellent beds of brick earth and white sand were said to be under the property. A further advertisement for the Cottage on Shoulder of Mutton Hill appeared in 1857, with the same physical characteristics as it had in 1845.

The 1851 tithe map for the manors of Bromkinsthorpe and Westcotes identified Shoulder of Mutton Close as containing 13 acres three roods and 12 perches of pasture while Stone Pit Meadow Cottage's area is ten acres one rood and 33 perches. This map indicates buildings in the top corner of Shoulder of Mutton Close, presumably

86 Fox and Russell, p.71

87 Abstract of the Title of the Right Honourable Sir John Mellor to property forming part of the New Parks Estate in the County of Leicester, 1911

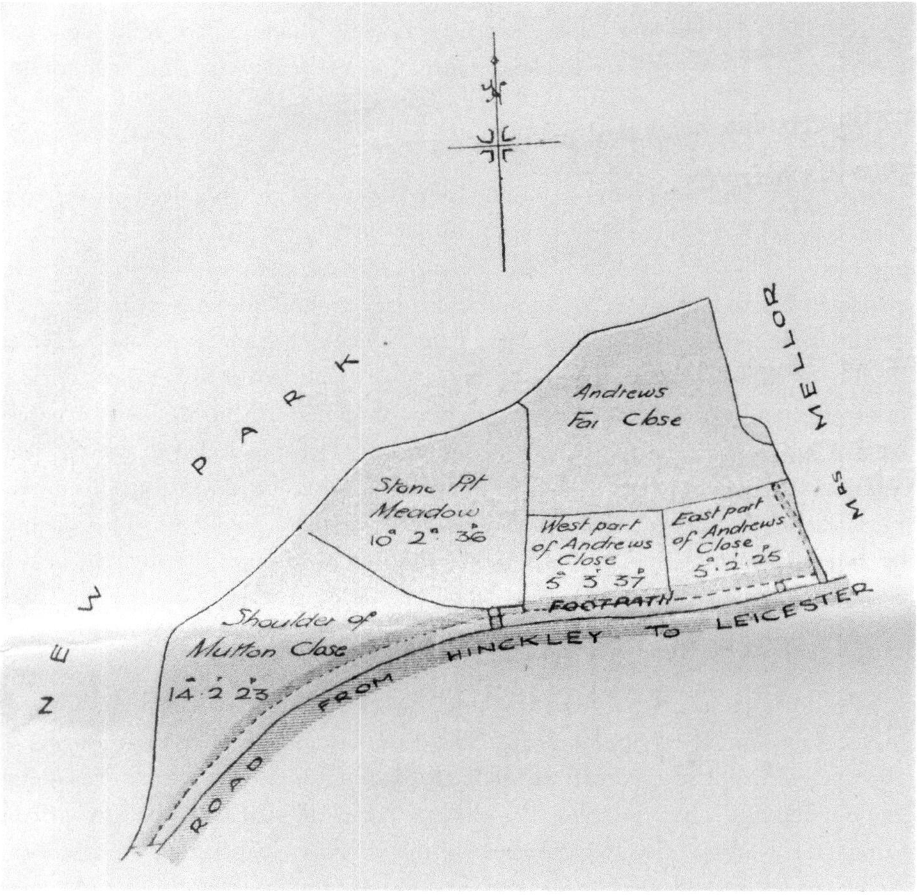

Field plan showing Shoulder of Mutton Hill, from property deeds.

the Cottage bearing its name. Census data from 1871 and 1881 shows that this Cottage was continuously inhabited throughout the Victorian period, in 1871 by four households but by 1881 there were just two. The tenants were not necessarily poor. Newspaper reports and Census data shows that in the 1870s William Mitchell, Mellor's agent and a registrar of births, deaths and marriages, was a resident and in 1890s, Mr Charlesworth the headmaster of Slater Street School and secretary of the Working Men's College, lived there. Other tenants were agricultural labourers, possibly working on New Parks Farm.

Cartographic evidence shows that the Cottage was on the site that became 459 Hinckley Road, on the plot of land where the park keeper's house, later transformed into the EcoHouse, was built in the 20th century, but slightly to the east of that building. There was an outdoor water pump on the south-west side of the cottage. When Leicester Corporation purchased land from the Mellor Estate to create Western Park in 1899, Shoulder of Mutton Close and the cottage do not seem to have been

The former Entrance Lodge to New Parks Farm, Hinckley Road.

included in the sale. Plans from 1902 show new drains being installed on the site by the Mellor Trustees. During the following decade, Leicester Corporation took ownership and William Ashton, the park attendant for Western Park, lived in the cottage with his family.[88] Sometime during the mid-1930s, a new house with a rectangular footprint was built for the park attendant, to the west of the Cottage which was then demolished. This new building became the EcoHouse in the 1990s. Another survivor of the early 19th century is the entrance lodge to New Parks Farm, now 445 Hinckley Road, where the original driveway joined the road. Its style is distinct from the later housing around it, featuring a rendered finish with decorative timber barge boards around its slate roof. At the time it was built, this house was in the countryside.

When the extension to the Swannington to Leicester Railway was under construction, not far from Shoulder of Mutton Close a kiln to fire the bricks used to build the bridge over the railway was in use. This was the site of a tragic accident in 1849 when three tramps sleeping inside it for warmth were killed when it collapsed. This was not the only tragedy to take place there. In 1856 a young man was killed by a cannon explosion in the ballast hole, presumably blasting in the sand pit. In another incident in the ballast pit, a man wheeling a barrow fell 12 feet from a plank and sustained an elbow fracture.The only cartographic evidence of the use of the site

88 *Kelly's Directory for Leicester*, 1912

for quarrying is in deeds produced in the 19th century which refer to and indicate on field maps Stone Pit Close. No quarrying or earthworks appear on Ordnance Survey maps, the first of which was published in 1888. However, further evidence of industrial activity in the form of brick making is provided by field names. Plans accompanying a sale catalogue for New Parks Farm of 1901 indicate Brick Kiln Close and Brick Kiln Meadow nearby.

Agriculture and employment

Local newspapers, such as the *Leicester Chronicle* and *Leicestershire Mercury*, contain reports on magistrates' court cases which provide evidence of the relationship between the town and countryside in the 19th century and also the class relationships of that time. As we have seen, these stories also give information on local agriculture, shown to have been a mixture of arable and pastoral farming. For example, as farmers both Thomas Stokes and his neighbour at New Parks Farm, George White, raised animals to be slaughtered as meat. Among the Christmas fare for sale in Leicester at the cattle market in 1855 were 14 half-bred sheep fed by White and five by Stokes.[89] In 1857 there was a superior heifer (young cow) fed by Stokes and 12 Shropshire Downs sheep fed by White on their New Parks farms.[90] The livestock were slaughtered at Sheen and Russell's butchers at West Bridge. At the next year's Leicester Christmas Meat Show, a Shropshire Downs sheep fed by White was slaughtered by the same butcher, while two heifers fed by Stokes were killed by Mr Snow on High Street.[91]In an earlier example, a strayed wether sheep had been in a New Parks field belonging to Mr Worthington for three weeks in May 1811.[92] A wether sheep is a ram that has been neutered by castration. Tenant farmer Worthington advertised in the local press for the owner to come forward and claim the animal by describing its identifying marks, and covering his expenses. Worthington occupied 240 acres of farmland in the area where New Parks House was later built, where the primary school is now.

One of the crops on Worthington's farm was potatoes. Potato picking or harvesting was a seasonal job which employed extra labour to get the crop in. In 1839 three men, Samuel and Thomas Lewin and William Smith, agreed to get up about three acres of potatoes for £3. They did some of the work, worth 15 shillings, but Worthington had paid them an advance of £1. They failed to come back to finish the job for two days as it was raining. When they did return Worthington was out, so they did no work. After that the three did not return at all.

Worthington took the men to court. They pleaded that Worthington had not wanted them to work and as they couldn't afford to be out of work any longer, they

89 *Leicester Chronicle*, 28 December 1855
90 *Leicester Chronicle*, 19 December 1857
91 *Leicester Chronicle*, 18 December 1858
92 *Leicester Journal and Midland Counties General Advertiser*, 10 May 1811

had taken another job. The men agreed to finish the work a couple of weeks after their court appearance, Worthington agreeing not to deduct his costs if they finished the work properly.[93]

It appears from this story that finding casual farm labourers was difficult, probably because of the proximity of Leicester and alternative employment which was better paid than farm work. This incident took place in November 1839, a time of year when more work was available in the seasonally cyclical framework knitting industry, as hosiers stocked up on items for winter. This may have caused a scarcity of people available for agricultural labour. In Leicestershire many workers were engaged in framework knitting, hiring a frame from a master hosier and working in their own homes with wives and children seaming, sewing up the finished items. They could supplement their income by taking seasonal work in agriculture, important as framework knitting was subject to seasonal fluctuations and slumps. Later in the century, boot and shoe manufacturing increased the opportunities for alternatives to agricultural labour.

Agricultural labourers, other than those in casual employment, usually agreed to work for an employer for a whole year at a time. Hiring fairs were annual events where farm workers offered themselves for hire as well as being market places and holiday occasions for fun. Leicester's fair took place annually on Humberstone Gate. In 1853 William Robinson was in court for absconding from the service of James Davenport of New Parks. Robinson denied he had been hired by Davenport for a full year, saying he only worked from week to week. The court was told Robinson had gone to work on Monday morning and left off without finishing his work or giving notice. A compromise was reached; Robinson was ordered to pay the legal expenses while agreeing to return to his master, Davenport, who consented to give him a pay rise of ten shillings a week. In effect Robinson's refusal to work was a strike over pay. In areas which were close to towns where there was alternative employment to lure labourers away from agriculture, wages were relatively higher than in more isolated rural areas where poverty was the norm.

Crime and conflict, poaching and punishment

Newspapers from the 19th century give some insight into the kind of life experienced by people living in or close to New Parks and elsewhere. After the end of the Napoleonic Wars prices for agricultural produce dropped, affecting the incomes of many farmers. At the same time, in Leicestershire, innovations in the hosiery and worsted industries coupled with changes in fashion from knee-length breeches with stockings on display to long trousers, combined with former soldiers returning from the wars seeking work, led to unemployment, under-employment and very low wages

93 *Leicestershire Mercury,* 30 November 1839.

New Parks farm buildings, early 19th century, by John Flower (1793-1861). (Image Leicestershire)

in the framework knitting industry, one of the district's chief employers.

Many urban dwellers were people who had moved into the town from the countryside or their children. Reliance on working for wages on piece rates in the small houses of the courts and terraced streets of Leicester meant that, in times of hardship, the countryside could be seen as a source of free food for those with the skill and nerve to trespass on the privately owned farm land and forage, rustle livestock or poach game. For poor people, subsistence poaching was an important way of supplementing their diet with meat.

Throughout the 19th century the local press reported on the trials of those who were caught stealing or killing wildlife for food or to sell as meat. As so many were arrested and imprisoned it can be assumed that these were the unlucky ones and that many more got away with it. In June 1823 ten unshorn sheep, belonging to John Clarke, were stolen during the night from a field on his New Parks farm. At that time, victims of crime had to pay for the costs of taking a felon to court. To protect themselves from the potential expense and to ensure more criminals were brought to justice, locally an organisation called the Leicester Association for the Prosecution of Felons was set up, a sort of insurance in case of crime. Clarke was a member and the Association allowed him to offer a reward of £30 to anyone who could help catch the sheep rustlers, even if it was one of their accomplices who turned in his co-offenders.[94]

94 *Leicester Chronicle*, 21 June 1823

To protect property, livestock and game on their land, land owners employed game keepers to help maintain wildlife and to police the area by keeping watch and apprehending trespassers and poachers. Gamekeepers were usually classed as servants but others had higher status. Lists of persons who had obtained game certificates for the year, the Game Lists for the County of Leicester, were published in local newspapers. According to the list, John Clarke's gamekeeper was John Turner.[95] A fee of £4 0s 10d was charged for this certification in 1841, so it was not cheap.

Poaching was always deemed to be a serious crime against the ruling class, as evidenced by the strict Anglo-Norman Forest Laws which restricted hunting to landowners. Hunting was only for the Norman lords and any commoner caught doing it could be hanged. The Swanimote Court proceedings of 1599, mentioned earlier, pronounced that no firearms should be carried or any borderer (bordar) carry a crossbow, gun or tiller to kill or disturb the Queen's game, or face a fine of 3s 4d, a lot of money for a poor person but a relatively light punishment compared to draconian penalties of later years.

Following the Restoration of Charles II in 1660, laws against poaching were tightened up after the lack of enforcement during and following the Civil Wars. Beginning with an Act in 1671, laws were passed restricting hunting and shooting rights on private property to landowners and their sons. Gamekeepers were hired to protect the land, while mantraps and spring guns were laid to catch poachers. The so-called Black Act of 1723 made poaching with a blackened face, a disguise or camouflage at night, a capital offence. Anyone caught could be hanged or face transportation to Tasmania or Australia if they were found to be carrying equipment for poaching.

These laws against poaching continued into the 19th century when new laws to control it were introduced. The Night Poaching Act of 1828 forbade the taking or destroying of game or entering private lands by night. Game included hares, pheasants, partridges, game birds and bustards. This law was added to in 1831 by Section 30 of the Game Act which stated it was an offence for any person to trespass in the day time, an hour before sunrise until an hour after sunset, by entering land to search for or pursue game, including rabbits. People could be charged with trespass if they fired a shot from a footpath where there was a right of way.

The Poaching Prevention Act of 1862 gave constables or peace officers the power to stop and search anyone they suspected of coming from land where they might have been poaching and also anyone suspected of aiding and abetting them in this crime. Vehicles and equipment could also be searched. This was the background to the arrest of many Leicester people over the years.

In 1833 Albert Gilbert, a labourer, was fined £1 plus costs of 11s 6d after his dog chased and caught a rabbit in New Parks. Gilbert, who pleaded guilty, said in his

95 *Leicester Journal*, 10 September 1841

defence that he didn't know his dog could do anything of that kind or he would not have taken it out. William Hyde, a brick-maker of Oxford Street in Leicester, was sentenced to a month in prison with hard labour after being convicted of using a snare to catch game.[96]

Henry Bright, William Orton, George Cox and John Hopkins pleaded guilty to trespassing in pursuit of game on 25 November 1841, the case being proved by the keeper. The poachers had come well-equipped with four game nets and two fine lurcher dogs. A hare was found on one of them. However, they swore that they did not own the dogs nor had they borrowed them, and they did not know how they came to be with them. They claimed the dogs belonged to John Clarke himself, in whose plantation, or wood, the poachers were caught. Orton and Hopkins had previous convictions for poaching. All four men were fined £5 plus costs. In addition Bright and Cox were sentenced to six weeks' hard labour, while Orton and Hopkins went down for six months.[97]

Poaching might be done to obtain meat but could also have been considered a sport. Men were well-prepared and organised to catch and kill game. Poachers came armed and tooled to carry out their work with a variety of implements. If caught with them they would find it difficult to deny the evidence that they were poachers. Penalties for those caught and convicted were relatively severe but as so many seem to have taken the risk, perhaps the odds were in the poachers' favour and many more went undetected.

Rabbits were particularly vulnerable. John Chapman was fined £1 after being convicted of trespassing in search of conies in 1865. He was caught when Thomas Highton of New Parks, a labourer working for farmer John Smith, saw Chapman on his master's land beating for rabbits. When asked his name by Highton, Chapman refused at first to give it. When Highton threatened to take him, he then lied and said it was Jackson.[98]

Poaching could be well-organised and involve large gangs. One Sunday, in March 1870, John Haywood, a gamekeeper, said he saw 17 men in a New Parks field occupied by Simeon Stretton. They were on either side of a hedge and were accompanied by ten dogs – snaps (whippets), greyhounds and terriers. The men were beating the fence for rabbits and hares. They chased a rabbit into its burrow, then one of the men pulled a ferret out of his pocket, put a line on it and put it into the hole. A lookout man gave the alarm and they ran away. Gamekeeper Haywood found the ferret still in the hole.

Samuel Fisher, a shoe finisher, and George Tow, a trimmer, were later arrested and charged with trespass in pursuit of conies. Fisher denied the charge, saying he

96 *Leicester Chronicle*, 16 March 1833
97 *Leicester Chronicle*, 4 December 1841
98 *Leicester Journal*, 13 January 1865

was in bed and hadn't gone out on the Sunday. A man called Bond provided Tow with an alibi. Bond claimed he had been out on Sunday for dinner and tea. Hannah Tow said Bond came to their house on Syston Street at about 3pm and stopped there until 6pm. George Tow said he had been out with Bond on Sunday morning and they had been for a walk round Cropston. They got back to Leicester at about 12.30pm and Bond went for his dinner. Tow went to the North Bridge Inn for some ale. Bond came back for him between 1.30pm and 2 pm. They remained in the pub until turning out time when they went to Tow's house until 6.15pm. Then they went to the Pack Horse, where they said they stayed until the early hours. The court did not believe them and they were fined £3 each plus costs or six weeks' hard labour. [99]

George White, according to the 1871 Census, was a farmer of 236 acres in New Parks, on the site of Western Park, where he employed seven labourers and two boys. His son-in-law, William Berry, worked with him as a farmer too. In 1861 Dean Williams, a hawker of Leicester, was caught with a gun on White's land. Williams was seen with the gun and several shots were heard. When caught and searched he was found to be carrying a partridge, a rabbit and a pigeon in his pocket. Special coats, with very large, interior pockets to carry the bodies of animals, were worn for shooting. Williams gave a false name to George White who followed him towards Leicester. Williams then took the gun from his pocket and threatened to beat White with it if he didn't go away. A struggle ensued, injuring White, but the gun was wrested from Williams who was brought to Leicester and identified. As it was his first offence he was fined £2 10s 0d or six weeks in gaol.[100] Although it was said to be Williams's first conviction, reports show he had actually had a brush with the law only a month earlier when, together with shoemaker Henry Monk, he was accused of stealing about 30 fowls, worth around £30, from Thomas Stokes's farm but there was insufficient evidence for a conviction.[101]

That same year there was another poaching incident on George White's farm. William Collins was charged with trespassing in pursuit of game on 24 March. A gardener called William Heyrick told a court he knew the land was occupied by White and owned by John Mellor. He had seen Collins on the land at about 11.30am, beating for conies with two companions and a dog. Heyrick told the men they were trespassing but they replied that they did not understand him. Heyrick only recognised Collins, so he was the one charged and fined £1 or 21 days' hard labour.[102]

Again on George White's land in May 1870, Leicester elastic weaver, Isaac Ward, was convicted of trespassing in search of conies. James Johnson saw him and seven

---

99 *Leicester Chronicle*, 19 March 1879
100 *Leicester Journal*, 7 June 1861
101 *Leicester Chronicle*, 2 March 1861
102 *Leicester Chronicle*, 20 April 1861

others with two dogs around a rabbit hole. When they saw Johnson they ran away but he managed to catch Ward and handed him over to PC Achurch. Ward was fined £2 plus costs or two months imprisonment.[103]

Not everyone accused of poaching was convicted. In 1837 John Breward was charged with trespass in pursuit of conies on James Wykes's New Parks Farm by Thomas Slater, a shepherd working for John Clarke. Breward admitted shooting rabbits but said he had the permission of his employer, Mr Wykes, who confirmed this. John Taylor, the gamekeeper for the liberty of New Parks, stated that Mr Mellor, the land owner, claimed the right to all the game on the land in question, a claim that Mr Wykes, the tenant, denied. Wykes asserted he had formed the warren himself and stocked it with rabbits from Bardon Park. As the gamekeeper was unable to prove the case, it was dismissed.[104]

William Harris, a dyer, and Joseph Cooper, a shoe finisher, were another pair who found themselves in court, accused of trespass in search of conies on land belonging to the Midland Railway where it crosses New Parks in April 1864. Joseph Smith's gamekeeper saw the men with five or six others with three terriers on the embankment where there were rabbit holes. When they saw Smith they all ran off, except for Harris who stopped and spoke to Smith and John Hayward, the gamekeepers. Harris told them he had been getting coltsfoot flowers but when the keepers searched him they didn't find any. Harris said he had seen the dogs, which were not his, at work on the bank. John Hayward told the magistrates he had seen the two defendants with six or seven other men, beating along the railway embankment with three or four dogs. They all seemed to be one party. Cooper had run off with the others. Both Harris and Cooper told the court they had been out for a walk and saw a large number of men getting violets. They thought there was no harm in it, so they joined in. They were down on their knees looking for flowers when the gamekeeper came. Harris added he was taking out his two children for an airing as they were recovering from illness. He was getting the flowers for them. Two witnesses said this was true and that they had seen the men go there in twos and threes, showing they were not all one party. The case was dismissed.[105]

Another case, which emphasises the class prejudices of the times, shows how a person's appearance could be an important factor as to whether defendants' excuses were believed or not. John Roberts and Alfred Collyer were two respectably dressed young men of Leicester who were charged with poaching in New Parks at the end of July 1876. John Haywood, the gamekeeper to Captain Pochin of Braunstone Hall, said he saw them both with a dog at around 7pm. They were beating a hedge and a startled rabbit ran out with the dog chasing it. When Haywood got up to them,

103 *Leicester Chronicle*, 14 May 1870
104 *Leicestershire Mercury*, 15 July 1837
105 *Leicester Chronicle*, 7 May 1864

Rural view of the Mellor Estate, Western Park Estate brochure, c.1908. (Records Office of Leicester, Leicestershire and Rutland)

Roberts was at a rabbit hole. Collyer said that he was visiting the farmer, Mr Johnson. After tea, he and Roberts went round Johnson's farm. They took Johnson's dog with them. He said they never saw a rabbit and had no intention of taking game. When they returned the house was locked up as Mr Johnson had gone out, so they decided to have a lie down but then the dog began to scratch at the hedge. They went to see what the dog had discovered and found a lot of hay and maggots. A rabbit had gone in the hole and died. Roberts corroborated this story. Mrs Roberts, the defendant's mother, and Mr Johnson told the court the defendants were on a visit to them. Johnson said that the young men had gone for an evening walk and let the dog loose without him knowing. He did not think they meant any harm. The case was dismissed.[106]

Only a year later, one of George White's employees, John Tilley, a waggoner, stole a fowl valued at eight shillings. William Berry, White's son-in-law, described to a court how Tilley had returned to the farmhouse after working in a field. Tilley was given his usual beer by Berry. In farming, workers were usually given beer as part of their wages, often brewed at the farm. Tilley should have gone home but when Berry crossed the farm yard he heard someone in the stable. He went inside and found Tilley in the dark, who told him to put the light out as he thought someone was about. Berry told him not to wait as he would see to them and went outside where he locked up before going back to the stable. There he found Tilley with a dead fowl in the manger, the trough for the animals' food. The bird was warm, showing it had been killed recently. Somehow, perhaps by sending a messenger, the police were called and PC Goodman

106 *Leicester Chronicle*, 19 August 1876

arrived. PC Goodman told the court he had been watching Mr White's premises at about 6pm. He saw Tilley come out of the stable carrying a basket on his arm with a lid on it, covered over by his coat. Inside the basket was a dead fowl. In his other hand he held an empty basket. Tilley said he had found the dead bird in the gutter, picked it up and threw it in the manger. Now he was taking it home to pluck.[107]

Frederick James, a machinist, was charged with stealing six fowls worth 11 shillings from Thomas Cufflin's barn in New Parks in April 1863. This was just five days after he had stolen five other birds belonging to Ezra Peel Smith, also of New Parks but who lived on Friar's Causeway according to the 1861 and 1871 Census. James had broken into Cufflin's and Smith's barns by taking the slates off the roof and taking away five hens and a cock. The birds were sold to Charles Bailey, a fishmonger of Wharf Street who plucked and sold them. The heads of the birds were found in his dust-hole.

Samuel Ward, a shoemaker, was charged by Thomas Highton, a labourer, of trespass in search of game and conies on Ezra Peel Smith's farm in 1865. Highton said he was at work on Peel Smith's land when he saw Ward and three others with two dogs, beating for rabbits in the hedge separating Smith's land from that of Mr Stokes. When he went to them they ran into Mr Cufflin's field. Highton found a purse net at the bottom of a ditch, not far from where he first saw the men. Ward said he had gone to catch rats in the stack, with Mr Cufflin's permission. Not finding any, he threw down his ferrets and coat then sat down. While he was sitting, Ward said his dogs found a rabbit hole in Mr Stokes's field, so he went to get them back. He said he didn't actually go into Mr Stokes's field. He wasn't believed by the magistrates and was fined £1 or 14 days' hard labour.[108]

It wasn't just rabbits, game and livestock that tempted poorer people to take a chance on taking foodstuffs from the land. Two boys, Julian Marvin Bullivant and Edward Burbidge, were accused of stealing strawberries from a New Parks garden in 1866. A warrant for the boys was dropped when the costs were paid.[109] Another young boy, William Headley, was charged with stealing 3d of walnuts from one of White's trees in October 1871. He was fined 5s 3d or ten days imprisonment.[110] October was clearly walnut season as another youth, Arthur Hunt, was also charged with stealing walnuts in the same month as Headley. He and two other boys were seen by William Berry under Mr White's walnut tree, knocking them off and picking them up. Arthur was caught with nuts in a pocket handkerchief by Berry. He was fined five shillings or seven days in prison.[111]

107 *Leicester Chronicle*, 30 September 1871
108 *Leicester Chronicle*, 7 October 1865
109 *Leicestershire Mercury*, 20 July 1866
110 *Leicester Journal*, 20 October 1871
111 *Leicester Journal*, 13 October 1871

A case against William Lagor, a shoehand, accused of stealing mushrooms belonging to farmer Francis Stafford of Braunstone Frith was dismissed. Lagor was caught in the field with a 3lb bag of mushrooms by one of Stafford's employees in August 1900. He pleaded not guilty, saying he had bought the mushrooms from another man for 6d outside a pub. A witness came forward to support this and the case was dismissed. A similar excuse did not help apprentice Percy Bambury, also accused of stealing mushrooms from Stafford at Braunstone Frith. The lad was seen picking them and had a bag of them weighing one and a half pounds on him, worth 6d, when he was caught. Percy said he had bought the mushrooms from another lad for a penny. He wasn't believed and was fined 15 shillings including costs.[112]

After Thomas Stokes moved into New Parks House in 1846, not only did he do some farming himself, he also rented out some of his land to tenant farmers. One of these was William Key who lived at Enderby Grange. Like the other farmers, Key often had trouble with trespassers and poachers. Thomas Morley, alias Sutton, a shoemaker and James Knott, a framework knitter who both lived in Leicester were charged with trespassing in search of game by Thomas Gamble, a New Parks wagoner, perhaps employed by Key. Gamble saw Morley and Knott at 4am on 27 April 1866. Knot had a gun and was carrying a hare. Gamble went up to them and asked what they were doing. Knott swore at him, 'You b.....! What have you to do with it, when we were on the footpath?' Knott then threw stones at Gamble. The two headed to Fosse Road, followed by Gamble, where they threw stones at him again. Knott pointed the gun at Gamble and threatened to shoot him. John Thomas Gamble, the son of the wagoner, corroborated his father's story so must have been there too. Morley was fined £1 plus costs, Knott 40 shillings plus costs. As Key's landlord, Mr Stokes, one of the magistrates, retired from the bench for the hearing.[113]

In late December 1867, three men from Leicester, Joseph Beadsworth and George Middleton, who were shoe riveters, and William Cave, a shoe finisher, were arrested and charged with trespassing on William Key's farm. Key's son gave evidence that he had seen the men on his father's land accompanied by two dogs and a ferret. Two of the men were down in a dyke at a rabbit hole, drawing a ferret out of the hole with a string. They told Mr Key they'd come to catch rats. Key told them to go to the Lodge and give their names. Cave said he was Roland Manship and Beardsworth claimed to be George Cox. Only Middleton gave his real name. Key searched them and found a ferret and a rat bag. Thomas Gamble, the wagoner, corroborated this evidence. The three men were fined one pound each or 14 days in prison.[114]

Stealing three hen's eggs, valued at 3d, from William Key was the charge faced by William Manship and Alfred Clark of Leicester in 1876. James Johnson, a shepherd

112 *Leicester Chronicle*, 1 September 1900
113 *Leicester Journal*, 18 May 1866
114 *Leicester Journal*, 11 January 1867

saw the two men in Key's yard early in the morning. He saw Manship come out of the cow house and close the door. Manship had three eggs in his hand and Johnson was following him out. Johnson said he challenged them and charged them with stealing the eggs. Manship then threatened him, saying if he had a pebble he'd break his head. Manship was later arrested by PC Bott and charged with stealing eggs. On his way to gaol, Manship told Bott he had taken the eggs out of the nest as he thought they had been laid by a stray hen. He had given some to Clark. As they had been in gaol before, the men were refused bail and committed for trial.[115]

Offences involving firearms seem to have been a regular occurrence. Thomas Davis, a shoemaker, was charged with using a gun to kill game in August 1867. Gamekeeper Haywood saw Davis with a gun in a shooting position looking for game in a field of beans belonging to Simeon Stretton. When Davis saw the keeper, he laid down his gun among the beans but he was caught and charged. Davis said he was sorry to Haywood, it was his first time and begged him to let him go, claiming his name was John Williams of Braunstone Gate. Haywood didn't trust him and so he took him to PC Jones of Braunstone who recognised him and knew his real name. Davis's excuse was that rather than hunting game, he had gone to shoot small birds for stuffing, and seeing an owl, he wanted to shoot it and stuff it. That was why he had gone along the path in the bean field. He was fined 12s 6d including costs or ten days' hard labour.[116] Taxidermy was a popular hobby in Victorian times so the excuse was not as outlandish as it might appear in the 21st century.

Thomas Cort, a nail maker, failed to appear in court when he was charged with having a hare in his possession at New Parks in July 1878. Two policemen, PC Mantle and PC Carter, heard the report of a gun at around 4am on 12 July. They had walked nearly to the Glenfield footpath when they saw Cort in a field near a spinney belonging to Sir William Henry Salt. Cort had a gun and ran away. The police told him that they knew him so there was no point in running. Cort told them he had shot a leveret (a young hare) and offered them a shilling to say nothing. PC Mantle took both the gun and the hare. Cort told the policemen he had got up at 2.30am to go out with his gun. In his absence he was fined £5 plus 12 shillings costs or two months' hard labour.[117]

Sometimes guns could be the cause of tragedies. In 1877 Thomas William Thomas, 16-year-old son of Cadwallader Thomas who succeeded George White at New Parks Farm, was at home with his family cleaning an old gun ready to go out shooting. A candle was on the table and when Thomas blew down the barrel near the flame a spark caused an explosion. Some gunpowder left in the barrel exploded, injuring the poor lad so seriously he died in the Infirmary the next day.[118] The inquest at the Swan and

115 *Leicester Chronicle*, 12 August 1876
116 *Leicester Chronicle*, 24 August 1867
117 *Leicester Chronicle*, 27 July 1878
118 *Leicestershire Daily Mercury*, 1 September 1877

Rushes heard that Thomas was cleaning an old gun barrel that he planned to fit with a different stock. He said to his brothers and another boy who were present, 'See me blow the candle out,' as he placed the end of the gun near the flame and blew down the barrel. Older brother Samuel had warned him to check there was no powder in it. Another brother, John Lewis Thomas, and George Murby, a lad working on the farm corroborated the tragic story.[119]

Another gun tragedy that shocked Leicester was when Richard Shirley Harris, eldest son of Richard Harris of Knighton House and nephew of John Dove Harris MP, was killed in November 1857. Married for just two years, 23–year-old Richard Shirley Harris was a young man who lived at Newfoundpool, in the building that was to become the Empire Hotel. He had gone out shooting one Saturday afternoon on a farm at New Parks. When he didn't return home as expected, a search party which included Thomas Fielding Johnson set out to look for him after Richard's brother, George Shirley Harris, asked for help. Fielding Johnson was a manufacturer living in another of the Newfoundpool houses at that time. They met several policemen at the Ashby Toll Gate on Groby Road who joined the search, scouring the fields and hedges around New Parks Farm and the neighbourhood. A small party went to search near the Glenfield Tunnel at 4.30am, then the search was abandoned until it was light.

The search began again at 6.30 the next morning, a Sunday, and within a few minutes of leaving Thomas Scotton Clarke's house, Harris's body was found with his faithful pointer dog beside him, in the field called the Bird's Nest, next to the Cottage Field. The dog showed the searchers where his master lay by galloping to the middle of the field 200 or 300 yards from the house and then back to the corner of the field. The party went after him and found Richard's body near the hedge. He was lying on his back by a small plantation, within two or three feet of some rails in front of a low, quick set fence. His gun and cap were on the other side of the rails. A gunshot through his right arm and then into that side of his body had killed him. As there was no sign of a struggle, the opinion was that he was coming out of the plantation when the gun accidentally went off as he was climbing the fence. There was a place in the hedge within a yard of the body where his loyal dog had been lying all night. Both barrels of the gun had been fired. Richard's gold watch and money had not been taken and his hands were clean. There was a hare in his coat pocket. His gun rod, which he carried by his side, was on the ground about two feet away.

Thomas Scotton Clarke was a farmer and grazier, who lived in a house on a farm in the liberty of New Parks, which had previously been the home of Richard Harris's maternal grandfather, Mr Shirley. This was probably Bird's Nest Farm. Scotton Clarke came from Great Bowden where he was listed as 'in Trade' rather than being Gentry in Post Office Directories of 1849 and 1855.[120] When he moved to New Parks with

119 *Leicester Journal*, 7 September 1877

120 *Post Office Directory of Leicestershire and Rutland*, 1849 and 1855

his wife, Drusilla, he was farming 205 acres and employed five labourers and three boys. He appears to have had no connection with John Clarke. Harris had permission to be on the land hunting and had been seen by Scotton Clarke crossing the Cottage Field with his dog and his gun. They spoke and Harris told Clarke he had shot one hare, then wounded another. The wounded hare had gone towards the Bird's Nest and Harris had set off that way to look for it. This was where the body, which was carried to Clarke's house, was discovered. One of Scotton Clarke's servants, William Webb, told the inquest that he had heard two shots of a gun while he was in the stack-yard the day before, coming from the direction where Harris's body was found. The shots followed one another quickly. The tragedy was not being suicide but instead an awful accident was the verdict at the coroner's inquest.

Life in Victorian times could be harsh and sometimes brutal. Nevertheless, there was a growing sense of awareness of the need for kindness, compassion and social change, not just towards people but animals too. In 1890, John Ainge, a butcher of Gresham Street in Leicester, was summoned by Inspector Alexander of the RSPCA for cruelty to sheep in New Parks. Alexander had gone to inspect premises in New Parks and found the poor creature in a small outhouse. On the floor were several inches of dung, there was no food or water in the place. The sheep had several bad sores which appeared to be dressed with lime as there were full buckets of the substance there. The sheep was hungry and when the inspector let it into an adjoining outhouse where there was some hay, it ate ravenously. In the field was the carcass of another emaciated sheep which had been dead for about five weeks. In his defence, Ainge said that the live sheep was only suffering from maggots and that treating it with lime was the best thing in the world for it, but the court heard the animal was neglected and a bag of bones. Ainge had shown a butcher-like hardness of heart in not having properly cared for his sheep.[121]

Evidence from court case reports gives information about what was produced on the farms of rural New Parks. Cattle for meat, sheep, poultry and pigs were reared. Crops mentioned included beans, strawberries, mushrooms, walnuts, potatoes and cereal. Evidence in a trial from 1848 shows that oats were grown as Thomas Bowley was charged by PC Job Glover with stealing a quantity of oats, the property of the Midland Railway Company in the district of New Parks. Glover said he saw Bowley cutting the oats with a sickle on land through which the railway was to pass. He said Bowley had cut about 130lb of the cereal and had an ass and a cart ready to carry the crop away. Bowley said he hadn't been aware he was doing anything wrong. He had been working on the line and seeing the oats trampled down, he cut some to give to his ass. The cart had been used to bring fencing to the railway. Whether he was aware he was committing a crime or not, Bowley was ordered to pay costs of 20s 6d.[122]

---

121 *Leicestershire Daily Mercury*, 17 December 1890
122 *Leicestershire Mercury*, 26 August 1848

Fields around New Parks House. (Records Office of Leicester, Leicestershire and Rutland)

Further evidence of the kind of farming activity that took place in the area can be seen from reports of auction sales. Hay was commonly sold by auction as fodder for the horses owned by town dwellers. John Abell was bailiff and farmer at Bird's Nest Farm between the 1860s and 1881. Much of his work appears to have been raising and caring for animals on behalf of Sir William Henry Salt. Salt was the son of Sir Titus Salt, famous as the textile mill owner and founder of Saltaire in Yorkshire, a model community for his workers. Sir William's connection with New Parks was due to his wife, Emma Dove Octaviana Harris, daughter of John Dove Harris, former MP and mayor of Leicester and Emma Shirley who owned land in the area. The Salts were tenants at Kirby Frith Hall before moving to Maplewell.

In May 1876 an auction at the farm offered for sale livestock from a pedigree herd, perhaps a hobby of Salt's. The shorthorn cows and heifers in the sale were of two 'tribes' or bloodlines, Gwynnes, said to be 'fashionable' at the time and Blanches. The advertisement shows that these valuable animals were treated and respected as individuals with names that reflected their pedigree: one cow among those being sold was described as 'the favourite', named Duchess Gwynne, who sold for 265 guineas, and her female heifer calf. Another was Flossy Gwynne (sold for 100 guineas) and her seven descendants. From the Blanche line was Lady Blanche II (sold for nine guineas) and her three calves, Blanche Kale and her four descendants, plus other choice animals. The fathers or sires of the calves were also sold and were advertised as having been bred by a Mr Bates. These bulls had the aristocratic-sounding names

Baron Waterloo, Marquis of York (son of the 7th Duke of York), and Lord Oxford, a fine red bull imported from the US, the fifth beast to bear that name.

Demonstrating that this was an auction of special interest, the sale was conducted by a London auctioneer, John Thornton of Hanover Square.[123] Before the sale, a luncheon hosted by Salt was served in a large marquee on the farm. The auction attracted members of the aristocracy, including Lord Faversham, Lord Skelmersdale, the Earl of Bective, Sir Curtis Lampstone, as well as many untitled genteman farmers. Shorthorn cattle were a relatively new breed in England, originating in the late 18th century; the Shorthorn Society of Great Britain and Ireland had only been founded two years earlier. Other cattle in the sale were owned by Mr Cheney of Gaddesby and Mr Lister of Kirklevinton.[124]

The beginning of the end

Many of the stories related so far happened in the 1850s and 1860s, the period of Victorian High Farming, dubbed the 'golden age of English agriculture' by Lord Ernle.[125] The term High Farming referred to agriculture using the most advanced methods of the time. Farming was profitable: land values and rents were relatively high as farmers worked hard to keep up with the growing demand for food during the time of industrial expansion which caused urban population growth. From the 1850s onwards, more people lived in towns and cities than lived and worked in the countryside and had become dependent on wages to buy food. Prices of grain remained high because of the impacts of the Crimean War between 1853 and 1856, which prevented exports from Russia, and the American Civil War between 1861 and 1865 which stopped imports arriving from the USA.

The 1870s was a tough decade for farmers. The agricultural golden age came to an end from the mid-1870s with the Great Depression that saw prices for produce falling, rents and land values dropping, farmers forced off the land and much former arable land converted to grass for less labour-intensive pasture. After the American Civil War much of the Midwest was settled and connected by railways to the east coast. New inventions, like the reaper-binder of 1873, helped the prairie farmers double production. Wheat and flour imports to the UK increased by 90 per cent between 1871–1875 and 1896–1900 while meat imports rose by 300 per cent and for butter and cheese by 110 per cent. At the same time, faster shipping and refrigeration on board ships facilitated this growth in North American exports. In Britain there were bad harvests in 1875, 1877, 1878 and a very wet summer in 1879. The price of wheat in Britain dropped from 56 shillings a quarter between 1867–1871, down to 27s 3d

123 *Leicester Guardian*, 15 March 1876

124 *Leicester Guardian*, 17 May 1876

125 P. J. Perry: *High Farming in Victorian Britain: Prospect and Retrospect*, Agricultural History, Vol. 55, No.2, April 1981, pp.156–166, p.156

Boundary marker, 1891, in Newarke Houses Museum.

between 1894 to 1898. More and more agricultural workers left the land and moved to find work in the expanding towns and cities. Many people from the surrounding counties moved to Leicester to work in the hosiery and boot and shoe industries.

Of course, New Parks was not immune from what was happening nationally and in the rest of the world. Thomas Scotton Clarke left New Parks and moved to Leire in around 1870 where he worked a much smaller farm of 82 acres, assisted by just two labourers and two boys. The size of his property in Leire reduced further, to 57 acres by the time of the 1881 Census. Although not part of the area under discussion, the population of Leire fell from 406 in 1841 to 354 in 1871 and just 286 a decade later, showing the impact of rural depopulation in those years.[126] George White had been a tenant farmer and after he died in 1876, New Parks Farm was advertised to let by John Mellor the landowner.[127] The excellent farm, which was 'Close to the town of Leicester, abutting on the Hinckley Road', consisted of upwards of 245 acres of arable and grass land. Prospective tenants could view the farm by applying to William Mitchell of The Cottage, Shoulder of Mutton Hill.

The new tenant who moved into New Parks Farm did not have such a prosperous business or lifestyle as George White. Just five years later a distress warrant was issued against this next tenant, Cadwallader Thomas, for the sale of his animals on New Parks Farm, including a yearling bull, 12 dairy cows, 29 lamb hogs and five cart horses. Cadwallader Thomas had debts totalling £4,665, including unpaid rent.[128] The Thomas family had moved to New Parks from Montgomeryshire in Wales where Cadwallader had farmed 510 acres. Cadwallader and his family's time at New Parks was not a happy one. His 16-year-old son, Thomas William Thomas, had died suddenly and shockingly in a shooting accident soon after they moved in. Possibly as a result of this trauma, Cadwallader developed mental health issues. He was also plagued by conflicts with people perceived to be trespassing on his land, resulting in several court cases. The first of these incidents was on 13 April 1877 when Robert Moore and Thomas Atkins, two militiamen, were summoned for breaking fences at New Parks. Samuel and Thomas William Thomas followed the militiamen through a spinney and saw them break down six hedges, causing ten shillings worth of damage. The incident happened at 1pm but the case was dismissed as witnesses said the two men were at home at that time.[129]

As we have already seen, poaching was an issue for New Parks farmers and teenage Samuel Thomas had his own encounter with some vicious ones a few days after the above incident. On 17 April Samuel had been out at 5am crossing a field where he saw the tracks of three men. He followed and found two of them, shoehand William Webster and bricklayer George Sutton. Sutton shot a hare, Webster picked it up and put it in Sutton's pocket. They threatened Samuel and threw stones at him. Webster pointed the gun at the boy and threatened to blow his brains out. In court Samuel claimed to have known Webster for two and a half years, which seems unlikely as Webster had been in prison until only six months before. The trial, in which the

126 Census data 1841, 1851, 1861, 1871, 1881
127 *Leicester Daily Mercury*, 16 March 1876
128 *Leicester Journal*, 15 April 1881
129 *Leicester Journal*, 27 April 1877

poachers were fined £5 each and 10s 6d costs or two months imprisonment, didn't take place until five months later.[130]

Just over a week following the encounter with the poachers, on 26 April 1877, William Pettitt, a factory hand, and framework knitter John Bailey damaged a fence worth 15 shillings. They had been seen going in and out of the spinney 'where they had no business to be'. The trespassers were each fined 2s 6d with 14 shillings costs and 7s 6d damages or a month hard labour.[131] The following month, on 31 May, two lads, Leonard Harvey and Frederick Tidmarsh, were charged with damaging wheat worth five shillings. Young Samuel and Thomas William Thomas had seen them wandering over the farm causing the damage. In court the defendants denied the charge but were found guilty and fined 6d each plus 12 shillings costs or seven days in prison.[132]

Just a month after Thomas William Thomas's horrific death when cleaning the barrel of a gun, there was another incident, involving confrontation. William Dyson and two others were charged with stealing walnuts belonging to Cadwallader. Samuel caught hold of Dyson who tried to hit him with a stick. Dyson pleaded guilty and was fined £1 2s 6d, including damages and costs of 14 shillings or 14 days' hard labour. His two accomplices got away.[133]

There were more incidents the following year. On 23 June William Carter and William Muggleton were lying drinking in one of Cadwallader's fields. They refused to move and used 'uncomplimentary language' when asked to do so. Carter was a 47-year-old brickmaker who lived in one of the courts off Sanvey Gate and his neighbour Muggleton was a shoehand. They were both fined five shillings plus two shillings for damage they had caused to the grass which was for mowing. In court on the same day another case brought by Cadwallader was against William Ward, another shoehand who had done a shilling's worth of damage to the mowing grass. Cadwallader was a minute late entering the court and so the case was dismissed as he was judged to have failed to appear. He ended up having to pay costs for the case.[134] Autumn brought out people after the farm's walnuts. Samuel Thomas caught Joseph Snow, another shoehand, stealing walnuts. Snow was convicted and fined 2s 6d.[135]

The summer following the incident involving Carter and Muggleton, there was a particularly nasty incident involving Cadwallader and Samuel Thomas who were charged with assault. Thomas Ward and his wife were going for an evening walk on the Dane Hills on 25 June 1878 when they saw Cadawallader and his son, each holding a bitterly crying child. Ward asked them what they were doing to the children. The

130 *Leicester Journal*, 28 September 1877
131 *Leicester Journal*, 11 May 1877
132 *Leicester Journal*, 15 June 1877
133 *Leicester Journal*, 10 August 1877
134 *Leicester Weekly Post*, 6 July 1877
135 *Leicester Daily Post*, 15 October 1877

Thomases said the children were trespassing and they were taking them to the police station. Ward said he thought it would be better if they took their names and addresses and let them go. Samuel then replied that the Wards were trespassing themselves. 'Oh bring him on too,' Cadawallader was said to have responded. Samuel seized Ward who got away but not before being hit on the head with a stick and kicked twice. A witness, John Scotney, was accused by Samuel of hitting him but this was dismissed as an attempt to prevent Scotney giving evidence. In Cadwallader Thomas's defence it was claimed that the assault was caused by Ward resisting arrest and after that it was a free fight. The judge's verdict was that Thomas had no right to arrest Ward or the children. Ward was awarded £5 damages.[136]

In a later incident, Samuel Thomas successfully prosecuted two men for trespassing in search of conies on 26 January 1881. Fines of 40 shillings were imposed on Edwin Jackson, a labourer, and William Sleath, a shopkeeper.[137]

Cadawallader Thomas was in trouble with the law again in April 1881, for violence against perceived trespassers when he was charged with assaulting Cots Day. The newspaper report named her as Cots Day, either a nickname or a mistake as Dora Cotes Day was a milliner at P. Wardle & Company on Cheapside, where she lived above the shop with 13 other women.

Being able to go out for walks was important as a leisure activity for young women, like the many live-in shop workers who had no personal space of their own. Dora told the court she was walking through a field on a pathway with a friend when she heard someone shouting. It was Cadawallader, telling her she was trespassing. Dora said she hadn't realised and apologised but she was kicked on her hip and hit with a stick by Cadwallader who aggressively told her not to dare speak another word. This was witnessed by William and Ann Lawrence, a couple also out walking. Dora's friend, Eliza Chamberlain, was looking the other way and couldn't say she had seen what happened. As she was closest to the incident and Cadwallader's defence claimed the story was made up, the magistrate decided there was doubt and the case was dismissed.[138] This alleged violent incident against Miss Cotes Day took place on 18 April, just three days after a distress warrant had been issued against Thomas, compelling him to sell up, perhaps coinciding with the breakdown of his marriage, so was a time of considerable stress for him. Earlier incidents had occurred shortly after the death of his son, Thomas.

What happened to Cadwallader Thomas and his family after they lost New Parks Farm? At the time the farm had to be given up, younger son, 18-year-old John Lewis Thomas was still living in New Parks with his mother Elinor, who the 1881 Census, taken on 3 April, describes as a farmer of 340 acres (not a farmer's wife), employing

---

136 *Leicester Chronicle and Leicestershire Mercury*, 27 July 1878

137 *Leicester Journal*, 11 February 1881

138 *Leicester Chronicle*, 7 May 1881

eight men. Younger sisters Catherine and Lizzie and eight-year-old brother William lived with them. Cadwallader appears to have found work as a groom in Twycross and was separated from his wife. The separation seems to have happened before the insolvency proceedings. Their landlord John Mellor's agent put 150 acres of valuable summer grass on the farm 'lately occupied by Cadwallader Thomas' up for auction by Warner Sheppard and Wade in May 1881.[139] This was not the end of his troubles for Cadwallader, whose mental health problems saw him admitted to Carlton Hayes asylum where he died after many years as a patient in 1915.

It wasn't only New Parks Farm that changed hands around this time as Bird's Nest Farm was put up for sale in 1881.[140] John Abell of Bird's Nest Farm was selling a pure-bred herd of shorthorn cattle, a flock of Shropshire sheep belonging to Sir William Henry Salt, and Monarch, a 'well-known' cart horse stallion, because the farm was being given up.[141] Another farmer of New Parks, William H. Key, also gave up his farm at the Lodge off Groby Road around this time. In March 1880 and April 1881 Key's and Abell's livestock was offered for sale by auction in preparation for Abell leaving the farm and starting a new career as a beer and later coal agent on Grape Street off East Bond Street. He was still working as a coal agent at the age of 75. The beasts listed for sale show the kind of farming carried out on the farm. There were ten fat shorthorn bullocks, four three-year-old shorthorn steers, 14 Welsh runts, three calving Welsh cows, a Welsh heifer 'in full profit', two Welsh heifers in calf, four barren Welsh heifers, 14 porklet pigs, 40 couples of fowls, a flock of 230 sheep, Monarch a cart stallion, and various agricultural implements including a chaff cutter and pulper. Five other horses were also among the lots offered for sale: these horses were not anonymous creatures but all had names which were included in the advertisement: there was 'Captain' who was chestnut; brown mare 'Gilliver'; 'Blossom' who was a black mare; 'Billy', a grey; and 'Emma', a roan mare.[142] Let us hope they found good homes where they were well-treated and not overworked.

When the substantial land owner Sir John Mellor passed away in 1887, followed by his widow in 1894, the land was put up for sale by the trustees of his estate. Mellor's trustees began offering land on the New Parks Estate for sale in lots for building purposes from July 1887. There were several splendid sites on the estate for villa residences, the fields having a frontage on to Hinckley Road, within the boundary of the borough. Potential purchasers could see the plan of the estate at the offices of surveyors R. J. and J. Goodman on Friar Lane.[143] This was the beginning of the end of New Parks as an agricultural district. However, the end did not come

139 *Leicester Journal*, 20 May 1881
140 *Leicester Journal*, 11 February 1881 and 15 April 1881
141 *Leicester Chronicle*, 26 April 1881
142 *Leicester Journal*, 26 March 1880, 16 April 1881
143 Leicester Journal, 22 July 1887

View from Braunstone Avenue towards Gimson and Wyggeston lands, c.1935.

suddenly. Bird's Nest Farm was purchased by the Harris family's (not part of the Dove Harris family) Westcotes Estate and continued as a working farm well into the 20th century, as evidenced by the bills and receipts of tenant farmer John Harding. In June 1933, Harding purchased plough pads from A.E. Julian of Highcross Street and paid £1 11s 0d for repairs to his cart performed by William Harrison. In March 1935 Harding renewed his commercial vehicle insurance premium with the Yorkshire Insurance Company Limited and received an invoice for shoeing a horse, paring a mare's foot and repairs to a chain harrow from blacksmith R. Thompson of Glenfield where he had an account. His June account showed he had several horses reshod and repairs made to a mower and seed hopper. He also paid R. Newland, a cultivating contractor, to do some work on 12 acres of clover land for £6 12s 0d.[144] Birds Nest Farm was sold by the Westcotes Estate to Leicester City Corporation in 1936, under the threat of compulsory purchase.[145]

The 1939 Register, which recorded everyone in preparation for wartime measures, shows that most of the area's farms were still inhabited and operational as agricultural businesses on the eve of and during World War Two, although now the occupiers were tenants of Leicester City Corporation. Braunstone Frith Farm was a dairy farm, the home of farm foreman William Barfield and his family. The relocated or renamed

144 Receipted bills for services or goods supplied to John Harding, of Bird's Nest Farm, New Parks, ROLLR DE3181/2/1–6

145 Records of the Westcotes Estate, Leicester, ROLLR DE9149, DE9128/176

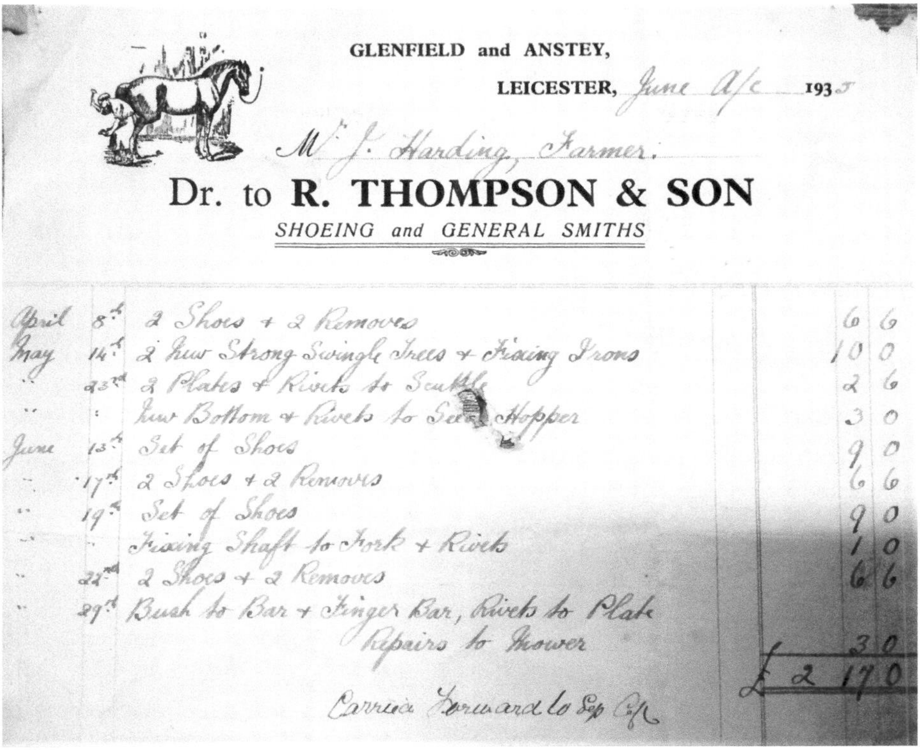

GLENFIELD and ANSTEY,

LEICESTER, June A/c 1935

Mr J. Harding, Farmer.

Dr. to **R. THOMPSON & SON**

SHOEING and GENERAL SMITHS

April	8th	2 Shoes + 2 Removes	6	6
May	14th	2 New Strong Swingle Trees + Fixing Irons	10	0
"	23rd	2 Plates + Rivets to Scuttle	2	6
"	"	New Bottom + Rivets to Seed Hopper	3	0
June	13th	Set of Shoes	9	0
"	17th	2 Shoes + 2 Removes	6	6
"	19th	Set of Shoes	9	0
"	"	Fixing Shaft to Fork + Rivets	1	0
"	22nd	2 Shoes + 2 Removes	6	6
"	29th	Bush to Bar + Finger Bar, Rivets to Plate Repairs to Mower	3	0
			£2 17	0

Carried Forward to Sep A/c

Blacksmith's bill, 1935. (Records Office of Leicester, Leicestershire and Rutland)

New Parks Farm in Dane Hills was the home of grazier and farmer, Walter Howkins and Edith, his wife. Western Park Farm Cottage was home to farmer Horace Cooper, his wife Hilda, son William and farm labourer Thomas Brewster. New cow stalls were built for Cooper during the 1920s. Western Park Farm House, the building of which survives on Park View, was the exception as it was occupied not by farmers but by Hetty and Henry Woodgate, a car and motor cycle sales and service manager. The farms were demolished as house building began after the war.

3

KIRBY FRITH

Kirby Frith Hall and estate

Tucked away between an industrial estate, the M1 motorway and Glenfield, Kirby Frith is an area that was separated from the rest of Leicester Forest as part of an area emparked by William, Lord Hastings, after he was granted its stewardship by Edward IV. The area came under the control of generations of the Hastings family when Sir Robert le Herle, whose family had been lords of the manor of Braunstone and Kirby Muxloe in the Middle Ages, had no male children. Herle left the property to his sister's son, Sir Ralph Hastings, in 1364. It remained with the Hastings family until around 1628. Documents in Leicester, Leicestershire and Rutland Records Office and the National Archives record some of the transactions relating to ownership and occupancy of the land at Kirby Frith, following the first enclosure in this area of Leicester Forest in 1526 and in the early modern period.

Kirby Frith Hall, a large country house with gardens and farm buildings, was built three and a half miles from Leicester, sometime following the enclosure, perhaps during the reign of Queen Elizabeth I, although no record of its construction has been discovered. As a sales catalogue from 1821 describes Kirby Frith Hall as having moats and a field called Draw-Bridge Close, it could be that the house was on the site of an earlier medieval building, perhaps a lodge of Leicester Forest, similar to the one called Bird's Nest. The description also refers to pasture fields called The Park and Free Bord, a reference back to when it was a deer park. At some point, probably in the 1720s or in 1730, Kirby Frith Hall was rebuilt, either on the same site or nearby, replacing any earlier building. A description of 1731 refers to the property as newly built.[146] The house and gardens survived into the 20th century and were situated in what was to become, after 1950, Western Park Golf Course.

In *Glimpses of Ancient Leicester*, Agnes Fielding Johnson, who may have been familiar with Kirby Frith Hall, describes a tablet on its walls bearing the initials E.R., with the royal arms and a fleur de lys, which she felt might be evidence that Queen Elizabeth I may have visited. Mrs Fielding Johnson also says that John Throsby mentions that in the Act of Enclosure in the early 17th century, one of the entrance gates to the hall, on

146 Jonathan E. O. Wilshere: *Old Kirby*, 1986

the Oaks Farm and Kirby Muxloe side, was called the Queen's Gate. Throsby related that 'a pavement of large forest stones, wide enough for two carriages to meet' was found there, supposed locally to be part of the old road traversed by Richard III and his army on the way to Bosworth. At the time of his writing in the 1790s, Throsby claimed to have been told by a local man that the road was still clearly visible and 'no doubt Queen Elizabeth, arriving from Kenilworth or Ashby, would pass along it to Kirby Frith Hall'.[147]

Commoners of the area complained to the Forest Court in 1623 that the ancient 'Queensyate' or Queen's Gate had been cleared and set back 240 yards by Sir Henry Hastings who had enclosed part of the land to the west of the road but his title was removed by the Enclosure Act of 1628.[148] However, no evidence exists that Queen Elizabeth ever visited Kirby Frith, an event that would surely have been recorded if she had. The description of Queen's Gate as 'ancient' in 1623 perhaps confirms this as any visit of Elizabeth I might still be within living memory or that of the previous generation.

The name may not have anything to do with Elizabeth at all, but could refer to the other queens associated with Leicester Forest who received an income from it: Margaret of Anjou who received lands around the Forest as part of her marriage settlement in 1465 or John of Gaunt's wife, Constance of Castile, who had claims to the throne of Castile. A document of 1705 said that rents from some lands in Leicester Forest formed part of the jointure, the financial provision for a widow, paid to the dowager Queen Catherine of Braganza (1638–1705), who had been the wife of Charles II. The document said that these lands were included in leases dating from 1628, following the enclosure.[149] Alternatively, the track or gate may have just been given the name in honour of a royal event. These regal references were also mentioned in an Historical Note in the sales particulars of 1915, '

The Hall possesses some considerable historical interest. In the courtyard is a tablet bearing the initials ER with the Royal Arms and fleur de lys. It is probable that Queen Elizabeth visited the house when making a progress through the country. It is also more than likely that King Richard III when marching his army to Bosworth Field passed through the Park. The old road from the Bow Bridge at Leicester traversed a section of the Park and one of the avenues of trees is still called King's Avenue.'[150]

As well as the Hall, other dwellings in Kirby Frith were a lodge and a gardener's cottage for people who worked for the occupant of the Hall, and farm buildings, sometimes owned by the same person who owned the Hall but leased or rented to a tenant farmer. Not many people lived in Kirby Frith during the 17th, 18th and 19th

147 Fielding Johnson, pp175–176
148 Fox and Russell
149 Fox and Russell, p.139
150 Kirby Hall and Manor Farm sales catalogue, September 1915, ROLLR DE182/19

centuries: there was just the gentleman's residence at the Hall with its household, and one or two farms occupied by tenant farmers, their families and servants. In 1846, according to *White's Gazetteer* there were just 20 souls residing in Kirby Frith's 300 acres.[151]

Wills and parish records for neighbouring villages, Kirby Muxloe and Glenfield, offer some clues as to who lived at Kirby Frith Hall but do not give a clear picture and are incomplete. Sometimes the actual owners had homes elsewhere. The earliest known occupiers of Kirby Frith Hall in the 16th century were the Styan family.[152] It is not known if the Styans had the Hall built or whether they moved into an existing property. Charles born in 1543 in Normanton in Yorkshire or his son Henry born in 1575 appear to have been the first to live in Kirby Frith. The evidence for this can be found in parish registers which show that another Henry Styan was baptised in Kirby Muxloe in 1598, followed by siblings Dorothy (1599), Annie (1603) and Thomas (1606). Christopher Styan's (brother of the older Henry, born in 1590) daughter was baptised in 1609, showing that a large family of more than one generation was living in Kirby Frith before 1600. Kirby Frith Hall may already, by 1613, have had other buildings associated with it around the estate as a bond, a legal document, was endorsed by Thomas Smyth of the 'Gotte House', Kirby Frith, probably a lodge at the entrance to the drive to the Hall.[153]

The baptism of the younger Henry Styan's eldest son and heir, a third Henry Styan (1628–1703), is recorded in Glenfield parish registers in 1626 as are those of his brother Thomas in 1630 and sister Jane in 1631. This younger Henry married Catherine (or Katherine) Tuke and had four daughters. Other records show that he was a landowner in that area and the west of Leicester. On his tomb in Glenfield Church was written, '

Here lieth the body of Henry Stain, late of Kirby Frith, Gent, who intermarried with Catherine, only daughter of Thomas Tuke and Mary his wife, by whom the said Henry had issue four daughters. He died the 3rd day of July 1703, aged 75 years.'[154]

An inventory of Henry and Catherine's possessions gives an impression of what their home was like in 1703; it gives details of their furniture and some of their farming and business activities, typical of the lesser gentry and yeoman farmers of the early modern period. The itemised list of property indicates what rooms there were in the house and what they contained and gives an idea of the layout of the house.

The kitchen is the first room on the list. The main feature of the room was a fireplace used for cooking which had fire irons and jacks for roasting meat, a long table which

---

151 *White's Gazetteer for Leicester*, 1846

152 Wilshere

153 Records of the Herrick family of Beaumanor Estates, 8 May 1613, ROLLR DG9/142

154 Nichols, *Bibliotecca Topographica Britannia, Vol. 8, Antiquities of Leicestershire.*

would have been used for food preparation, stools, brass and pewter items as well as other things. Having a separate cooking place was an innovation of Tudor times, when houses were built with fireplaces and chimneys for the first time. In a period that became known as the Great Rebuilding, many older domestic buildings were reconstructed or remodelled during the second half of the 16th century to include this new development, moving away from the smokey interiors of medieval homes which had a fire in the centre of the main hall and little ventilation. It also looks like coal, as well as wood, was used for cooking, another innovation of the mid to late 1600s.

The house had a new parlour, evidence of some recent reconstruction, which contained two tables, 12 chairs and hangings and next to this a lodging parlour with two beds, presumably a place for guests. In earlier times, the master of the house and his wife would have slept downstairs but this modern house had an upper floor now used for sleeping, rather than storage. Over the kitchen was a chamber with a bed, bedding and six chairs, a table and a coffer. In a chamber over the parlour were two beds and bedding, a chair, a chest with drawers and two more coffers. At the top of the stairs were bedrooms, two little chambers containing two beds, a cupboard and two chairs. Whether these were arranged as a connecting suite of upstairs rooms is unclear, but they do illustrate the emerging and growing importance of personal privacy, at least among the wealthier classes. Out buildings included a dairy with a table and pounding tub, glass bottles and some pots, next to this a cheese chamber, containing cheese and shelves, and also a buttery, with barrels and brewing equipment. There was an additional little parlour with a chamber over it, perhaps used by servants, which had a bedstead and other items stored in it.

Outside in the fields, hay and corn were growing, the crops worth £16 12s 6d. There was malt and pease (a local food staple, probably beans) wood and coal. The Styans' livestock consisted of a mare, three cows, six ewes, six lambs and a swine (pig), valued at £19 1s 6d. Farming equipment and lumber were also included in the inventory. It appears that the Styans, or at least one of them, were literate as their home contained two Bibles and other books. What is a striking aspect of the inventory comes at the bottom of the list: in a hard to decipher couple of sentences, it shows that most of Henry's monetary wealth was loaned out to others in the form of two mortgages, described as 'good debt'. One for £200 and another for £220, the bulk of the value of the entire estate which totalled £536 9s 6d, evidence that their wealth was not just derived from farming but also from financial investments.

Henry Styan's widow Catherine continued to live in the Hall until 1715. Their daughter, also called Catherine (1665–1734) (or Katherine, spelling wasn't consistent) married Edward Muxloe of Desford (1663–1729) but as he is described in a document as 'of Kirby Muxloe Frith' it indicates that he took possession of the property through his wife and that they perhaps lived there with her family after their marriage. When their eldest son, also Edward Muxloe, died aged 39 in 1727, he was buried at Kirby

Muxloe rather than Desford, so he was probably living at Kirby Frith when he died. Although described as the owner, the younger Edward Muxloe may have been confused with his father as both parents were still living at the time, meaning he would not yet have inherited the property, although he could have made his home there in anticipation of his legacy or had it given to him.[155]

As well as Edward, the couple, Catherine and Edward Muxloe, had other children: Henry, John, Ellen and Katherine (born 1685). The younger Edward also had six children of his own, including perhaps an illegitimate son, as Freeman Muxloe is mentioned in his will, with instructions for him to be sent to sea or apprenticed to a trade, rather than share in any inheritance. Already a widower, Edward, whose wife Elizabeth had died in 1723, left instructions that a chest of linen and 'rings left by their late mother, which she desired them to have' were to be shared by his daughters Elizabeth and Katherine. All household goods were to remain in the house until his eldest son, another Edward, reached the age of 21. If their two brothers died before coming of age and left no children, the girls would inherit their father's personal estate. If they also died and left no children as heirs, Edward's property would pass to his nephew, Henry, son of his late brother Henry, otherwise to his sisters. There must have been a string of untimely deaths as the estate at Kirby Frith eventually went to his sister, the younger Katherine Muxloe who had married and become Katherine Bakewell.

At the time of Edward Muxloe the younger's death, his parents Catherine Styan and Edward Muxloe were still living. When the older Edward married Catherine, her property and inheritance, including Kirby Frith Hall, would have come under his control and ownership. His will, made in 1729, proven the year following his death, is less complicated than that of his son. In Edward Muxloe the elder's will his freehold and copyhold estate in Desford, where he was from, was left to his son Henry Muxloe of Quorndon, and his grandson Robert Bakewell of Loughborough, born in 1705, the son of daughter Katherine. The surplus after paying any debts was to be given to his wife, for her to share among any grandchildren as she thought fit. The estate at Kirby Frith was ultimately left to grandson Robert Bakewell, whose own father, also called Robert, left an interesting will, which explains how the property was transferred to the next generations.

Other members of the Styan family, active in the area around the same time, were Mary Styan, a daughter of Henry of Kirby Frith who was born in around 1686. A man called Muxloe Styan left a will in 1684 and in 1701 Benjamin Styan left a yearly rent charge of ten shillings to be paid out of the income from land at the intriguingly

155 Deeds, bills and papers concerning the estate of Edward Muxloe of Kirby Frith, including his will of 1727 1698–1727) , National Archives, C112/167; Jonathan E.O. Wilshere, *The Place-Name Kirby Muxloe,* LAHS Transactions,Vol. 42, 1966–67, p.83

Francis St John memorial in Kirby Frith Church.

named Cuckold's Haven, to be applied every sixth year to apprentice a poor boy. Widow Katherine Styan died in 1715 and Mary Styan, perhaps a daughter, in 1718.

During the period between about 1727 and 1732 Kirby Frith Hall was the home of Francis St John, originally of Cold Overton. Kirby Frith Hall appears to have been rebuilt around this time as in 1731 it was described as 'new built, neatly furnished, with Convenient outhouses, Gardens and Orchards'.[156] There was also a newly built farm nearby. Did the St John's move into a new house or did they live in the old Hall while a new one was constructed nearby? Described as a gentleman of Kirby Frith,

156 Wilshere, p.23

Francis St John died in 1732, with his will granted probate in 1733.[157] Francis's wife, Eliza or Elizabeth, had been buried in the chancel of St Bartholomew's Church in Kirby Muxloe only a few months earlier. Elizabeth St John may have had the maiden surname Needham. An Elizabeth Needham, daughter of John and Sarah Needham was christened at Kirby Muxloe in 1694. In his will Francis left all of his lands and tenements to his son, Needham St John. Needham St John was studying at Emmanuel College, Cambridge, in 1743 when he was 18 years old. He died in 1762, aged just 37 and, like his parents, was buried in the chancel of Kirby Muxloe church.[158]

Francis's executors were instructed to sell his personal estate for the best price that could be got and put out the money at interest, to pay his daughter Sylena (Selena) £1,000 at the age of 21 or on her marriage if she married before reaching that age, in the meantime the interest was to be used to pay for her maintenance and education. If Francis's son were to die before reaching the age of 21, the estate was to go his nephew Sir John Fifield of Southampton. The will did not name the property to be passed on or where it was, so St John was probably a tenant, renting Kirby Frith Hall as his older brother, Rowland, had inherited the family home at Cold Overton in 1705. Whether or not the Hall was occupied by its owner or a member of their family after Francis St John died in 1732 is unclear. However, Robert Bakewell inherited the property in 1734 but he died in 1737.

Katherine Bakewell's (nee Muxloe) husband Robert Bakewell, of Swepstone, died in 1707, when his son was an infant. The detail of his will gives an insight into the lifestyles of his class at the time. All Robert's goods and stock in his estate in the parish of Normanton were left to his father Thomas. Maybe he had inherited them through his wife as her great great grandfather Charles Styan had been baptised in Normanton in Yorkshire, although it could have been either the village in Nottinghamshire or Rutland. He left a horse called Flower to a brother, and a filly known as the Blazed Filly to his brother-in-law Henry Muxloe. A guinea to buy a mourning ring, or 'whatever else they please', was left to each of his fathers and mothers (natural and in-laws), grandmother Katherine Styan and all his brothers and sisters. His widow was to receive all his household goods and plate, and his servants received gifts of money, £5 or £1.

The poor of Normanton and of Swepstone were also left legacies: £4 to be put out at interest by the overseers of both parishes with the interest shared and distributed among the poor each year on 21 December. He left £400 to his son, Robert, if he reached the age of 21, and or to any of his children and possible future heirs. If his wife were pregnant at the time he died, £400 was to be paid out of the Swepstone estate by his son Robert to his new brother or sister when they reached 21. Widow Katherine was to have use of Swepstone, their home, for the rest of her life. An additional estate at Markfield was left to his parents, Thomas and Mary Bakewell or

157 Will of Francis St John, 1733, National Archives, 11/662/248
158 Cambridge University Alumni, 1261–1900

their heirs. The Swepstone property would go to his brothers, Thomas, Joseph and John. There was still a Bakewell living at Swepstone in the 19th century. Robert left £100 to his brothers-in-law, Edward and Henry Muxloe, who were still alive in 1707, and his sister in law, Ellen got £200. If his brothers failed in their obligation to pay out the various legacies within six months, Robert made a provision that all their rights under the will be revoked and his father in law, Edward Muxloe, who was also an executor of the will, would take control of the estate.

When the younger Robert, the son, died in 1737, after also inheriting from his grandparents at Kirby Frith through his mother, it appears that all his Styan and Muxloe relatives and potential heirs were already dead, despite their large family with several sons and daughters. The property was now bequeathed through his Bakewell grandfather and then uncle Joseph to a cousin, Richard Bakewell, described as a gentleman of Kirby Frith. He was born in Tollerton in Nottinghamshire in 1714 and married Prudence Shears in Glenfield in 1740, which suggests he was already living at Kirby Frith Hall. Richard Bakewell made his will shortly after his marriage, although it was not needed until he died in 1772, a year after his wife. The will refers to an estate including messuages, cottages, closes, tenements, and hereditaments situated, standing and lying in the counties of Leicester, Nottingham, Derby and Lincoln and his possessions in Cosgrave and Clipston in Nottinghamshire.

With an eye on good management of the estate, Richard cautioned against any improvement of woods, wilful waste in pulling down houses and buildings, but trees for timber were exempt from this condition. In his will Richard left his wife a lifetime's interest in his property, with any as yet unborn sons inheriting at the age of 25 or on their marriage if that was sooner. If there were no sons, then a daughter would inherit when she reached the age of 21 or married if that happened first. If he had more than one daughter, the estate was to be inherited between them as tenants in common, which means they had shares independent of each other. If there were no surviving children at all, then his estate would pass to his siblings.

Prudence Bakewell died the year before her husband Richard, but he had thought of that possibility and included as alternative heirs his brother Joseph and sisters Joanna and Ann who was already married to Richard Barber. From the details in the will it would seem that Richard Bakewell was a relatively wealthy man. The furniture in his house at Frith, 'wherein I now dwell', and all his plate and linen he left to Prudence who was to be entitled to occupy the house, and for his two executors, one of whom was Thomas Pares, to sell his pasture and kine (cattle) to pay his debts, funeral expenses and to provide £50 a year to support his wife and any children.

The story of the Bakewells now takes a very sad turn into misfortune. The couple had at least four children: Prudence born in April 1742 who died after just three months; another Prudence born in 1743 who died in 1747, a son Richard born and buried in 1745, and a second son, John Shears Bakewell, baptised in 1747 but who died aged 18 in 1765. By the time his will was proven in 1772, none of Richard's immediate family and heirs were still living. Richard had requested that he be buried in Tollerton near his father, but this request was not carried out. Instead he was buried in St Martin's in Leicester, where Prudence had already been laid to rest.

When Richard Bakewell died in 1772, his sister Ann Barber was his only surviving heir. She and her husband moved into Kirby Frith Hall and Richard Barber gained a place on the electoral roll though his property qualification, as owner of his wife's property and his status as a gentleman of Kirby Frith.[159] The Barbers had three daughters: Hannah who married Stephen Wilkinson in 1766 but who died in 1772, leaving two daughters, Ann and Frances Wilkinson; Joanna whose husband was John Spencer and who had at least three children, Hannah, William and Samuel; and Ann (1741–1819) married to Elijah Riley from 1764. The Rileys had at least ten children who lived into adulthood, the eldest ones born in Duffield where they originally lived. The five youngest were baptised at Glenfield, indicating that the family had moved to Kirby Frith.

Ann Barber predeceased her husband Richard in 1777 but he was not alone for long. He quickly found a new partner, Ann Willatt (or Willott), with whom he had a son, William Barber, whose baptism is recorded at Glenfield in August 1778. The birth of an illegitimate baby half-brother must have come as a shock to the adult daughters of Ann Barber who now had children of their own, especially as the new parents seem to have been cohabiting. As heirs to the estates in Nottinghamshire and Derbyshire, as well as Kirby Frith, their and their late sisters Hannah Wilkinson's and Joanna Spencer's children must have thought their futures secure, but then there came another upset: on 21 My 1786 their father Richard married Ann Willatt at Kirby Muxloe, both of them giving their address on the marriage license as Kirby Frith Hall, and in doing so legitimised William and provided a male heir. In 1776, Richard Barber had increased his land property in Leicestershire when he took out a mortgage for £700 to buy enclosed land near Stoney Stanton.[160] This mortgage was paid off in just two years.[161]

Richard Barber didn't live long after his second marriage. In his will, he left his first wife's property in Nottingham to his son William for his life and then to William's heirs, along with his Derbyshire estates. As an adult William Barber became a clergyman, vicar of Duffield where his father had lived before moving to Leicestershire and perhaps controlled the living. Richard Barber's new wife, Ann Willatt, was to receive £50 a year in two payments, on Lady Day and Michaelmas. She was also to live in the house, although the will doesn't say which one, with use of the furniture as long as she remained a widow. Richard's daughters, no longer heirs to the wealth and land they must have anticipated all their lives, were left the real estate of their late

159 Poll Book, 1775
160 East Sussex Records Office, FRE/8707
161 East Sussex Records Office, FRE/8710/11

mother, except for that in Nottingham which also went to William, the son of the mistress and later second wife. Hannah, Joanna and Ann became tenants in common of Kirby Frith, owning a third share each, which they could use and dispose of as they wished. Hannah, who had married Stephen Wilkinson, the son of John Wilkinson of Hillcote Hall in Derbyshire, had already died but her daughters, Frances and Ann, inherited her share.

Frances Wilkinson had married Charles Mellor of Derby, and she and her husband, together with his parents Charles and Ann, brother James Mellor and sisters Dorothy and Frances, moved to Kirby Frith where the elderly parents died and were buried in the chancel of Kirby Muxloe church, Charles senior aged 75 in 1809 and Ann aged 70 in 1812. Frances Mellor born in 1778, married John Lucas of Knaptoft in 1808. Frances Wilkinson and her husband Charles Mellor moved away. Perhaps they or James went to France for a while, as when Dorothy died in 1831, she was at the home of her brother in Dieppe.[162] They later lived in Margate where Frances died aged 66 in 1837.[163] Charles and Frances had three children, Stephen Wilkinson Mellor who studied at Oxford University, and Harriet and Maria, neither of whom married. The family never returned to live at Kirby Frith but Charles' brother James continued in residence and farmed the land, mostly as sheep pasture until he too moved away.

Engaged in local affairs, in 1815 James Mellor, subscribed two guineas to the Leicester Infirmary.[164] James married Mary Waterhouse of Humberstone in 1817, whose farm property there he sold shortly afterwards. In 1817 James was selling a share, or moity, in some of his land.[165] Mellor owned enough property to make it worth his while to join the Ansty (sic) Association, which in 1818 offered a reward of ten guineas for the capture of whoever had killed a sheep in a close near his home and taken away its hind quarters.[166] James's name also appears in contemporary legal documents, such as a conveyance of May 1820 relating to Park Close in Westcotes.[167] James Mellor and his family lived in Kirby Frith until 1821 when the estate was sold. There is no apparent relationship between this family and John Mellor of New Parks, the elder of whom was born in Oldham in 1780 and moved to Leicester where he married Elizabeth Mitchell in 1806.

The Rileys continued to live in the area, perhaps sharing the Hall or in one of the other houses on the Kirby Frith Estate. The Glenfield parish registers record five of the Riley children being baptised there in the years immediately following the death of great uncle Richard Bakewell, four of them bearing given names emphasising

162 *Leicester Chronicle*, 15 October 1831
163 *Kentish Gazette*, 7 February 1837
164 *Leicester Journal*, 8 September 1815
165 *Leicester Journal*, 15 August 1817
166 *Leicester Chronicle*, 28 November 1818
167 Conveyance, 10 May 1820, ROLLR DE9128/70

their Bakewell kinship: Prudence Riley in 1774, Richard Riley in 1775, Elijah Riley baptised in 1780, Elizabeth Bakewell Riley in 1782 and a son Bakewell Riley in 1787. As the ten children grew up, they too married. The eldest son, Adam, born in 1769 in Duffield, was apprenticed to the hosiery trade in 1783. Richard, baptised in Glenfield, may have emigrated to the United States and his brothers born in or near Kirby Frith, Elijah (1780) and Bakewell (1787) were apprenticed as plumbers and glaziers in Leicester. The younger Rileys, Elijah, Prudence and Mary, became involved with the Great Meeting in the town, perhaps where they met their marriage partners. Two of the sisters, both baptised in Glenfield, Prudence (1774–1845) and Mary (1777–1842), married brothers Joseph and William Whetstone, in business together as wool staplers, in a firm founded by their father. Mary and William had no children but Prudence and Joseph had six, all but one, Helen, living to adulthood.

It wasn't only the countryside that was the scene for class conflict to be played out between those who controlled access to resources and those often desperate to feed themselves and their families. There were struggles between employers and the emerging working class in the town of Leicester. The Whetstone's wool trading business in Northgate Street in Leicester prospered, despite having been the focus of attacks by crowds of framework knitters and other workers in 1787, in protest at the introduction of a new method of spinning worsted, invented by Joseph Brookhouse of Church Gate.[168] Spinning was a process that had traditionally been done by women workers, usually the wives and families of the knitters. Brookhouse had gone into partnership with the father of the brothers, Joseph Whetstone (1725–1811), and leading hosier John Coltman, after the pair of his fellow Unitarians paid for his release from prison for debt. Whetstone fired on the angry crowd after his house on Northgate Street was attacked. The mayor of Leicester died after being fatally injured while trying to read the Riot Act. The new spinning machinery was installed in Market Harborough and in Melton Mowbray but was destroyed by angry groups from Leicester. No worsted spinning by machine took place in Leicester for at least a decade after that.[169]

William and Mary Whetstone made their home on London Road in Leicester, while Prudence and Joseph moved to Red Hall at Barwell. William Whetstone was involved in the sale of Kirby Frith Hall as his wife probably still retained an interest in the family property although with so many heirs as tenants in common, it must have become difficult to administer and ensure fair payments. Both couples were buried at the Great Meeting, Unitarian church in Leicester.

---

168 *The City of Leicester: Social and administrative history, 1660–1835*, British History Online, (British-history.ac.uk) accessed 14 August 2020

169 David L. Wykes: *The reluctant businessman: John Coltman of St Nicholas Street, Leicester (1727–1808)*, Transactions of Leicestershire Archaeological and Historical Society, LXIX, 1995, pp.71–85, p.81

Kirby Frith Hall, c.1915. (Records Office of Leicester, Leicestershire and Rutland)

Other members of the Riley family were by no means well off, despite the large estate described in Richard Bakewell's will of around 30 years earlier. Newspaper records show that young Elijah and Bakewell Riley were plumbers who became involved in petty crime, theft and fraud for which they were imprisoned several times.

A son or grandson of the other sister, Joanna Spencer, may also have moved to Leicestershire from his birthplace in Pentrich in Derbyshire, to occupy a share of the inheritance, as the auction of the Kirby Frith Estate in 1821 was in two lots. As well as Kirby Frith Hall and its adjacent fields, Lot 2 was Red Hall Farm occupied by John Spencer. Was this purchased from him by Prudence and Joseph Whetstone and kept in the family, or maybe the farm and Red Hall were separate premises, excluded from the sale or brought privately within the family by the Whetstones?

Evidence that the residents of the Hall were not living in complete isolation is provided by documents that give the address of signatories as Kirby Frith. Some of them may have been servants or tenants. One of these is an agreement to lease land there in 1657, for 26 years for £40 a year, made between William Francks, a mercer of Leicester and George Somerfield of Kirby Muxloe. It refers to an area of land divided into two closes or fields, one arable and one pasture, at Kirby Frith or Kirby Pastures. On the rear of the document are the signatures of witnesses, Thomas Wadland, John Swynton, Jane Kirke, and Francis Cooper. Jane Kirke may have been a widow or heiress of the Kirk family, who gained land in the area during the enclosure earlier in the century.[170]

170 Lease re land at Kirby Frith, 25 May 1657, ROLLR DE571

Other Kirby Frith residents were wool stapler of Castle View in Leicester, Thomas and Mary Wightman, whose daughter Maria Hannah was baptised in Kirby Muxloe in 1764, soon followed by another daughter Elizabeth the following year. The family later moved into Ravenstone Hall. Both of Wightman's executors were involved in the key local industries, as a worsted maker and hosier.[171] A legal document drawn up by their father's executors, for Maria Hannah and Elizabeth Wightman shows that the sisters continued to own land they had inherited in and around Braunstone and the Frith which was later owned by the Winstanleys.[172] Were they tenants of Kirby Frith Hall while the Bakewells were staying at another property they owned or did they live in one of the neighbouring houses or farms on the estate? Another document is a marriage settlement agreed between Samuel Miles and Justina Sutton of Kirby Frith in 1768.[173] The Jordan family were other neighbours. Thomas Jordan of Kirby Frith married Ann Mee of Leicester Forest in 1786. Their children Martha and John were baptised in the same place in 1787 and 1795. Another mention of the area is in a title deed for the sale of land to the Leicester Meeting House for a burial ground in Soar Lane, dated October 1790, in which one of the signatories was Dan Woodland of Kirby Frith, possibly an alternative spelling of the surname Wadland.[174] The Cramp family were farmers, whose residence was given at different times as Kirby Frith House and Kirby Frith Farm. Joseph Cramp was also referred to as the occupant of Mares Gap Close along with John Marston who occupied a garden adjoining a field called Bottom Close.[175] Generations of Cramps lie in Kirby Muxloe Church burial ground.

When the Kirby Frith Hall estate was offered for sale by auction in February 1821, at the George Inn in Leicester, the lot was described as comprising, 'A capital mansion, called Kirby Frith Hall, a good farmhouse and requisite outbuildings in the several occupations of James Mellor esq, Mr John Spencer and others. The mansion commands beautiful and extensive views, is well calculated for the residence of a genteel family, is in the neighbourhood of the Quorn and Lord Anson's Hunts, and within three miles of that excellent market town, Leicester.'[176] The estate was tithe-free and, together with another property called Cramp's Farm, it was a parish or liberty in its own right, responsible for maintaining its own Poor, although at the time there were said to be none chargeable to it. The family occupying Kirby Frith Hall had its own pews in both Glenfield and Kirby Muxloe Churches. Other information in the

171 Will of Thomas Wightman of Ravenstone Hall, 1784, National Archives, PROB 11/1116/165

172 Lease and release, Maria Hannah and Elizabeth Wightman, 1787, ROLLR 16D 66/213–214

173 Marriage settlement 1768, ROLLR Box 11/2

174 Title deeds of Leicester Meeting House and burial ground in Soar Lane. 23 October 1790, ROLLR 12D39/V/1(41/9)

175 Collection of sale particulars and catalogues, 13 February 1821, ROLLR, L333

176 Sale particulars of a capital messuage called Kirby Frith Hall, Leicester 1821, Derbyshire Record Office, D5336/2/25/72

sales particulars indicates that a 'fee farm rent' was paid to the Earl of Radnor, at that time Jacob Pleydell-Bouverie, the 4th Earl who became Viscount Folkestone in 1828, who seems to have no other local connections. This vestige of feudalism, that required £80 1s 0d to be paid to the Earl every 21 years, for nothing in return despite it being a freehold property, remained payable into the 20th century.[177] The 168 acres, one rood and 24 perches of agricultural land was a mixture of arable and pasture. Field names forming the estate included Thistly Close, Gusset Close, Pump Close, Woad Close, Oak Tree Meadow and Shoulder of Mutton Close, next to the Hinckley Turnpike.

Kirby Frith Hall was sold to Leicester lawyer and partner in a bank, Thomas Pares (1746–1824), but he soon died and the estate, along with many other properties in Leicestershire and Derbyshire passed to his brother, John (1749–1833), a hosiery manufacturer, who also leased the adjacent 230 acres of Braunstone Frith Farm. The property then passed to John's son also Thomas Pares (1790–1866). Educated at Eton and Trinity College, Cambridge, this Thomas was called to the bar at Lincoln's Inn in 1816 but never practised law. However, he continued the banking partnership, with James Heygate and Thomas Paget. Thomas was Member of Parliament for Leicester between 1818 and 1826. As part of the Whig opposition, Thomas voted for liberal policies such as parliamentary reform, Catholic relief and presented petitions for the abolition of slavery. In 1830, it emerged that partner James Heygate junior had been embezzling funds and the bank was in difficulty. The situation reversed in 1836 when the banking business changed from a partnership to a joint stock company, Pares's Leicestershire Banking Company, and as a major shareholder, Thomas became a director. He seems to have lived at Kirby Frith Hall until 1832 or 1833 when the Robinson family moved in; perhaps he moved to another family home after his father's passing.[178]

Different generations of the Pares family, many of whom were called Thomas, seem to have had an interest in Kirby Frith, even before they actually owned it. Thomas Pares the grandfather (1716–1805), was one of the executors and administrators named in the will of Richard Bakewell in or shortly after 1740. The younger Thomas was MP for Leicester between 1818 and 1826. During 1825, local farmers, including Pares together with Clement Winstanley of Braunstone, John Clarke and Thomas Worthington of New Parks and T.W. Oldham of Leicester Frith were offering a reward of £100 for the capture and conviction of sheep thieves who were active in the area.[179] This appeal continued to be published in local newspapers

177 Sales particulars of Kirby Frith Hall and Manor House Farm, 1915, ROLLR DE182/19

178 Samuel Tymms, *A Compendium of the Ancient and Present State of Derbyshire, Leicestershire, Lincolnshire, Northamptonshire, Nottinghamshire, Rutlandshire, Warwickshire, Cheshire*, London, 1832

179 *Leicester Chronicle*, 10 December 1825

Kirby Frith Farm, c1935. (Records Office of Leicester, Leicestershire and Rutland)

throughout the following year.[180] Other evidence of the economic activity of Kirby Frith is an advertisement offering for sale ash, elm and willow trees at Glenfield and Kirby Frith plus larch and willow poles cut down and prepared for purchasers who were invited to apply to the gardener at Kirby Frith House.[181]

Like the Mellors and Whetstones before them, the Pares family were involved in the life of the local community and good causes. Mrs Pares subscribed a guinea to the British Society for Promoting the Reformation of Female Prisoners in 1826 and her husband donated £1.[182] In 1828, the couple suffered when their infant son, John, born at Kirby Frith, died there.[183] Thomas paid for the building of Glenfield School in 1831. Soon after this, the Pares family moved to one of their other properties, Hopwell Hall in Derbyshire. In 1833 a ten-year lease at an annual rent of £129 was agreed with John Briggs Robinson of Halifax who made Kirby Frith Hall his family home until the late 1830s.[184] His daughter Charlotte Robinson married at Kirby Muxloe in 1835. His business was J.B. Robinson and Son, wool staplers of Talbot Lane in Leicester. By 1842, the Robinsons had moved on to Rothley Grange but did not enjoy their new, prestigious home for long as John died there in 1843.

Sometime in the late 1830s, Thomas Pare's cousin, the daughter of his maternal aunt, Elizabeth Lightbody, came to live at Kirby Frith Hall with her husband Isaac

180 *Leicester Chronicle*, 12 August 1826, 23 December 1826

181 *Leicester Chronicle,* 3 February 1827

182 Fifth Annual Report of British Society for Promoting the Reformation of Female Prisoners, 1826

183 *Leicester Herald*, 14 May 1828

184 Wilshere, p.23

CAPITAL FREEHOLD MANSION AND ESTATES
IN THE COUNTY OF LEICESTER.

PARTICULARS

OF VALUABLE

FREEHOLD ESTATES,

SITUATE AT

KIRBY FRITH and BARWELL, in the County of Leicester,

ABOUT THREE MILES DISTANT FROM THE MARKET TOWNS OF

Leicester and Hinckley,

CONTAINING IN THE WHOLE

Upwards of 259 Acres

OF

SUPERIOR ARABLE, PASTURE, AND MEADOW LAND,

DIVIDED INTO

TWO ELIGIBLE FARMS,

WITH A

CAPITAL MANSION, CALLED KIRBY FRITH HALL,

AND GOOD FARM HOUSE AND REQUISITE OUT-BUILDINGS,

IN THE SEVERAL OCCUPATIONS OF

JAMES MELLOR, ESQUIRE, MR. JOHN SPENCER,

AND OTHERS;

Subject to Land-Tax, and part to a Fee-Farm Rent and Tithes;

WHICH WILL

BE SOLD BY AUCTION,

BY MR. HOLLIER,

On TUESDAY, the 13th Day of FEBRUARY, 1821,

AT THE

GEORGE INN, IN LEICESTER,

AT THREE O'CLOCK IN THE AFTERNOON,

IN TWO LOTS,

(Unless disposed of in the mean time by Private Contract, of which due Notice will be given,)

SUBJECT TO CONDITIONS TO BE THEN PRODUCED.

For further particulars and Inspection of Maps of the Estates, as also to Treat for the purchase of the same, apply to Mr. WILLIAM WHETSTONE, *North Gates, Leicester; or to Mr.* COWDELL, *Solicitor, Hinckley, Leicestershire.*

Kirby Frith Hall and Manor Farm sale catalogue, 1821. (Records Office of Leicester, Leicestershire and Rutland)

Hodgson. Hodgson, born in 1783, was the son of a Liverpool merchant, Thomas Hodgson. His father had been involved in the slave trade in Gambia and had owned his own fort off Sierra Leone but pulled out of the evil business and instead became involved in the textile industry. Both Isaac and his brother Adam were active abolitionists. Isaac became secretary of the Liverpool Anti-slavery Society through which he proclaimed that slavery 'was the greatest practical error as well as the greatest calamity, that has ever disgraced and afflicted human nature'.

Both brothers were on the founding committee of the Liverpool and Manchester Railway. As well as being related by marriage to Thomas Pares, Isaac Hodgson was also a business associate of his. He was deputy chairman of the Leicester and Swannington Railway and a partner in Pares's bank. Hodgson attracted criticism in the local Tory supporting newspaper, the *Leicester Journal*, because of his radical, liberal political activities. Hodgson was put on to the list of voters in Leicester by using the address of the bank, claiming it was his home in order to qualify as a burgess in the town to meet the property qualification to vote. The local Tories' agent, John Johnson Adams, complained that it breached the rules of the recent 1832 Reform Act and Hodgson was removed from the list of voters in 1838.[185]

The Provident Society he was involved with gave bread as charitable relief to the poor which annoyed the mayor of Leicester as he claimed it attracted imposter beggars. The mayor believed it would be best to give beggars one of the Society's tickets that could be exchanged for food, rather than give relief at the door to anyone who called.[186] As a Liberal, Hodgson was often attacked by the Tories, but was said to pursue 'the even tenor of his way, uninfluenced by the petty attacks of men who, like dogs that bay at the moon, are ever ready to snarl at that excellence of character which they cannot appreciate and to which they will never attain'.[187] In his turn, Hodgson could be outspoken in his own criticism of political opponents, including accusing Gladstone of corrupt electioneering practices by 'swamping the votes of honest electors by bribery'. Isaac Hodgson died in 1859 and the Pares family moved back to Kirby Frith soon afterwards.

In 1846 there was an auction of the farming stock, implements and furniture on the premises of Jonathan Cramp at Kirby Frith House, presumably the farmhouse, who was said to be leaving his farm. Things for sale included dairy cows, heifers, lambs, three horses, a couple of fat pigs, wagons and carts, a winnowing machine, harrows and an excellent scuffer.[188] Perhaps he had a change of heart or couldn't find a buyer because in May 1859 the farm and fields, still occupied by Jonathan Cramp, were put up for auction once more. Cramp may have already moved out

185 *Leicester Journal*, 19 October 1838
186 *Leicester Chronicle*, 16 February 1839
187 *Leicestershire Mercury*, 16 April 1842
188 *Leicester Journal*, 6 March 1846

but perhaps continued to farm the fields as in the advertisement of 1859, the farm was described as a 'Compact Freehold Estate', comprising 80 acres of arable and pasture land, pleasantly situated at Kirby Frith. Potential buyers were informed that the estate was well timbered and connected to the mains of the Leicester waterworks, which pass under it. The property was promoted as 'well worthy of the attention of builders and capitalists'.[189] The property being auctioned, probably only the farm and not the Hall, doesn't appear to have attracted any buyers and was advertised again in July 1859. Farm labourer William Arguile, with his family of six children, including eight-year-old ploughboy Richard whose 12-year-old brother William was still in school, had moved into Kirby Frith Cottage by 1861. The gardener's cottage was occupied by William Chamberlain, whose 14-year-old son, another William was a pupil teacher, perhaps learning and assisting in the school at Glenfield supported by Pares. Chamberlain was still working as the Kirby Frith gardener in 1875.

The next generation of the Pares family, Eton and Cambridge educated Thomas Henry (1830–1878) and his wife Mary with their three children and four servants, moved back into Kirby Frith Hall, where they were on the night of the 1861 Census. At the time, his parents were at another Leicestershire property in Ulverscroft. Before moving to Kirby Frith, Thomas and Mary lived at The Oaks off Hinckley Road at Leicester Forest West where one of their children was born. The family joined in the life of the local community: Captain Pares won first prize for the best brood mare which he entered into the Sparkenhoe Farmers' Club Show held on Leicester Race Course, now Victoria Park, in 1862.[190] The grounds of Kirby Frith Hall supplied holly and other greenery to decorate the local church at Christmas.

After a few years, the Pares family moved to Hopwell Hall, perhaps when Thomas senior died in 1866. By the end of the decade the Hall was occupied by William Henry Salt, son of Sir Titus Salt, the textile manufacturer who had created the model community of Saltaire near Bradford. Salt's wife, Emma Dove Octavia Harris, was born in Leicestershire and so they had land and local connections, mentioned in the previous chapter. Salt engaged with local agricultural life and in 1869 some of his pigs won a prize at the Leicestershire Agricultural Show at Ashby de la Zouch.[191] Salt's gardener, Charles Chamberlain, entered some of his produce in the Glenfield Flower Show and won two shillings in August 1875.[192]

Described as a landowner and magistrate in the 1871 census, only ten years earlier Salt's occupation had been declared as an alpaca manufacturer, a branch of the woollen textile industry and in trade. By 1881, Salt identified himself as a farmer and lived at

189 *Leicester Chronicle*, 21 May 1859
190 *Leicester Journal*, 5 September 1862
191 *Leicester Guardian*, 15 September 1869
192 *Leicester Daily Post*, 27 August 1875

Maplewell Grange. The Salts probably moved from Kirby Frith to Maplewell in 1875 as the Hall was advertised to let with early possession in July that year. The advertisement gives a description of what comprised the property at that time. 'The Mansion House called Kirby Frith Hall, with good gardens, hot house and green house, consisting of seven loose boxes and two stables of two stalls each, all well drained and ventilated, a coach house, saddle room and other buildings, five acres of grass land (additional land to be had if required). Also a gardener's house or entrance lodge.' The house contained a dining room, drawing room, library, billiard room, breakfast room, housekeeper's room, good kitchens, servants' offices, five principal bedrooms, four dressing rooms, four attics and a man servant's bedroom. The property was within reach of the Quorn and Atherstone Hunts and Mr Tailby of Skeffington Hall's hounds, an important factor for anyone aspiring to live the life of a country gentleman.[193] Tailby was master of the Billesdon Hunt from 1850 to 1876.

Tenants of Kirby Frith Hall in the later 1870s were the Stephen family. James Young Stephen (1843–1909), a Major in the Leicestershire Militia, was the eldest son of Oscar Leslie Stephen, a director of the London North Western Railway Company. James married Augusta, the daughter of Vice-Admiral Sir Cornwallis Ricketts of Grosvenor Place and Beaumont Leys, a granddaughter of the Duke of Newcastle, at St George's Hanover Square in London in May 1876.[194] James brought his bride to Kirby Frith Hall where their son, Douglas Clinton Leslie Stephen, was born exactly nine months later.[195] From Kirby Frith, the Stephens moved to Elmodesham Hall in Amersham.[196] By this time Thomas Cope, Justice of the Peace and a barrister, had moved into Kirby Frith Hall, where he was living in 1881.[197] Later, Cope inherited and moved to his own home at Osbaston Hall, the family seat since 1827. He became leader of Leicestershire County Council between 1908 and 1922. In 1918 Cope was created a baronet, becoming Sir Thomas Cope.

The occupiers of Kirby Frith Hall lived the life of country gentleman, despite owing their wealth to business. Strictly speaking, those who were tenants did not qualify as gentry as the status was dependent on owning land. The younger Thomas Pares owned the estate until he died in 1878: this entitled him to vote in local elections for the constituency, despite his address being given as Hopwell Hall. Standing in a beautifully timbered and undulating park, the property was said to command fine views of Bradgate and Charnwood Forest. Continuously improved over the years, in the late 19th century the mansion possessed stabling for 11 horses, a gardener's house, entrance lodge and covers for rearing and shooting game birds.

193 *Leicester Chronicle and Leicestershire Mercury*, 3 July 1875
194 *Cheltenham Looker-On*, 6 May 1876
195 *Pall Mall Gazette*, 10 February 1877
196 *Northampton Daily Echo*, 18 August 19099
197 *Leicester Chronicle and Leicestershire Mercury*, 15 January 1881

2

THE capital MANSION called *Kirby Frith Hall*, and *Farm Buildings*, are in excellent repair, and the Lands in a high state of cultivation, and in the occupation of JAMES MELLOR, Esq.—This Mansion commands beautiful and extensive Views, is well calculated for the residence of a genteel Family, is in the Neighbourhood of the Quorn, and Lord Anson's Hunts, and within Three Miles of that excellent Market Town, Leicester.

This Estate is Tithe-free; and together with another called *Cramp's Farm*, is a Parish or Liberty, and maintains its own Poor, but at the present time none are chargeable or known to belong to it.—The Land-Tax charged upon the whole Parish, is £21. 8*s*. 8*d*. of which this Estate pays £14. 5*s*. 9½*d*.—It is also subject to an Annual Fee Farm Rent of £16. 1*s*. 8*d*. of which this Estate pays £10. 14*s*. 5½*d*.; and to a Fine of £80. payable every 21 Years to the Earl of Radnor, of which this Estate pays £53. 7*s*. 4*d*.—This Fine was last paid in 1813.

N.B.—The above Payments do not amount to 3*s*. 4*d*. per Acre, per Annum.

A Pew in each of the Parish Churches of Kirby Muxloe, and Glenfield, belong to this Estate.

To view this Estate, apply to Mr. JOHN SLATER, of GLENFIELD PASTURES.

The BARWELL ESTATE consists of an exceeding good FARM HOUSE and BUILDINGS in excellent repair, and 90A. 2R. 20P. of superior Grazing Land, in a good state of cultivation, called or known by the name of *Red Hall Farm*, and now in the occupation of Mr. JOHN SPENCER.

This Estate is subject to a Land Tax of £7. 1*s*. and Tithes; it adjoins the Town of Barwell, is distant from Hinckley Three Miles, and from Leicester Nine Miles, and within Two Hundred Yards of which the Coaches from Leicester to Coventry pass daily.

To view this Estate, apply to the said Mr. SPENCER.

An undivided Twenty-fourth Part or Share of these Estates is vested in a Minor, of the Age of 18 Years; but his Guardians will guarantee the Purchaser or Purchasers of these Estates for his performance of the Contract, on his attaining the Age of 21 Years.

Possession of these Estates may be had at Lady-Day next.

3

FARM and LANDS at KIRBY FRITH, containing 168A. 1R. 24P. or thereabouts, (be the same more or less,) in the occupation of *James Mellor, Esq.*

LOT 1.

NOS. ON THE MAP.	STATE.	QUANTITIES. A. R. P.	A. R. P.
1.—Kirby Frith Hall, Out-Offices, Garden, and Moats,		2 0 11	
2.—The Park,	Pasture,	16 1 23	
3.—Draw-Bridge Close,	Ditto,	5 3 20	
4.—Nine Acres,	Ditto,	9 1 2	
5.—Pump Close,	Ditto,	10 3 24	
6.—Thistly Close,	Arable,	10 3 33	
7.—Gusset Close,	Ditto,	4 1 30	
8.—Shoulder of Mutton Close,	Pasture,	5 2 38	
9.—Bottom Woad Close,	Ditto,	6 2 27	
10.—Far Bottom Woad Close,	Ditto,	6 3 17	
11.—Far Middle Woad Close,	Seeds,	6 0 26	
12.—Middle Woad Close,	Arable and Pasture	6 1 9	
13.—Top Woad Close,	Pasture,	7 2 18	
14.—Far Top Woad Close,	Arable,	7 2 5	
15.—Stevens's Close,	Pasture,	15 2 2	
16.—Two Acres,	Ditto,	2 3 8	
17.—Barber's Close,	Arable,	10 3 30	
18.—Seven Acres,	Pasture,	7 3 10	
19.—Four Acres,	Ditto,	3 2 36	
20.—Oak Tree Meadow,	Arable,	11 1 10	
21.—Spinny and Lane,	Pasture,	0 3 19	
22.—Barn Meadow,	Ditto,	5 3 11	
23.—Buildings, Farm Yard, and Stack Yard,		0 3 1	
24.—Allotment in Glenfield Parish,	Ditto,	1 2 26	
25.—Free Bord,	[illegible]	[illegible]	
			168 1 24

RED HALL FARM and LANDS, at BARWELL, containing 90A. 2R. 20P. or thereabouts, (be the same more or less,) in the occupation of *Mr. John Spencer.*

LOT 2.

NOS. ON MAP.	STATE.	A. R. P.	A. R. P.
1.—Bottom Hall Close,	Pasture,	4 3 16	
2.—Near Newlands,	Ditto,	5 1 25	
3.—Far Newlands,	Ditto,	4 3 20	
4.—Long Close,	Ditto,	6 2 6	
5.—Little Hall's Close,	Ditto,	2 1 10	
6.—Top Hall's Close,	Ditto,	5 3 22	
7.—Top Cow Close,	Ditto,	8 2 21	
8.—Bottom Cow Close,	Ditto,	7 2 30	
9.—Little Cow Close,	Ditto,	3 1 33	67 1 9
10.—Barn Close,	Ditto,	4 2 1	
11.—Red Hall Buildings, Garden, & Orchard,		2 2 25	
12.—Spinny and Ponds,		2 0 19	
13.—Crow Tree Close,	Ditto,	5 0 32	
14.—Little Plat,	Ditto,	3 0 29	
15.—Far Berry Hill,	Ditto,	3 2 28	
16.—Oak Tree Berry Hill,	Ditto,	6 0 26	20 1 23
17.—Middle Berry Hill,	Ditto,	5 1 18	
18.—Dawson's Berry Hill,	Ditto,	5 0 31	
CLAMP, JOSEPH, Occupier.			
19.—Mare's Gap Close,	Ditto,	2 3 13	2 3 13
MARSTON, JOHN, Occupier.			
20.—Garden adjoining Bottom Cow Close,	Garden,	0 0 15	0 0 15
			90 2 20

By this time the house had been modernised and was supplied throughout with water from the Leicester Waterworks Company. A five-horsepower Hornsby engine that generated electricity for lighting was installed in 1913. Indoors, Kirby Frith Hall contained a dining room, drawing room (32 feet by 18 feet on the first floor), smoking room, a library, billiard room, breakfast room, a housekeeper's room, good kitchens and servants' offices and outbuildings, nine bedrooms, including the Oak bedroom, three dressing rooms, four attics and a man servant's room. Three bathrooms were installed, a change in hygiene practices since the 1870s. In the many greenhouses grew melons, peaches and vines. Situated in the centre of the Quorn and Atherstone hunts' territories, according to *The Field*, the country gentleman's newspaper, it was within reach of the meets of Sir Bache Cunard's hounds.[198] Baron Cunard, grandson and heir of the founder of the shipping line but more interested in polo and hunting, lived at Neville Holt, quite a way for a horse but by that time more accessible using the railway network. Fox hunting was an activity that took place regularly, with local meets, such as in 1876, when the Quorn Hunt chased a fox from Braunstone Spinney, a covert owned by Captain Pochin of Braunstone Hall, along the Leicester and Burton Railway, towards New Parks and then to Kirby Frith Hall, where it seems the poor creature escaped after outrunning the riders and hounds.[199]

198 *The Field – The Country Gentleman's Newspaper*, 3 March 1883
199 *The Field,* 23 December 1876

Kirby Frith Hall was offered for rent again in 1883 by the next generation of Pares offspring to inherit it, but seems to have attracted no one wishing to take on the tenancy as the next year it was on the market for sale.[200] Only one of Thomas and Mary Pare's five children had survived into adulthood. This was Edward (1854–1931) who lived in Ivy House in Glenfield before transferring to Hopwell Hall when his father died. The adjacent property to Kirby Frith Hall, Manor Farm in Glenfield parish, was sold separately by Edward Pares to John Harris Cooper of Evington Hall in 1884 for £5,690. At this time the property, like Kirby Frith Hall, was subject to a 'fee farm rent' of £9 14s 6d, this time paid to the Colston Hospital in Bristol, the school established by the endowment of slave-trader Edward Colston. Colston Hospital had other interests in land in the area as it received fee farm rents from New Parks Farm and Western Park Dairy, as well as from Manor Farm. The obligation to make this payment was finally extinguished in 1921.[201]

In 1895, Edward was divorced by his wife Muriel for adultery with Alice Taylor, the parlour maid, and his subsequent desertion of her and their five children.[202] After a visit to Canada Edward returned and put Hopwell Hall up for sale, without informing his wife, disobeying an order for the 'restitution of conjugal rights'. Edward was soon remarried to Agnes Heard in 1896, leaving Hopwell Hall and moving into Hopwell Hall Farm, run by Mary's farmer brother. Edward Pares had lost most of the wealth built up by his family, leaving only £1,098 when he died in Bedford in 1931.

The Kirby Frith Hall estate was bought by Leicester solicitor, Samuel Francis Stone in 1884. Stone was involved in local government as Town Clerk. Politically he was a Conservative, nominating the Conservative candidate, Gerald Holbech Hardy, in the Harborough election in May 1891.[203] Stone's home at Kirby Frith was the venue for the Primrose League fête in 1889. The Primrose League, founded in 1884, named after the favourite flower of Benjamin Disraeli, was an organisation set up to obtain the support of working-class people, including women, for the Conservatives. At Kirby Frith Hall's fête there was an open air concert featuring Major Brindley, billed as 'the cleverest amateur comic singer in England' and a substantial tea. Speakers included Thomas Tapling, member of parliament for the Harborough Division. Primrose League badges were presented and there was plenty of music and dancing.[204] Fêtes were regular events at Kirby Frith Hall during Stone's residence there. Continuing the relationship with the school endowed by the Pares family, as a benefactor of the Glenfield National School, Stone played host to fêtes and bazaars to raise funds.

200 *The Field*, 3 March 1883, Leicester Chronicle, 28 June 1884; *Leicester Journal*, 11 July 1884

201 Sales Catalogue 1915, ROLLR DE182/19; Abstract of Title, 1925, ROLLR M1090

202 *Derby Mercury*, 1 May 1895

203 *Leicester Chronicle and Leicestershire Mercury*, 9 May 1891

204 *Leicester Journal*, 9 August 1889

In 1895 a 'fancy fête costumée' (presumably fancy dress) event on Whit Tuesday, Wednesday and Thursday, 4, 5 and 6 June, raised funds in aid of the extension of the school. Visitors were welcomed to a marquee containing stalls, a refreshment tent, games under the direction of Samuel's son Leonard Stone, and a 'café chantant', presumably singing entertainment.[205]

During the year 1901 to 1902, Samuel Stone was High Sheriff of Leicestershire.[206] As well as his civic, political and business activities at Kirby Frith Hall, like his predecessors, Stone took on the life of a gentleman farmer. In the autumn of 1891, he sold some of his livestock in an auction. He offered for sale 46 head of shorthorn cattle, comprising two newly calved cows, four fat cows and heifers, 23 two- to three-year-old steers, three heifers due to calf the next spring, six 18-month-old steers, four yearling steers and four rearing calves. He was also selling 121 Shropshire and long-wool sheep, including 41 tupping ewes, 79 ewe and wether lambs, a Shropshire ram and six fat pigs.[207] Stone's farming interests were expanded in 1902 when he bought Manor Farm from John Harris Cooper.[208]

As in New Parks and Braunstone Frith, conflicts between the urban poor and the landowners of Kirby Frith were made manifest by poachers. Sergeant Hall and constables Kirby and Harding were on fixed point duty at about 1am in June 1898 when they were met by Charles Baskett, the butler at Kirby Frith Hall. The four of them saw five poachers enter the hall grounds where they laid netting. The butler had called on the policemen for help as the poachers were likely to put up a fight. One of the poachers, a shoe hand named Parker, offered no resistance and Sergeant Hall secured another of them. The other three mercilessly attacked the other two policemen with bludgeons. PC Harding was thrown violently to the ground but managed to secure a third poacher, despite receiving a terrible blow to his temple from a sharply pointed stone with which he had been pounded on the head. A second poacher had beaten Harding on the head with a thick stick. The seriously injured constable was taken to Leicester. Two of the poachers managed to escape, but Parker, James Cook a framework knitter and Thomas Simpson, a labourer were arrested and brought to Leicester with their spoils as evidence of their guilt: 15 rabbits, 250 yards of netting, pegs and sticks.[209]

Looking at the history of Kirby Frith Hall over the years before the 19th century reveals a set of circumstances that saw the estate passed down through the female line of inheritance and collateral descendants as although the owners had large families, their sons and daughters died either in childhood or as relatively young adults. This seems to be especially true in the 18th and early 19th centuries, although the Riley

205 *Leicester Daily Post*, 25 May 1895; *Leicester Chronicle*, 8 June 1895
206 *Yorkshire Post*, 3 September 1915
207 *Leicester Daily Post*, 3 October 1891
208 Abstract of Title, ROLLR M1090
209 *Central Somerset Gazette*, 25 June 1898; *The Chronicle*, 22 June 1989

brood was the exception. However, with so many children to provide for it seems that this meant it was difficult to establish each of them within the lesser gentry as the inheritance of their mother could not provide for them all and so the sons were apprenticed into trade, an investment in itself that was not usually available for the poorest. It is easy to imagine why some of those of the next generation could feel dissatisfied with their lot in life and become involved in crime. Despite this, two of the Riley daughters made good marriages into the Whetstone family of wool staplers who had made their way through a trade. The wills show a difference in the treatment of eldest male heirs where primogeniture kept estates intact and female ones who inherited property that had been their mothers and shared it with their sisters. There is also evidence of female agency although husbands became the legal property owners when a woman married. Younger sons might also inherit property that had been their mother's when she married.

What is apparent is that the owners of Kirby Frith Hall did not rely on the land for their income, even as early as 1703 the majority of Henry Styan's money was invested in mortgages loaned at interest to others. This idea of capital investment recurs in other wills, where instructions are left for executors to sell disposable property and invest the money to provide for widows and children and even the poor with annuities, annual incomes paid out of the interest at traditional quarter days in the year, such as Lady Day, Midsummer, Michaelmas and Christmas. Sales and purchases of land or lending money for others to do so, played an important part in the accumulation of wealth to pass on to future generations and also to provide legacies for younger children rather than the oldest male heir who would inherit existing estates which were usually left intact. The complexity of the wills, which covered every possibility for the deaths of various heirs, shows that uncertainty over the survival of children was always present in the consciousness of parents, a fear of loss perhaps only ameliorated by religion and faith, as reflected in the customary protestant opening paragraphs of most of the wills, with their emphasis on salvation and the assured expectation of an eternal afterlife.

Compared with the great estates of the aristocracy, Kirby Frith was relatively modest at only about 200 acres. A substantial landowner would have owned around 2,000 acres. However, the owners of Kirby Frith usually had land and other homes elsewhere, so before Pares's time Kirby Frith, often brought into the assets of the nominal owner by marriage to one of the heiresses, did not provide the only income for the occupier. By the late 18th century and through the 19th, the occupiers' income was derived from trade or industry. For example, Thomas Pares (1716–1805) was a Leicester attorney who purchased Hopwell Hall in Derbyshire in the 1780s. He was Richard Bakewell's executor and so the Pares were already familiar with Kirby Frith when it was bought by his son. Thomas Pares's sons Thomas (1746–1824) and John (1749–1833) were hosiers but John's son, another Thomas, became a partner and then director of a bank, working with Thomas Paget and Isaac Hodgson.

The growing wealth through finance and industry of this new and prosperous middle class contributed to a lively market for medium-sized country estates with fine houses that could enhance the status of these newly affluent men, whose farming activities were secondary to their businesses, as seen not only at Kirby Frith but in New Parks where hat maker John Mellor and hosier Thomas Stokes purchased property and land in the 1830s and 1840s. As well as a home and farm income, Kirby Frith Hall frequently provided a rental income from tenants. Francis St John moved in as a younger son from a family with an aristocratic background. As such he had almost no prospect of inheriting his family estates at Cold Overton but living at Kirby Frith Hall allowed him to maintain some social status as his immediate social position declined to the level of gentry. Other tenants of the Hall were young men like Thomas Cope, waiting to inherit the family residence at Osbaston Hall. Others were successful in business, rising in wealth, for whom Kirby Frith Hall was a step upwards from living near their business, on the way to renting or owning a grander property of their own, such as Thomas Wightman, John Briggs Robinson and James Young Stephen. Kirby Frith Hall's status as a respectable home for a member of the lesser gentry, either by birth or aspiration, came to an abrupt end with the death of Samuel Stone in 1915.

Kirby Frith in the 20th century

Samuel Stone died suddenly on 18 July 1915, at the age of 81, at home at Kirby Frith Hall. His funeral was held at St Peter's Church in Glenfield, followed by interment at Knighton Churchyard.[210] He was relatively well off, leaving £103,297 in his will, including bequests to his servants.[211] Following the death of Samuel Stone, his trustees instructed local estate agents, Warner, Sheppard and Wade, to sell the Kirby Frith Hall estate by auction on 25 September 1915. It was marketed as a well appointed, freehold, residential property, occupying a retired situation in charming pleasure grounds and gardens with ornamental flower beds, a rose garden with pergola, winding walks, tennis and croquet lawns and a profusion of ornamental trees. The Hall was approached by an extensive carriage drive, through a splendidly timbered and undulating park of 50 acres. A picturesque entrance lodge guarded the entrance to the drive, with a gardener's cottage nearby. A small farm was located within the grounds, surrounded by 171 acres three roods 29 perches of land plus neighbouring Manor House Farm, a productive holding of over 178 acres close to the village of Glenfield which was occupied by John Randles.[212] The estate does not appear to have found a buyer straight away as in the Kelly's Directory for Leicestershire of 1916, it says that the trustees of the late Samuel Francis Stone were still the chief landowners at

210 *Leicester Daily Post*, 21 July 1915
211 *Yorkshire Post*, 3 September 1915
212 *Leicester Journal*, 10 September 1915

Kirby Frith, where in 1911 only 11 people had been living, fewer than in the 1840s, as people moved from the countryside and agricultural labour to work in towns.[213]

Perhaps illustrating the social changes during World War One, Kirby Frith Hall was sold, not to a wealthy person hoping to enjoy the life of a country gentleman but to Arthur James Cart, a retired cattle dealer who let out rooms in the mansion as a house in multiple occupation, to use the modern term. Manor Farm was also purchased by Cart for £14,000 in 1919. Cart seems to have been a rather shady character and also cruel, even by the standards of the time. Life was miserable for the tenants who were bullied and exploited by Cart in collaboration with Matilda Sims who seems to have been his unacknowledged partner, normal for those days when cohabiting was frowned upon.

The first incident involving Cart at Kirby Frith Hall, which ended up in court at Leicester Castle, took place in July 1920, and was reported in the local newspaper under the headline 'Liveliness at the Hall', and 'County justices hear stories of rumpus at Kirby Frith'.[214] A series of assaults were alleged to have taken place on 17 July, when Matilda Sims, aged 45 and Arthur Cart aged 47, whose occupation was cattle dealer and whose address was given as 9 Trafford Road in Leicester, were summonsed for attacking 68-year-old John Hale.

John Hale was a commercial traveller whose wife Betsy had died in 1918 and soon after he left her family home in South Croxton where he had been a grazier for a short time. Hale had lived at Kirby Frith Hall where he rented two bedrooms, a sitting room and kitchen for ten shillings a week since December 1919. Sims had also issued a summons against Hale for an alleged assault on herself. Hale was also accused of assault by Albert Bassett, a Leicester shoe hand. After being away for a few days, he returned to find his rooms had been entered and drawers ransacked. He asked Mrs Sims for an explanation but she responded by delivering 'a vicious and violent blow' to his forehead. Then Cart appeared and when he was asked about the incident had struck Hale a heavy blow in the chest, declaring he should not go into the house again alive. Then, Hale claimed, he was set upon by another man, Bassett, who hit him on the head with a stick. They struggled and Hale claimed they fell, his throat was grabbed and his head forced into the gravel. He was left 'groaning with pain and not caring whether he was dead or dying'. When he went to the police, Hale said he took an unloaded rifle to frighten his attackers and so offer some protection.

The defence lawyer disputed the charges against his clients, referring to Hale's great energy and physical strength, despite his years. Mrs Sims claimed she got the stick because of Hale's 'dirty talk'. She said she would have given him a good hiding if she had had the chance, but he had wrenched the stick from her and struck her several times before threatening 'to put her lights out'. Sims claimed she had not been in

213 *Kelly's Directory for Leicestershire*, 1916
214 *Leicester Daily Post*, 19 July 1920

Hale's rooms; they might have been entered by someone looking over the Hall with a view to purchase. A boy named Rogers said he had heard Hale threaten 'to chop Mrs Sims' ears off'. Cart denied the assault or getting anyone else to carry it out. Bassett denied fetching a stick or having been fetched himself, claiming that it was Hale who had grabbed his throat. It was unlikely, Bassett said, that they would fetch a one-legged man with a bad arm. He claimed that Hale had pointed a gun at him and he had been trying to get it off him. In their verdict, the magistrates decided that all charges against Hale should be dropped, but Sims was fined 20 shillings and Cart 40 shillings.

On 23 September 1920, Cart claimed possession of Hale's rooms and the case again went to court which did not find in Cart's favour. Outside the court, Cart began to threaten Hale, using bad language censored by the reporter, saying, 'No matter what that ... old judge had said, he would have him out of that ... house. I'll put a man in who will chuck you and your furniture on to the lawn.' Hale told the court that he had once found a man named Hart, Sims, and a carpenter in one of his rooms. He claimed that Sims turned to the carpenter and said, 'Throw his furniture out of the other rooms. He can go and see the damned old judge again.' May Smith, Hale's niece, said she had seen her uncle bullied by Sims and heard her refer to the 'damned old judge'. Now she and her uncle had to sleep in the same room. Sims claimed she had bought some furniture from Hale and had gone to look at it. She swore she had not threatened him. Sims said she had been the tenant of the whole of the Hall since May, paying £25 a year in rent to Cart, although another tenant was already paying £26 a year in rent. As she and Cart were living together, the court deduced, the business of one party was naturally known to the other. A defence witness for Sims, Emma Kinton, a charwoman at the Hall, said she knew Mrs Sims had bought some furniture from Hale and put it in a bedroom, which she had heard Hale say he was giving up as he had no use for it. The court again found in favour of Hale, and Sims had to pay £50 in damages.[215]

Just a month later, in October 1920, Matilda Sims summoned John Hale to court for alleged threats made against her. She said she was in the kitchen when Hale came through. Sims claimed she told him to stop knocking about a woman who lived with him and whose screams frightened her. Hale abused her, she alleged, and he had threatened to fetch his gun to shoot her if she said anything else to him. Sims was said to have asked, 'Are you a wicked man to that woman?' 'No, I'm not,' replied Hale. 'Why is it she keeps screaming?' asked Sims. 'Because you make her. You're enough to drive anybody mad; you're a virago,' retorted Hale in response. The case was dismissed as it was shortly after Cart and Sims previous conviction in the court for assaulting Hale, so presumably judged by the magistrates to be vexatious.[216]

215 *Leicester Daily Post*, 25 November 1920
216 *Leicester Daily Post*, 18 October 1920

The feud between Cart, Sims and Hale continued for about a year. Another report in the local newspaper in November 1920 echoed the earlier proceedings. John Hale sued Arthur Cart and Matilda Sims, claiming £100 in damages for trespass and £10 for damage to articles of his property. Cart and Sims trespassed in the three rooms Hale occupied in the mansion, preventing him having proper use of them. The pair had filled one of the bedrooms with furniture and threw out the furniture from his other bedroom, putting him to such inconvenience that he had to occupy the sitting room as a bedroom, sharing with his niece who lived with him. His furniture was damaged, his life was made very unhappy and his health was affected.

Two years later, Cart was charged with threatening another of his tenants, Sarah Frost, who rented a cottage in an acre of ground from him at 12s 6d a week. In February 1922, Mrs Frost said she was in the spinney when Cart came up and told her the spinney was not hers. 'What am I paying 12s 6d a week for?' she asked. Cart went into the house, she claimed, and threatened 'to cleave her with the stick'. She ordered him out and said she would punch his head, so Cart then threatened to kick her. Cart said in his defence that Mrs Frost had been asked not to connect a hut to a tree so, in response, she had threatened to punch his nose and declared she intended to get some money out of him. Witnesses were called, Albert Johnson, a carpenter of Prospect Hill who corroborated Frost's story and John Taylor, a bricklayer of Court C Grunden Street, off Abbey Gate in Leicester. Taylor made the court laugh when he said that when he heard Mrs Frost using bad language, he was so disgusted he 'went to a beer shop and had a pint'. He said that later, Mrs Frost came to his house and they 'had a pint apiece'. Both witnesses declared that Mrs Frost had offered them £1 to give evidence on her behalf and so the case was dismissed.[217]

Other stories of the ill treatment of Cart's tenants and their poor living conditions appear in the autobiography of Reg Twigg, *Survivor on the River Kwai*. Twigg's family had lived in Kirby Frith Hall when he was a boy. The Twiggs had moved to Kirby Frith when Reg's father couldn't pay the rent on their previous home. It 'was a dreadful place, made worse … because it had once been a rather grand Georgian country house with a cobbled courtyard and stables. The house was falling apart when Cart had bought it and converted it into flats.

'Beneath the house and out buildings were old cellars and in the stables was an ancient landau, a reminder of the Hall's more peaceful, genteel, past. Like Hales, the Twigg family lived in a sitting room, two small bedrooms and a tiny kitchen. The floors were flagstone and freezing in winter; only the sitting room had a fireplace. Water came from a communal tap in the yard. For toilets there were buckets in an outhouse, emptied daily into a huge tub on a cart to be spread on nearby fields. The

217 *Nottingham Journal*, 6 March 1922

whole place stank. Once Reg chopped down a young oak tree for the fire and Cart went ballistic, threatening to evict everybody if no one owned up.'[218]

Conditions were even worse for the family of Twigg's friend, Bob Hillier. The Hilliers had moved from Shropshire to Kirby Frith Hall when the father got a job there working for Cart. Cart rented them a ramshackle hut in the corner of a field with a leaking corrugated tin roof. It had just one room for two adults and six children. There was no toilet, water or kitchen and so Mrs Hillier had to cook outside on an open fire. Twigg wrote of Cart's viciousness, describing him as a stranger to scruples, who rode about the place in a pony and trap, like a lord of the manor. He whipped his horse for no reason. Once it lashed out with its hind legs, which got tangled in the shafts. Cart was purple with fury and whipped the poor pony even more.

In the spring of 1923, there was a sale of horses and property, advertised for immediate disposal by A. Bayard, of Kirby Frith Hall. On sale were two heavy cart mares which were in foal and three heavy cart colts aged two, three and four years old, 'broken to all gears' or types of work. Also for sale were cobs, horses, vans, carts, harness etc and a 'very useful hunter', all guaranteed with 28 days' trial given. He was also selling two touring cars, a Ford and an American Hupmobile.[219] Bayard was probably another of the tenants.

Further evidence of the cruelty and horrific conditions of life at Kirby Frith Hall under Cart's ownership is found in another case, reported in the local press in 1920. Arthur Cart was convicted of running an unlicensed slaughter house on the premises, following a raid by P.C. Webster on 11 October. In a cowshed, about 200 yards from the Hall, he found the carcass of a beast hanging up, dressed in two pieces as if it were in a butcher's shop. There were also two heads, one of a beast (cattle) and one of a donkey, an ox tail, two plucked fowl and butcher's tools. When he returned the next day, he found the hide of a donkey on the floor and its feet and shins in a corner. Cart made the excuse that it was for the pigs, although he did not have any pigs. The donkey had been owned by Matilda Sims, who Cart said rented the hall and let rooms.

A boy called Leslie Price gave evidence, telling the court he had been near Kirby Frith Hall when he saw a donkey lying in a field. He said he told the woman at the Hall that the donkey looked ill. He then killed it with a pick, skinned and dressed the poor thing. Young Leslie then divulged that he had helped John Cart to kill horses. John Cart was Arthur's brother who rented the field and who was also on trial for running an unlicensed slaughterhouse at Kirby Frith, with a previous conviction for the same offence at Thurnby. After an eight hour hearing, both Cart brothers were convicted not just of running an illegal slaughter house, but also of possessing

---

218 Reg Twigg: *Survivor on the River Kwai*, Penguin, 2013. An extract of the book appears on the Bygone Glenfield website.

219 *The Advertiser*, 22 March 1923

diseased meat, including the donkey, intended for human food.[220] He was sentenced to two months' hard labour following this latest conviction. The court heard that Arthur Cart's brother John and Mrs Sims were both undischarged bankrupts. By 18 November 1920, Arthur Cart had 25 convictions for various offences, including breach of the peace, bad language, assault, furious driving and cruelty to animals. In an earlier case in Lincoln in 1913, Arthur Cart was described as a buyer of worn-out horses for the export trade but he often had difficulty in getting enough to make up a load. In one batch sent to Antwerp, the horses were of such inferior quality that one died on the journey to Hull.[221]

Arthur Cart appears to have been no better as an employer than he was as a landlord, tradesman or keeper of animals. In retaliation for not being paid his wages, in the spring of 1920 a young farm labourer, 16-year-old Walter Henry Stirrup, stole a horse with its saddle and bridle from Cart. Stirrup was apprehended in Kibworth Harcourt, after stopping in Oadby to ask his way to London where he planned to sell the horse. Cart, he told the court, owned the horse but owed him 15 shillings, a week's wages.[222] Stirrup was not the only young man owed money for work done for Cart. A boy named George Franks, described as a farm labourer of 70 Maynard Road, giving evidence as a witness in one of the court cases, claimed Cart owed him £1 for a week's wages. This was despite Cart being described by his solicitor as a 'well-to-do man with a large business'.[223]

Arthur Cart himself lived in the Manor Farm house, close to Kirby Frith Hall, which stood on the Glenfield side of the property. Matilda Sims lived with him and was described as his housekeeper. Cart sold part of the land associated with Manor Farm to Mr A.H. Harvey in 1925, to provide building land for part of the Dominion Suburb housing development in Glenfield.[224]

One of the men who worked for him, Joseph Robey, an army deserter, lived in a van near Manor Farm, for which he paid rent. In 1925 Robey burgled the house while Sims was out, by breaking through a bricked up doorway, from an unused part of the property. He stole £63 in gold sovereigns, a gold brooch, a gold watch and other items from a chest. The sovereigns belonged to Cart and the jewellery to Sims.[225] Robey admitted the theft, perhaps a sign of another disgruntled employee. Another example of Cart's disrespect for the law and those who worked for him was when he was in court in 1927 for failing to pay the insurance contributions of Walter Gadd, to whom he also owed £13 5s in wages. Gadd said he took a job with Cart in

---

220 *Leicester Daily Post*, 18 November 1920
221 *Grantham Journal*, 15 March 1913
222 *Leicester Mercury*, 10 April 1920
223 *Leicester Daily Post*, 20 November 19120
224 Abstract of Title, 1925, ROLLR M1090
225 *Nottingham Journal*, 13 August 1925

July 1927 at an agreed wage of 50 shillings a week. To Gadd's dismay, he was at Cart's 'beck and call from morning to night' and for several weeks was only paid 25 shillings in instalments. He told the court that once he was working in a field when Cart drove up in a trap to tell him to clear out of the field as insurance inspectors were around and gave him two shillings as a bribe. Cart claimed that Gadd did not work for him but was a tenant in a van rented for ten shillings a week. At the same court appearance, Cart was also charged with inciting a youth to steal a barrel of tar and with receiving the tar as stolen goods.[226] Cart referred to sheds and caravans as a use for the tar, so the vans that were rented out were likely to have been caravans. For the charge of receiving stolen goods and procuring a youth, Cornelius Davis to steal it for him, Cart was sentenced to six months' hard labour.[227]

Cart continued his life of petty crime, and in 1934 he was charged with a long series of fraud offences after conspiring with five accomplices, including Matilda Sims and her 17-year-old daughter, Edith. These crimes included tricking someone out of a caravan without paying for it the previous year. Sims was charged under her real name of Rhoda Matilda Simms. She was sentenced to two years' hard labour and her daughter to three years in borstal. Both women had their convictions quashed after an appeal.[228]

Cart was arrested after fleeing to Ireland with Edith Westacott, after being on the run. By now Cart and Sims had left Manor Farm and were living at 445 Hinckley Road. Even in his old age, Arthur Cart was still living a life of crime and dishonesty. He was again in court, this time in Northamptonshire charged, with two other men, with robbery with violence against William Wilkinson, from whom they stole 18 shillings and a horse-drawn float at Wooton, using 'personal violence'.[229] Just a year before he died, banned from sending livestock to Leicester Cattle Market, Arthur was in court for fraud again, after forging the signature of Joseph Hallam of Glenfield Farm on cattle market forms. Cart tried to convince the magistrate that he was in fact Joseph Hallam as it was his trade name and so no fraud had been committed. His older brother John, now over 80, was charged with a similar offence.[230]

Despite their dysfunctional life and dubious associates, Arthur Cart and Matilda Sims spent the rest of their lives together. Their first appearance together in court reports was in February 1916 when Rhoda Matilda May Simms (her full name) of 9 Trafford Place in Leicester appeared in a bankruptcy hearing. She was described as a cattle dealer although she claimed she only ever dealt in horses and wardrobes. She was living apart from her husband, although she had a baby daughter, Edith Agnes Simms, born in 1915. Arthur Cart was the tenant of the house and, she said, John Cart did the dealing

226 *Nottingham Journal*, 7 November 1927
227 *Nottingham Journal*, 4 January 1928
228 *Nottingham Evening Post*, 11 August 1934
229 *Grantham Journal*, 17 August 1935
230 *Leicester Evening Mail*, 6 April 1943

for her. She had opened a butcher's shop in Loughborough but had paid no rent. 'Jack' Cart provided the meat for the business. She had also bought a motor car which she had not paid for. In response to a tale of bad luck, the Registrar responded, 'Mrs Simms, you have been very unfortunate. The bullocks you bought went wrong, the motor car you bought went wrong, the furs you bought went wrong.' The Official Receiver remarked, 'And the shop at Loughborough went wrong, Sir.'[231] At some point during World War One, Matilda's life, and Arthur's, had clearly gone wrong and deteriorated into one of petty crime and dishonesty, what can be described as a chaotic lifestyle. How they came to be in possession of a country estate is difficult to explain, unless it was a consequence of the war and its uncertainties so that no other purchasers were willing to invest in a Georgian manor and farm.

The 1939 Register that recorded all UK citizens in preparation for wartime measures shows that Arthur Cart, farmer, cattle and horse dealer, born in 1866 was still living with Rhoda Simms (Matilda Sims) at 489 Aylestone Road, an Old Mill. Daughter, Edith Agnes Simms, born in 1915 and now a motor car dealer, was living with them. Next door someone was living in a caravan, so perhaps the pair continued to rent them out as accommodation. When Arthur Cart died in August 1944, leaving £15,758, probate was granted to Edith Agnes Simms and Edith Westacott, one of his co-accused in the fraud case.

The sad story of the latter years of Kirby Frith Hall, which had deteriorated rapidly since Samuel Stone's time, ended in a fire in the early hours of 1 June 1931. At the time of the fire there was only one family living in a flat in the Hall, Mr and Mrs Percy Bayliss and their four-year-old son, Victor, who escaped the fire. They were in bed when Percy heard something falling. When he went to the next room to investigate, he was met by a sheet of flame and a wave of intense heat. Neighbours from nearby cottages helped rescue property from the flat, including the Baylisses' bed and the cot which were saved from the flames along with Victor's treasured toy car. Leicester Fire Brigade battled the flames through the night. Percy Bayliss, a keen photographer, lost his expensive camera in the fire and also the family's holiday money of about £10, which Percy had put aside, 'For weeks I had been saving up for a summer holiday unknown to my wife. I had got about £10 in notes, but when I searched for the money it was gone, and must have been burned up very quickly – so we won't be able to go to the seaside this year.'[232] The rear of the Hall escaped the flames and so the Bayliss family were able to move temporarily into a room at the back of the building. Despite only part of the Hall being damaged in the blaze, it was never restored.

A glimpse of an otherwise unrecorded and hidden past is revealed when, in his book, Reg Twigg describes his walk from Kirby Frith Hall to the village school in Glenfield, across the fields, passing by the gypsy camp where there was always a fire

231 *Leicester Journal*, 18 February 1916
232 *Leicester Evening Mail*, 1 June 1931

and where a fox was kept tethered to a caravan wheel.[233] This camp could have been shared with some of Cart's caravan tenants, romanticised in the eyes of a child or perhaps it indicates the area's long tradition as a site for travellers. Kirby Frith Farm continued as a working farm and in 1926 suffered when there was an outbreak in the area of foot and mouth disease.[234] Life on the farm continued after Cart moved out, and in 1931, Ivan Smith of Kirby Frith Farm, the other side of the Hall to Manor Farm on the south, was advertising for a strong girl to do housework. Let us hope she fared better than those who worked for Arthur Cart.[235]

Approximately 51 and a half acres of the Kirby Frith Estate was sold by James Arthur Cart to 'The Lord Mayor Aldermen and Citizens of the City of Leicester' in around 1930. Leicester Corporation desperately needed land for housing but in 1935 competing ambitions for a municipal aerodrome won, described in another section of this book. This meant that in late 1932 some of the footpaths from Kirby Lane to Frith Farm had to be diverted to avoid the airfield.[236] This path may have been closed temporarily the following summer as there was another outbreak of foot and mouth disease among Kirby Frith livestock.[237] In 1935, the city of Leicester's boundaries were extended to include most of the area, although the section nearest to Glenfield remained in Blaby District. The majority of the land around the Hall was on the city side of the boundary and was acquired by Leicester Corporation.

By April 1950 a pile of stacked bricks was all that remained of the ruins of Kirby Frith Hall. Its orchard had been uprooted in preparation for the work to create Leicester's new municipal golf course, to replace the existing one at Western Park by Glenfield Road, which was required for the new schools to serve New Parks housing estate. Local people complained of the loss of a nice walk through the fields, a lovers' lane, that ran by the drive of the Hall and over the fields to Braunstone Lane. The drive would have been in the area marked in the plans for the golf course's fairway, and some people were concerned that the substitute path that would be marked out would not mean quite the same thing in beauty or fond memories.[238] At a point known as the Gold Diggings, a wood on the Glenfield side, a new footpath was marked out, bearing a sharp right turn to the old drive. 'If this route avoids the ponds and portions liable to flood, it will be acceptable,' was the verdict of the *Glenfield Topics* local paper. The new path would not provide a direct route to the *Airmen's Rest* pub end of Braunstone Lane and it would be essential to reopen another path which was closed during the war years and had almost disappeared.

233 Twigg
234 *Leicester Mercury*, 2 February 1926
235 *Leicester Mercury*, 9 October 1931
236 *Leicester Mercury*, 29 November and 6, 13, 20 December 1932.
237 *Grantham Journal*, 26 August 1933
238 *Leicester Mercury*, 11 April 1950

In 2020 the 129 acres of the former golf course around what was Kirby Frith Hall, much loved by local residents since its closure as a place for country walks, was under threat again. Leicester's Local Plan consultation highlighted the competing demands of land for more housing and to provide employment in an expanded industrial estate, as opposed to preserving a popular area for recreation. At the time of writing, the Local Plan proposes to allocate space for 466 houses, 50 acres to an industrial area and the remainder as public open space.

4
TRANSPORT

Turnpikes and toll gates

Important routes to south-west Leicestershire and beyond traverse Western Park and New Parks. Hinckley Road follows the line of what used to be called Doveland Lane, which led to the Doveland Gate, one of the entrances to Leicester Forest. This stood just west of the present drive to Braunstone Hall, now Winstanley House. Until the late 18th century, roads were usually in very poor condition, deeply rutted by wheel tracks, boggy or flooded. The weather could be a determining factor in whether a journey could be made. With no national road network, most traffic was local. Since Tudor times, the maintenance of roads was the responsibility of the parish, under the provisions of the Highways Act of 1555. This left road repairs to unpaid labour, conscripted from among local residents who had no specialist skills or knowledge. Paid labourers were more efficient and some parishes began to commute their obligation to provide workers to a cash payment to fund the task.[239] The Chamberlain's accounts for the Borough of Leicester show a payment of £10 made towards the mending of the highways in Braunstone Gate and Doveland Lane during the year 1622 to 1623.[240]

Turnpike Trusts were created for the purpose of keeping roads in good repair to make them passable whatever the season. The first of these was formed in 1663 to manage a stretch of the Great North Road from London. During the 18th century the demand for road transport changed as trade grew in importance and goods were exchanged over wider distances. The word 'turnpike' referred to the gate or barrier, sometimes just a long pole or pike, placed across the road to prevent travellers passing through before they had paid a fee or toll. This was usually called a toll gate or toll booth.

Both the roads to Hinckley and that to Ashby de la Zouch, now Groby Road, were improved when they became managed as the Leicester to Hinckley Turnpike and the Leicester to Ashby Turnpike, as a result of an Act of Parliament procured by Leicester Corporation between 1752 and 1754.[241] The turnpikes trusts took responsibility for

239 Susan Barton and Allan Brodie (eds): *Travel and Tourism in Britain, 1700–1914*, Pickering Chatto, London, 2014, p.1

240 Records of the Borough of Leicester, Chamberlain's Accounts, 1622–1623

241 R.W. Greaves: *The Corporation of Leicester 1689–1836*, Leicester University Press, 1970, p.65

Dane Hills Tollgate, Hinckley Road. (Records Office of Leicester, Leicestershire and Rutland)

the surfacing and upkeep of the road, paid for by road users who had to pay a toll to travel along particular stretches of it. To collect the money, the turnpike trusts erected gates attached to toll houses which were rented to a keeper, who would open the gate in return for payment. The first toll gate encountered on the way out of Leicester on the road to Hinckley was the Dane Hill Toll Gate, which according to a map of 1828, was situated close to the present-day junction of King Richard's Road and Hinckley Road, opposite Westcotes Drive.[242]

Auctions took place early each year at the Three Crowns Hotel in Leicester where hopeful toll gate keepers would bid for a particular gate house, to be occupied from the beginning of April; for instance in 1829 the rent bid for the Dane Hill Tollgate was £310 for the year. For the one serving the road to Ashby, now Groby Road, at the junction with Woodgate, known as the Fosse Lane Toll, the price bid was £401. The successful bidder had to be able to pay ten per cent of the amount he had bid before taking up his position. Further out of town, five and a half miles towards Hinckley was another tollgate, the Forest Gate, where travellers paid to continue

242 A plan of Leicester shewing the limits of the borough, boundaries of parishes and extra parochial liberties, the whole laid down from an actual survey, in the year 1828, published by A. Cockshaw of Leicester.

along that stretch of the road.[243] By 1850 the cost of renting the toll gate houses had risen, to £540 each for the Dane Hill Toll and the Forest Gate. A more expensive, and perhaps more lucrative gate had appeared on Narborough Road which raised £692 for its rent.

The successful bidders, once they had paid the agreed rent for the year, could keep any additional amount they raised as profit for their own income. The keeper of the Dane Hill Toll Gate in 1861, Charles Hanger, was charged with having taken 4d toll on 31 July from John Carter, the carrier between Stoke Golding and Leicester. Carter should have been exempt from the fee as he had already paid and been through the gate that day, and now he was on his way back from Leicester carrying no goods in the cart other than his own sack of potatoes. Hanger refused to let him pass and took hold of the horse's bridle. Carter paid under protest but summonsed Hanger to court where he was fined ten shillings for falsely charging. The magistrate also ordered Carter to pay 2s 6d costs for attending court.[244] From this single reported incident, it is not possible to judge whether over charging was a regular occurrence to make more money or a one-off misunderstanding.

The Dane Hill Toll Gate sometimes witnessed events much more grisly than people travelling through on the way to or from Leicester. In April 1813, it was the site of the execution of three men, Daniel Lynn, Samuel Dickens and Thomas Langley. The previous February, Lynn and Dickens were members of a gang of five who had broken into and robbed the house of Miss Bakewell at Swepstone, a relative of the Bakewells who had lived at Kirby Frith Hall. Three of the gang held the female servants while the others plundered the house. Two of the robbers burst into the dining room where poor Miss Bakewell was reading and demanded money and plate while holding a pistol to her head. The men threatened to 'blow her brains out' if she resisted or made a noise. The burglars were given pewter and silverware worth about £300 and left. Three of the gang, Lynn, Dickens and a woman, were arrested in Birmingham with some of the stolen items in their possession. The other two, William Smith (aka S. Hunt) and Thomas Cook were caught in Leicester.[245] They were tried, found guilty and sentenced at the Assizes. For their part in the crime, Lynn, a 30-year-old tailor with a wife but no family, and Dickens, aged 26 and a blacksmith were sentenced to death for burglary. The third man to be executed at the Toll Gate, Thomas Langley, was judged particularly harshly as his crime was to use a forged £1 note, supposedly issued by Pares Bank. Langley had once been a hawker of earthenware but most recently he had been a street vendor who 'cried about the town pies and muffins'. Langley left a wife and five children.[246]

---

243 *Leicester Journal*, 6 February 1829
244 *Leicester Chronicle*, 17 August 1861
245 *Bell's Weekly Messenger*, 21 February 1813; *Leicester Chronicle*, 27 February 1813
246 *Northampton Mercury*, 24 April 1813

Public executions always attracted crowds and this one was no exception. 'An amazing concourse of spectators attended to witness the unhappy fate of these unfortunate men, whose conduct since their condemnation, and at the "fatal tree", was marked by great penitence and resignation.'[247] All three condemned men were said to have confessed the justice of their sentence. In an accompanying broadsheet addressed to the crowd and to his fellow prisoners, Lynn admitted that it was the breaking of the Sabbath Day that had first led him to commit crime, by mixing with others of a sinful disposition.[248] The broadsheet also featured two letters, written by the literate Lynn while he was awaiting execution. He tells his story, of how he had been a midshipman in His Majesty's Ships of War and had visited many places abroad, including the 'Newnighted States of America' (sic), before falling in with a bad crowd in prison, where he had been sent due to a misunderstanding involving an army sergeant, for which he was released. His final letter, printed on the broadsheet ended with nine lines of verse:

We shall but meet a few days more,
But may we meet above;
Where pain and parting are all o'er,
In that sweet world above.
Then we with Christ in Paradice (sic),
For ever more shall Dwell;
Then let us Pray both night and day,
And so my friends farewell.

Where the Dane Hill Toll Gate stood was still countryside surrounded by fields. In 1834, a horse, belonging to Mrs J. Scott, a butcher of High Street, was stolen from the adjoining close. The horse was identifiable as it was branded on all four hooves with J.S., the owner's initials.[249] Because all traffic was horse drawn, land to grow or store hay or other fodder was needed even by urban dwellers who were in trade or affluent enough to keep a carriage. Evidence of this comes from reports in local newspapers, such as the theft of three strikes of wheat belonging to Mr Needham of Dane Hills, stolen from a barn on Shoulder of Mutton Hill in 1868. That year arsonists set fire to two haystacks on Hinckley Road during the same night. The first belonged to Mr Peel, a maltster of Highcross Street, the other to a Mr Howgill. Fighting the fires was hampered as there was no nearby water supply, only that obtained from the pump outside Shoulder of Mutton Cottage.[250]

---

247 *Northampton Mercury*, 24 April 1813
248 The Dying Declaration and Address to his fellow Prisoners of Daniel Lynn, Printed Broadsheet, April 1813, ROLLR DE2625/2
249 *Leicester Chronicle*, 30 August 1834
250 *Leicestershire Mercury*, 15 August 1868

Milestone on Hinckley Road

Even before motorised traffic, road accidents were common as the road becomes quite steep at Shoulder of Mutton Hill. For instance, in October 1847, the *Leicester Journal* reports that the Hinckley and Leicester coach over-turned while carrying over 20 passengers, 18 outside and 5 inside, when the two horses, being unable to pull the weight up the hill, were dragged backwards and the passengers thrown into a ditch. Luckily no one was killed. The ditch was filled in around 1861 but accidents continued to happen, despite the hill being reduced in height by six feet as a safety measure in 1861.

From 1874 the turnpike system of toll roads around Leicester came to an end and local government took responsibility for their upkeep. The toll houses were dismantled ready to be removed, and the materials were sold on 27 October by auctioneers Warner, Sheppard and Wade, together with the gates, oak gate posts and timber. Potential buyers met at the Dane Hill Gate House at noon and at Forest Gate Toll House at 1pm.[251] The Dane Hill Toll Gate was taken down and rebuilt beside the Hinckley Road at Leicester Forest East by Benjamin Rhodes, a builder from Bradford.[252]

Road accidents involving horse-drawn vehicles, bicycles and, later, motor vehicles occurred regularly on this stretch of road. In an attempt to make the road safer and less steep, at the same time as creating labour for the unemployed, in 1894 the Corporation paid men who were otherwise out of work, to further lower the top of Shoulder of Mutton Hill and to take away the greensward, the grass verges, at the side of the road.[253]

Speeding traffic has always been a problem, both before and after the turnpike system of highway maintenance, and the introduction of powered transport which

---

251 *Leicester Journal*, 23 October 1874
252 *Leicester Daily Post*, 24 May 1919
253 *Leicester Daily Post*, 1 February 1894

superseded horse-drawn vehicles. An accident involving horse-drawn vehicles happened in 1895 when Urban Gurney, a builder, was driving his cart pulled by a spirited young horse at a brisk pace down Shoulder of Mutton Hill when some cattle came towards him up the road. The horse was frightened and bolted. As it galloped near the town there was a collision with a trap carrying the Scampton family in the opposite direction. All the passengers and drivers were thrown into the road and injured. Scampton's horse was harnessed to Gurney's cart to carry them all home to Ratby.[254]

A fatal accident occurred the following summer when a 21-year-old cyclist, shoe hand Alonzo Mold, collided with a trap coming the other way, driven by hay dealer Mr Mason. Mold's three cycling companions had already safely passed the vehicle. Neither the trap or Mold's bicycle had lights and it was after 10pm so quite dark. The badly injured Mold was taken on a passing ginger beer trolley to the Infirmary where he died.[255]

In the early 20th century, when both motor and horse-drawn transport shared the same roads, there were inevitably conflicts. Jacob Hardy Smith, a clerk, of Leicester Frith on the far side of Groby Road pleaded not guilty to riding a motor cycle in a dangerous manner in New Parks in March 1914. As he rode his motor bike down Groby Road, William Chambers driving a pony and trap, claimed he passed him at about 35 miles an hour. The motor bike sounded like a gun. A baker who witnessed the scene said he was watching to see if the biker would get into the tramlines and kill himself. Smith, who admitted travelling at 28 miles an hour, said he was not a danger to anyone, there were no children in the road and he was in control of his motor bike in the countryside and on a straight road. However he was fined 40 shillings and ordered to pay 30 shillings in costs. The speed limit had been 20 mph since 1903.[256]

Another incident involving a cyclist was when James Morris of Bendbow Rise in Braunstone was knocked off his bike by the hit and run driver of a motor car in May 1939. Morris was left unconscious in the road with a gash to his head. The driver, Mr Crane, was later caught at the Red Cow where broken glass from his vehicle provided evidence.[257]

During World War Two, Braunstone Park was in use by the military and from February 1944, the American 82nd Airborne unit was based there. Soon after their arrival there were a couple of road accidents on Hinckley Road. In March 1944 a US Army Jeep collided with a car driven by a civilian who was arrested for drink driving. The crash happened on Shoulder of Mutton Hill with the Jeep ending up falling down the railway embankment on to the tracks, where it was smashed to pieces by a train.

---

254 *Leicester Chronicle*, 19 October 1895
255 *Leicester Journal*, 7 August 1896
256 *Leicester Chronicle*, 7 March 1914
257 *Leicester Mercury*, 20 May 1939

Tram lines, Hinckley Road. (Image Leicestershire)

Luckily the American driver managed to leap to safety and escaped unhurt. In another accident, a six year old boy, Barry Gilbert, of Gallard's Hill was killed when he was hit by a U.S. Army lorry on the Hinckley Road.[258]

From 1904 Leicester Corporation's electric tram network extended to Western Park gates, with a regular service bringing the park within reach of people living outside the local area. Public transport also encouraged suburban development and was a selling point for houses built in new streets off both sides of Hinckley Road. Trams also carried children, accompanied by a teacher, from the city centre to attend the Western Park Open Air School from 1930. The art deco, 'moderne', tram shelter at the terminus for passengers waiting by the Western Park gates was erected in 1934, one of five around the city. It was designed by architects Bedingfield and Grundy, and funded by Leicester hosiery manufacturer, Robert Rowley JP. His initials, R.R., are incorporated into the metalwork design ornamenting the structure. The windows, characteristic of the art deco period of design, were made by Crittall. Although the tram service was discontinued throughout the city in 1949, the shelter remains and since then served to protect bus passengers from inclement weather, until the stop was moved.

Concerns about road safety, speeding traffic and its volume continue into the 21st century. Bus and cycle lanes, crossings with traffic lights and speed cameras have all helped reduce the number of accidents but there remains a small number of motorists who choose to drive too quickly to the danger of themselves and others, a serious issue

258 Vincent Holyoak: *But For These Things*, Matador, 2014, p.180

Tram shelter, Hinckley Road, taken 2020.

that residents have campaigned over, securing speed humps and 20 mile an hour zones for New Parks and Western Park in 2021.

Tram outside Western Park. (Postcard)

Railways

Swannington Railway

As well as main roads the routes of two railway lines pass through the New Parks and Western Park area. One of these is no longer in use and has all but disappeared, although traces of it remain. The other, closely connected with the first, forms the south-western boundary of the neighbourhood and is still in operation.

The first track to traverse New Parks was the Leicester to Swannington Railway, one of the earliest locomotive operated lines in the world. The Leicester and Swannington Railway Company was formed by William Stenson, mining engineer of Coleorton and founder of Whitwick Colliery. In 1828 Stenson visited George Stephenson who at the time was working on the first public railway, the Liverpool to Manchester. George invested £2,500 of his own in Stenson's project and his son, Robert Stephenson, was appointed as its engineer, working in conjunction with another Geordie, Charles Liddell.[259] Local surveyor Thomas Miles worked with them to survey and cost the 16-mile route. Businessman, John Ellis of Beaumont Leys, and other local colliery owners became involved in the project, forming a company which held its inaugural meeting at the Bell Hotel on Humberstone Gate in Leicester. A total of £58,250 was raised in subscriptions, with the rest of the £90,000 needed supplied by Stephenson's contacts in Liverpool. To build a railway required an individual Act of Parliament that received the Royal Assent in 1830 and work began in 1831. Writing in 1891, 60 years later, Agnes Fielding Johnson, said that the aim of Stenson and Ellis was 'mainly that of self defence against the large supplies of Derbyshire coal being brought to Leicester by canal; and also superseding the conveyance by road of their own coal from the Swannington district, a tedious and costly method, and often cruelly burdensome to the animals employed on the rough and hilly roads to Leicester'.[260]

The railway was to run from Swannington, close to the Leicestershire coal mines to the wharf at West Bridge, where a station would be built near the canal. To reach Swannington the railway would have to cross New Parks but the locomotives of the time lacked the power to travel up the hill. To solve this problem a tunnel, designed by George Stephenson, was dug under the supervision of his son Robert. This meant that trains from West Bridge travelled under New Parks, going into the tunnel and emerging near Glenfield where there was a station. The tunnel was only the second in the world built for a railway and at 1,796 yards (1,642 meters) was the longest.

To dig the tunnel, which needed to be too deep underground for cut-and-cover methods, and too long for boring directly from one end to the other, a different construction method was called for. Vertical trial borings mistakenly seemed to show that the tunnel would go through solid ground. The route of the tunnel was plotted

259 Grace's Guide to Industrial History
260 Fielding Johnson, p.371

Glenfield Tunnel shaft, Stenson Road, taken 2021.

overground and four large vertical shafts were bored to the required depth. The tunnel was then created by linking these shafts with horizontal tunnelling below ground.

The assumption that the tunnel would pass entirely through solid ground proved to be a mistake. About a third of the way through, the workmen discovered that the nature of the earth had changed and the tunnel was passing through running sand, a problem that would make it unstable and dangerous. The solution was to line the tunnel with bricks, to give it the strength to prevent it collapsing. At first the bricks were made from clay from Thomas Pare's estate, perhaps at Kirby Frith,

Shoulder of Mutton Hill or Brick Kiln Close. However the quality of these bricks was inadequate and they could not be supplied in sufficient quantities, therefore the bricks to line the tunnel had to be made in a kiln on site. The task of lining the tunnel was done using wooden 'shuttering' to hold back the sand while the brick lining was built inside the shuttering.[261] Timber from Braunstone was used in construction.

During construction work on the tunnel, the contractor Daniel Jowett fell down one of the working shafts in a section of the tunnel that burrowed through porous sandstone and was killed. Jowett was not the only person to meet a tragic end during tunnel construction. In October 1831 the Board voted to give £5 to Revd Irvine for the relief of Mrs Pegg, a widow whose husband had been killed in the tunnel.[262] Without any experience of a similar project, some local contractors felt out of their depth and quit the job. The tunnel was completed at a cost of £17,326 12s 2 1/2d, way over the budgeted amount of £10,000 due to the unexpected technical challenges.[263] The capital costs of the line between Leicester and Swannington eventually reached £140,000.[264] For security, there were gates at each end of the tunnel. The wide shafts used in construction and the narrower test bores remained after completion, providing 14 air vents along the course of the tunnel, which can still be seen today.

The first stretch of the line to be completed and in use was between Leicester and Bagworth. The railway opened as far as Bagworth on 17 July 1832, with much ceremony and excitement among local people who turned out to line the route. At the Leicester end, 'The banks of the Soar, a place out of all danger, were lined with females, decked in the gayest of colours, the men occupying the more dangerous situations. The tops of Kelly's and Raby's turreted factories were filled with flags and spectators', said the eye witness account of Mr W. Gardiner, who described the engine as a 'snorting monster' which 'began to fill his lungs, and try his strength.'

Tickets for the initial journey and the opening ceremony were sold to over 300 people. For the directors of the company, a covered carriage was made which would be used for future passengers on the line. Other travellers on that first journey rode in ten open wagons, with green baize-covered planks installed as temporary seating. Gardener was one of these lucky people, who was 'induced, at the hazard of broken bones', to place himself in one of the carriages on its destined flight to Bagworth. The train was 60 yards in length and decorated with flags and banners

---

261 *West Bridge Wharf and Station, The Story of the First Railway Headquarters in the Midlands*, Leicester Industrial History Society, 2018, p.6-7

262 C.R. Clinker, *The Leicester and Swannington Railway*, Leicestershire Archaeological Society Transactions, 1954

263 Story of Leicester website

264 *Leicestershire Mercury*, 25 November 1848

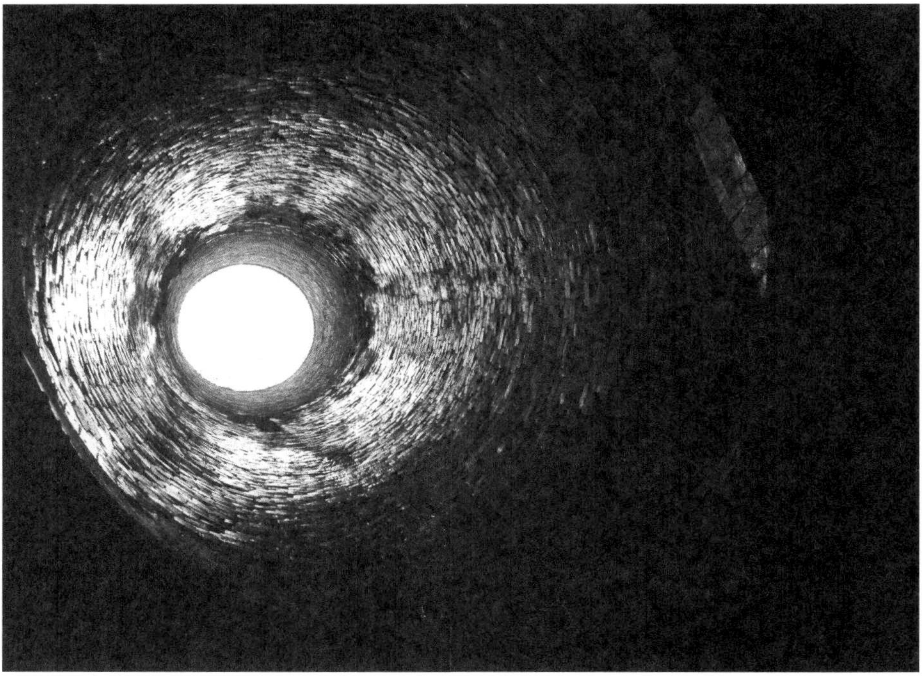

Shaft from inside Glenfield Tunnel, taken 2016.

bearing inscriptions, such as 'Success to the Leicester and Swannington Railway'; 'Cheap Coal and Granite, Warm Hearth and Good Roads'; 'We wish our efforts to promote the prosperity of all'; 'May the Triumph of Science prove the Blessing of the People'.[265]

At the opening ceremony the first locomotive on the line, Comet, was driven by George Stephenson accompanied by another driver, identified only as Weatherburn, but likely to have been Robert Weatherburn (born 1811), another native of Northumberland who had worked with Stephenson and taken part in the Rainhill Trials, and who subsequently moved to Leicestershire.[266] Comet had travelled to Leicester from the north-east by sea and canal. To the delight of the spectators in Leicester, when the train set off from West Bridge it travelled just a short distance before reversing back to its starting point and setting off again, at what would have been a 'killing pace' for a horse. Seeing the train go backwards would have surprised the spectators, as for a horse-drawn vehicle this was a difficult manoeuvre. When it reached the tunnel entrance, where there was a cottage for a railway worker and a water tank, Comet stopped to take on more water. Then, to the great joy of the passengers, the train bounded through the tunnel in just six minutes. It stopped for a few minutes when it reached a branch line from the quarries at Groby to be

265 *Leicester Chronicle*, 21 July 1832, p.103-104
266 Grace's Guide to Industrial History

Glenfield Tunnel, east end. (LAHS)

congratulated by the villagers, workers and Thomas Pares of Kirby Frith Hall, while a band played in celebration.

Around 60 years later, Agnes Fielding Johnson described how Comet set off to the accompaniment of ringing church bells and the firing of a cannon.[267] This cannon was carried on the rear wagon, and was fired to alert the villages on the route so they could greet the train with a peel of their own church bells. Frightened sheep and cows ran from the noise. In little more than an hour the train arrived in Bagworth, where several marquees and long tables with food, wine and champagne awaited them. The ladies were entertained across the road in the house of Mr Pickard, an agent for Stenson's company. There was an immense number of spectators at every point along the route and in adjacent fields, who enjoyed their own celebrations in the pubs of the villages through which the line passed.

How gay appeared the meadows of Glenfield, Ratby and Newtown. These were spread over with gazers, to see us emerge from the tomb! The landscape was beautiful, speckled with the white shirts of the hay-makers. Here the line runs through a series of flowery meadows, where the country lasses darted from their toil – the mower left his scythe – the ploughman his horses, and with the rickman, ran to behold the wondrous sight. 'Lord, what will the world come to,' said an old farmer as he leaned on his fork, 'to see wagons running without their tits [sic]*.'*[268]

267 Fielding Johnson, p.371

268 Presumably an archaic term for a horse.

A couple of trucks of coal and granite were added to the train for its journey back to Leicester, but it was still able to travel at over 20 mph, although at a slower pace in the tunnel which took ten minutes on the return.[269]

Contemporary accounts of the Leicester to Swannington Railway's opening in the local press stated that the journey passed without accident or incident, although one account contradicts this. A reminiscence by William Kelly, a man who had been on that first journey, related, 'All went well until reaching the middle of the tunnel, when a sudden shock was felt. The train came to a dead stop. The engine chimney was knocked down and the occupants of the open carriages were for some time in the middle of a moist and smoky atmosphere, which was odorous of anything but the perfumes of Arabia.' This accident was explained at the time, he said, as having been caused by one of the cross-timbers used in constructing the top of the tunnel having been left in by mistake. However, the late Mr E.S. Ellis had told him a few years before that it was really because of an error in the gradient of the line. Kelly described how, owing to the effect of the steam and dense smoke, the light bonnets, veils, and dresses of the ladies, and the shirt fronts and faces of the gentlemen were thickly covered with black spots. Where a brook crossed the line, the train stopped and most of the party descended and washed their faces in the stream using their pocket handkerchiefs as towels.[270]

Agnes Fielding Johnson repeats the story of a mishap, 'In the tunnel the engine chimney caught the low roof with an alarming shock, and on safely issuing from the darkness and smoke, the train was stopped to allow the company to alight and wash off the accumulated smuts in the adjacent Glenfield brook,' information she obtained from the records of Clement Stretton.[271] This story, retold to commemorate the line's Jubilee, contrasts with Gardiner's version of travelling through the tunnel 50 years earlier, '

In less than 200 yards we lost the light of day, and were immersed in utter darkness. Before we were half through, some of the passengers felt a great depression of breath, which was probably occasioned by the fumes of the engine, with a mixture of fear; but on bursting into the open day dismissed these sensations. It was truly sublime, extatic [sic] and delightful!'[272]

In its report on the opening, the *Leicester Journal* wrote, 'There was a slight delay by the chimney striking the roof of the tunnel,' and does mention passengers, particularly the ladies, washing.[273] This would imply that the striking of the roof was only a slight mishap, perhaps a scrape or coming very close, not giving enough space for the smoke to disperse. If the tall chimney had actually struck the tunnel roof, it would have needed repairing, most likely putting an end to or seriously delaying the journey.

269 *Leicester Chronicle*, 21 July 1832
270 William Kelly FSA: *Leicester Chronicle*, 22 July 1882
271 Fielding Johnson, p.372
272 *Leicester Chronicle*, 21 July 1832
273 *Leicester Journal*, 20 July 1832

wheels (a pattern now very generally employed) was designed and con-
structed by R. Stephenson and Co. for the Leicester and Swannington Railway Company.

LEICESTER AND SWANNINGTON RAILWAY COMPANY.
"ATLAS," No. 6. FEBRUARY 8, 1834.

	ft.	in.
Diameter of cylinders	0	16
Length of stroke	0	20
Diameter of wheels	4	6
Weight of engine in working order	17 tons.	

The driving wheels were without flanges. The "steam trumpet" in use upon that railway at the time will also be observed.

The "Atlas" proved a highly satisfactory engine, and a long and most complete series of experiments was made by Mr. Henry Cabry, the company's engine superintendent, to ascertain exactly its performance, the result being that several other engines of similar design were built for other railways.

Atlas, locomotive. (Image Leicestershire)

As there had been a fatality at the opening of the Liverpool to Manchester Railway, the owners would have been anxious to ensure that nothing made it look as if rail travel was unsafe, as it often was in those early days, with many accidents because of the public's lack of experience of how to behave while travelling at speed. To ensure passenger safety in the tunnel, where sticking one's head out of the window could result in decapitation, carriages for the line were built to be relatively narrow to give space in the tunnel and had bars fitted at the windows.[274]

Vandalism and trespass on the railway soon became a problem and in October 1832, just three months after the line opened, the company was compelled to make an announcement in the local newspapers, saying that in order to put a stop to the

274 Story of Leicester website

inconveniences and dangers which had arisen from pedestrians using parts of the line as a footpath and from mischievous people throwing stones, pieces of wood and other things, obstructing free passage of the railway, a fine of 40 shillings would be imposed for travelling on foot on the track. For throwing things the fine was £10, while transportation to the colonies was the possible penalty for breaking or taking any part of the railway.[275]

The railway achieved its objective of reducing the price of locally mined coal in Leicester. Using packhorses to bring the coal to the town cost 16 shillings a ton, but the new railway could deliver coal at just ten shillings a ton, cheaper than coal from Derby which cost 13 shillings a ton. An indication of the initial success of the railway, the locomotive Comet was joined on the line by further engines called Phoenix (in 1832), Samson, Hercules and Goliath (1833), and Atlas in 1834. So far all these locomotives had been designed and built by Robert Stephenson. The first by another manufacturer, 'Liverpool', by Edward Bury, joined them later in 1834 to be followed by Vulcan, made by Charles Tayleur in 1835, Ajax in 1837 made by the Haigh Foundry, and the more powerful Hector in 1839.[276] The line was soon extended to Swannington, making a total distance of 14 miles.

The Midland Counties Railway

In 1840 the Midland Counties Railway had opened a line that connected Leicester with the rapidly developing national rail network although it did not link with the Swannington line. Following mergers with other regional companies, this became the Midland Railway in 1844, with George Hudson as chairman of the company and John Ellis as deputy. For the coal, granite and other products carried along the line from Swannington to benefit from these links, the contents of its wagons had to be emptied into horse-drawn carts to be transferred to the new line, a time consuming and costly process that made Leicestershire coal expensive.

After several offers by other railway companies, inspired by the mania for railways that was taking hold among investors, in August 1845 the Swannington shareholders decided to sell their line to the Midland Company.[277] In January 1846, the *Leicestershire Mercury* reported that a short extension of the Leicester and Swannington Railway was needed to connect with the Midland Railway, which would cost between £70,000 and £80,000.[278] The shareholders of the Leicester and Swannington Railway attended a meeting in June 1846 at the Bell Hotel on Humberstone Gate, chaired by Clement Winstanley of Braunstone Hall. They discussed the vesting of their company in the

275 *Leicester Journal*, 19 October 1832

276 Paul Banbury: *The Leicester and Swannington Railway In a Nutshell*, Leicestershire Industrial History Society, 2014, p.26

277 Clement Edwin Stretton: *The History of the Midland Railway*, 1901, p.102

278 *Leicestershire Mercury*, 24 January 1846

larger Midland Railway, a resolution proposed by Isaac Hodgson and Edward Shipley Ellis.[279] Joseph Harris of Westcotes Hall objected to the proposal as it would give the Midland a monopoly with sole control of the railway communications of Leicester and of its coal supply. He reminded his fellow shareholders that the railway was originally formed to deliver cheap coal to the town. The shareholders were assured that the existing rate of charges, 2 1/2d a ton per mile, would continue. The shareholders voted by 336 votes in favour of the proposal to just 12 against the merger.[280]

This happened at the peak of the period dubbed 'Railway Mania' when speculators invested in railway shares, the price of which kept going up, creating a bubble. In the year that the companies merged and the Midland Railway applied to build the extension to the line, there were 272 separate Acts of Parliament establishing new railway companies and projects to build new lines. Samuel Smiles, wrote of the phenomenon in his *Life of George Stephenson,* which illustrates the incredible workload and demand for his skills that the great railway engineer experienced,

> 'The rapidity with which railways were carried out, when the spirit of the country was fairly up, was indeed remarkable. This was doubtless in some measure owing to the increased force of the current of speculation, but chiefly to the desire which the public now entertained for the general extension of the system. Railways became the topic of conversation in all circles; they were felt to give a new value to time; their vast capabilities for 'business' peculiarly recommended them to the trading classes [eg people like Ellis and Stenson]; while the friends of 'progress' dilated on the great benefits they would eventually confer upon mankind at large.'[281]

The newly merged company obtained the necessary Act of Parliament on 3 August 1846, amended a year later. Work was soon under way on an extension to the line between Leicester and Swannington and onwards to Burton from Coalville, a new route possibly devised by Robert Stephenson and Charles Liddell. As well as diverting the line around the lifts for wagons up the inclined planes of Bagworth and Swannington, it also bypassed the Glenfield Tunnel, now possible because of the technical improvements that had led to more powerful locomotives. It left the existing line near Desford, and then crossed New Parks, looping round to join the Midland Railway at Knighton Junction, a diversion of just over six and a half miles. This involved digging a cutting at Shoulder of Mutton Hill and building an embankment which, along with the construction of the 'Twelve Arch Bridge' across the Soar and canal, delayed the completion of the project.[282]

279 Stretton, p.102
280 *Leicester Chronicle*, 20 June 1846
281 Samuel Smiles: *Life of George Stephenson, Railway Engineer*, John Murray, 1858, p.348
282 Stretton, p.103-104

Midland Railway cutting, Shoulder of Mutton Hill.

The contractor appointed to carry out the work was Simms and Colpas and Company, whose previous work had been as dealers in timber and various other mercantile activities, for instance, in December 1847 the merchants Simms, Colpas and Company were selling a year-old steamer made of iron in Liverpool.[283] Judging by the number of court cases in which he was involved, Henry Colpas seems to have been the one responsible for negotiations and payments to subcontractors. Claims for payment by these subcontractors identify some of the smaller firms engaged in the construction of the railway and its supply chains. For instance, there were six cases involving suppliers and carriers of wooden sleepers. Goodman's boatmen claimed £686 for the carriage of sleepers by canal; the price agreed in London with an agent for Colpas was 10s 4d a ton but when the load reached Leicester they were only offered 8s 5d a ton, a significant difference.[284] In another case, a carrier called Mellor claimed £4 5s 3d that was owed him for bringing sleepers from London. The judge found in favour of all six plaintiffs in these cases.

Other claims for short payments were made by Shirley White for work by his business on the excavation and turfing of the railway. The first embankment built was 2,394 yards long, measured by Mr Attwood, an agent of Simms and Colpas, and a second one was 3,290 yards in length, measured by Mr Packer. White said he was paid by the day and did not know how long the job would take when he began. The court found in White's favour as the certificate showing the measurement of the second longer embankment had been altered to the same length as the shorter first one.[285]

Another disputed payment was made by subcontractor Shaw, for permanent and temporary fencing he had erected by the branch line at a fixed price per yard in

283 *Shipping and Mercantile Gazette*, 23 December 1847
284 *Leicestershire Mercury*, 16 December 1848
285 *Leicester Chronicle*, 13 January 1849

1848. The final bill came to £2,002 but by June 1851 he had only been paid £1,548 9s 8d on account.[286] Yet another claim, this time for £11 3s 8d, was made by a Mr Thompson, for levelling on the railway. Colpas alleged that the contract was to level and put soil on the slopes of the embankments and cuttings to a depth of six inches but Thompson's work had only been to a depth of three and a half inches. Thompson said that when he took on the contract nothing was said about the depth of soil. He had agreed to trim and soil the slopes in a workmanlike manner with what soil there was. He explained to the court he had been told by Mr Colpas himself to make the most of what there was. After it was finished it was examined by Colpas, who said it looked well. Thompson said all the soil provided had been used there and nowhere else. He had not been told to procure more from anywhere else and was not bound to procure it at his own expense. The judge thought Colpas had objected to the work in order to get out of paying the men for it.

Yet another claim against the contractor was made by Hill and others for £12 8s 3d, the balance owed to them on their account with Colpas for sawing wood. Hill alleged that the wood supplied was so old and full of nails and bolts that a lot of work had to be done to the edges before the serviceable wood could be sawn. It was yellow pine and not the Memel anticipated. Memel was lumber from the forests of what is now Lithuania, but at that time part of the Prussian Empire. Apparently, according to Colpas's witness, 17,000 feet of wood had been charged for but only 6,000 feet actually produced. Hill told the court that he considered he had only been paid in part because money was scarce.

Money owing for work done to carriages on the railway, £2 7s 6d, was claimed by Mr Ilford, another tradesman who had not received all the payment agreed in his contract. In every case the judges at Leicester County Court found in favour of the plaintiffs, showing either that Simms and Colpas suffered from acute cash flow problems as they had not been paid themselves, or they failed to budget correctly for the project, or perhaps were just trying to swindle the subcontractors to make more profit for themselves.

To transport materials around the construction site, a locomotive was needed to tow trucks of earth removed from cuttings to where it was needed to create embankments. In order to procure one, Simms and Colpas and Company placed an advertisement in the *Railway Times* for a four-wheel engine and tender, in good condition for earthwork and ballasting.[287] One was purchased, rather than hired, and was resold after the project's completion.

Apart from the on-site steam engine, all construction was carried out by the tough, physical, manual labour of a vast workforce of navvies. As well as cuttings and embankments, new bridges had to be built to carry the railway over existing roads

286 *Leicester Journal,* 13 June 1851
287 *Railway Times,* 30 December 1848

and the River Soar, including one at the top of Shoulder of Mutton Hill to carry the Hinckley Road over the railway, which at this point was in a cutting. The bricks for this bridge were made on site and fired in a kiln in Shoulder of Mutton Close. The *Leicester Journal* printed a story of a tragedy that occurred during construction in February 1849, when a woman and four men, described as tramps, were crushed by falling bricks. These bricks were piled up over the kiln's flue and fell on them as they slept in the hole of the brickyard furnace. Workers there said it was often occupied by tramps keeping warm during the night. The woman and two of the men were killed, their bodies taken to the Birmingham Tavern on Braunstone Gate. One of the men, who was wearing a blood-stained fur cap, was recognised as someone who had previously done some work on the railway. The second was a young man said to have slept in the draught hole of the kiln for two nights, who had told a witness that he had had no bread for three days; all he had eaten the day before were some Swede turnips which he had roasted at the fire hole. From his dress, he was thought to be a miner. The woman was dressed in an old black velvet bonnet, a figured gown and a shawl with a small check pattern. She had been seen begging with two children earlier.

Working on railways was a dangerous job, with no health and safety legislation to protect workers. Another fatal accident in the cutting at Shoulder of Mutton Hill took place after the line had opened in 1855, when George Slater, a labourer, died of injuries sustained when earth above gave way and fell on him.[288]

Progress on constructing the extension to the Midland Railway to Swannington was rapid. There were two sets of workpeople, on day and night shifts, with hundreds of navvies regularly employed.[289] The sheer scale of the project can be deduced from the list of items that had been used during the work by the contractors Simms Colpas, which were offered for sale by auction after completion of the project. In an advertisement addressed to railway contractors, farmers, horse-dealers, builders, blacksmiths, wheelwrights and others, the auctioneers Harris and Cooke offered the whole of the surplus plant, horses and materials from the contract and listed the following items for sale: a capital four-wheel locomotive and tender, in good working condition, by Stephenson and Company; 250 two-and-a-half-yard earth wagons; 300 flat-bottomed rails; 28 powerful draught horses; 70 sets of thiller and gear harness; 15 strongly built carts; two strong timber carriages; two stone drugs; a large quantity of sleepers, dobbin carts, wheelbarrows, wheeling planks, centring loggins, Baltic timber, deals and boards, crabs, blocks, ropes, chains, pile engines; blacksmiths' tools including bellows, anvils and equipment for six forges; and all temporary erections stored at Fosse Yard on Hinckley Road where the sale was to be held.[290]

---

288 *Leicester Journal*, 21 September 1855
289 *Leicestershire Mercury*, 15 July 1848
290 *Leicestershire Mercury*, 11 August 1849

A steam engine entering Glenfield Tunnel, May 1962. (R.C. Riley, Transport Treasury)

Foreign timber owned by Simms and Colpas, left over from the railway building project, was put on sale by auction in November 1849, at Swann's Wharf on Mill Lane. Wood on sale was 12,000 feet of dry white battens, 7,500 feet of red pine deals, 18,000 feet of yellow pine planks, 5,500 feet of spruce battens.[291] Wood for use in the massive construction project came from far and wide, not just Britain. Records from the Port of Gloucester show that a load of deal and sleepers were imported for Simms and Colpas from St John's, New Brunswick in Canada, carried on the ship Ella of Cork, an illustration of how colonialism was helping to fuel industrialisation in Britain.[292]

The improved section of the double line of rails between Desford and Long Lane, now named Coalville, was ready in March 1848 and opened to passengers from Leicester on 27 March.[293] The rest of the new stretch of the line opened on 1 August 1849, without the ceremony associated with the opening of the original Leicester to Swannington Railway 17 years earlier. It scarcely got a mention in the local newspapers, perhaps because the opening of new railways had become commonplace. Previously the coal had to be carted from one line to the other, but now the wagons could be loaded at the pit mouths or quarries and drawn to the stations where it was

291 *Leicestershire Mercury*, 17 November 1849
292 *Worcestershire Chronicle*, 18 August 1847
293 Stretton, p.103

Closed tunnel, 1965. (Nigel Tout, Wikimedia commons)

required without further trouble or expense. The line could now carry engines and carriages of the standard gauge, as there was no need for them to be made narrower to fit in the tunnel or have bars at the windows.

Beyond Swannington, the line extended to Ashby de la Zouch and Burton upon Trent. Diesel trains began to travel the route from 14 April 1958. Known as the Burton Line, it carried both passengers and freight until the passenger service ended on 7 September 1964. The line is still in use for freight, carrying mostly minerals. There have been discussions to restore a passenger service on the route, rebranded as the Ivanhoe Line, since the 1980s, when there were suggestions of a station at Western Park, off Ainsdale Road. This was nearly 100 years after the possibility of a station to serve Western Park had been raised at the opening of the park in 1899. A feasibility study into the possibility of a new passenger service was approved in May 2020.

With the opening of the extension by the Midland Railway, the portion of the original Leicester to Swannington line that passed under New Parks through the Glenfield Tunnel to Leicester remained as a spur, carrying mostly coal and other minerals, plus passengers to West Bridge. West Bridge station was closed to passengers in 1928 and the line to that point, used for freight only, closed altogether in 1966.

Although nowadays the New Parks end of the tunnel is sealed, the tunnel still exists beneath some of the roads, houses and gardens between there and Stephenson Court in Glenfield. Most of the shafts are still there, including the four large ones used during construction and the smaller ones that were probably the bore holes used to test the ground. Some of the shafts come up in the gardens of the houses built on top of the tunnel. The most easily visible to passers by can be seen beside New Parks Boulevard and at Amhurst Close, Weatherburn Close, and Kemp Road. Leicester City Council bought the disused tunnel for £5 from British Rail in 1969 and the entrance or portal at the eastern end was built over, the cutting leading to it filled in and houses built above the sealed entrance, creating Copeland Avenue.

In 2006 the Council tried to sell the tunnel but, unsurprisingly, had no takers. Following a collapse in a similar tunnel of the same age, built using the same techniques, between 2007 and 2008 the Council installed 31 concrete hoops to reinforce the structure and ensure safety, at a cost of around £500,000.[294] In recognition of the historical importance of the tunnel, it now enjoys statutory protection by being listed at Grade II by Historic England. The names of the early engines, Comet, Phoenix, Samson and Ajax, are commemorated in road names in New Parks, close to the route of the former railway line, as are Jowett, Stenson, engineer Stephenson, Hudson, Weatherburn and the destination of Swannington. Part of the route of the line can be explored in Stokes Wood Park and the Rally recreation ground off Tudor Road.

Leicester's airport

It may come as a surprise to read that Leicester was once at the forefront of the emerging field of civil aviation in the early 20th century. Leicestershire Aero Club was formed in 1909 at the Bell Hotel on Humberstone Gate, although at that time it possessed no planes of its own. It initially focussed, between 1911 and 1914, on inviting aviation pioneers to give displays at the Aylestone Aerodrome, which was at the Old County Cricket Ground, what is now the Grace Road Ground, during the period when the Cricket Club was based on the playing field on Aylestone Road. The aviator, Gustav Wilhelm Hamel, gave a display of his flying expertise there in January 1913, when he made three flights in his 50-horsepower Bleriot monoplane in front of 1,000 spectators.[295] During one flight Hamel is said to have closely followed a tram, though there are no reports of what any passengers on board might have felt about this. Flying was still a dangerous occupation and Hamel disappeared in May 1914 while flying across the Channel.

Leicester saw its first demonstration of a loop-the-loop at the Old Cricket Ground in May 1914, by Bentfield Charles (B.C.) Hucks, who in September 1913 became the first British aviator to perform the feat. Hucks flew a two-seater, 80-horsepower Bleriot, in a display described as 'ragtime flying' in the local press.[296] Hucks's trick

294 *Glenfield Tunnel and Glenfield Station,* Leicestershire Industrial History Society, 2018

295 *Leicester Daily Post,* 20 January 1913

296 Timeline of British Civil Aviation History in 1913, www.rafmuseum.org, accessed 1 May 2020

flying included vertical banking and diving. He also took up a passenger, Mr Green. Some spectators paid to enter the show but many more watched from the outside.[297] Displays such as these helped inspire confidence in aviation among witnesses.

During World War One, although the Leicestershire Aero Club was no longer active, by working with the Chamber of Commerce its members joined in the fund raising efforts to present a BE1 aircraft named 'The City of Leicester' to Canada as part of the Aircraft for the Dominions initiative. The presentation ceremony took place on Western Park in 1916, attended by an estimated 40,000 spectators.

The Leicestershire Aero Club reformed in the 1920s, with Harry Purt of the chamber of Commerce as secretary, World War One pilot Roy Winn of Winn's Cafes as chairman and Sir William Lindsay Everard as its president.[298] It wasn't until 1929 that the Aero Club acquired its own plane, thanks to Lindsay Everard, a DH60 Gypsy Moth G-AAIF, which was named 'The Quorn'. With a membership of 900, it was one of the largest such clubs in Britain. The plane was based first of all at an airfield rented at Desford, 20 acres known as Cart's Field and then later at Ratcliffe, the home of Lindsay Everard. Touring aeronautical displays, termed Flying Circuses, were arranged by the Club at Desford and on a new airfield with grass runway at Braunstone between 24 April and 3 May 1931.[299]

Leicester Corporation had purchased Braunstone Frith from the Winstanleys in 1925 and since 1928, the Aero Club had been in discussions with the council in the hope of being able to use the land as an airfield, but there were delays because the need of land for housing was thought more important than an airport by the Housing Committee. The Leicestershire Aero Club gained permission to use this land at Braunstone Frith, next to Kirby Frith, near the Hinckley Road, for an aerodrome in 1931. Eventually, in 1932, the Corporation designated 72 and a half acres of the 154 acre site for the aerodrome project, which was to become Leicester's municipal airport.[300] Footpaths leading from Kirby Lane to Braunstone Frith Farm were diverted in 1933, to prevent the public walking across the aerodrome.[301] It received its licence to operate in March 1935. A copy of this licence is in the National Archives at Kew.[302]

Thanks to the enthusiasm of Cllr Willford, the new airport was built and funded by Leicester Corporation but sub-contracted to Leicestershire Aero Club as its operator. At this time, aircraft did not have the distance range of later planes and had to stop regularly to refuel. This meant a network of small regional airfields was

297 *Leicester Daily Post*, 7 May 1914
298 Leicester Aeroclub History, https://web.archive.org/web/20070922201544/http://www.leicesterairport.com/ accessed 30 April 2020
299 *100 Years – a Celebration and History of the Leicestershire Aero Club 1909-2009*
300 Braunstone Frith – appropriation of land for municipal aerodrome, National Archives HLG 51/295
301 ROLLR QS48/1/300
302 Aerodrome licence for Braunstone Frith, National Archives AVIA 2/715

Leicester Airport or Braunstone Aerodrome, c.1935. (Records Office of Leicester, Leicestershire and Rutlad)

needed. The aerodrome provided an important link between London and the north for flights.[303] It had a hangar and a luxurious club house, with a roomy central hall, brick fireplaces and full length windows, built at a cost of £18,000 by the En Tout Cas Company.[304]

The clubhouse was run by a steward assisted by his wife. Members could enjoy toast and muffins by an open fire, hot lunches, and dinners, all served by white coated waiters. There was a lounge, a smoke room, a room for playing cards and outside there were tennis and badminton courts. On top of the Club House was a rotating and tilting 800,000 candlepower Chance Shadow Bar Floodlight that allowed planes to take off and land at night for an additional ten shillings charge on top of the one-shilling landing fee.[305] This light was a beacon that was said to be visible from 47 miles away.[306] The building stood in the centre of grass runways, 1,000 feet long in every direction, built with the specification that a car should be able to drive anywhere on the grass at 20 mph without its passengers experiencing any discomfort.

However, the airport had no wireless facilities as there were no available radio frequencies: to contact the ground, pilots had to call Heston Aerodrome in west London from where a telephone link put them in touch with Leicester. Aeronautical

303 *Leicester Mercury*, 13 March 1950
304 *Leicester Mercury*, 3 November 1950, 6 November 1950
305 *Leicester Aeroclub History*
306 *Leicester Evening Mail*, 5 January 1935

Planes at airshow, Leicester Airport, c.1935. (Records Office of Leicester, Leicestershire and Rutland)

equipment manufacturers Reid and Sigrist were conveniently based on site and were able to offer engineering skill to carry out repairs to aircraft. Braunstone was a satellite site to the Desford aerodrome from where Reid and Sigrist operated the Civilian Flying Training School, contracted by the Air Ministry to supply personnel for the Auxiliary Air Force.

Although the airfield was already in use, the opening ceremony on 13 July 1935 was performed by the Air Minister, Sir Philip Cunliffe-Lister, in front of thousands of spectators in temporary grandstands. There were speeches by the Lord Mayor, Alderman E. Grimsley, and Sir William Lindsay Everard. The opening of the airport was anticipated to be such a popular attraction for Leicester people and country residents, that a one-way system was introduced along Kirby Lane, with traffic regulated by police. Special bus services operated from Western Boulevard. There were four enclosures for spectators, which included parking for motor cars. One was reserved for Aero Club members, one cost five shillings, another 2s 6d and a one shilling enclosure was accessed from Hinckley Road. Bicycles were banned from the parking enclosures so had to be left at the road side. Tickets could be purchased in advance from the Municipal Offices in Leicester or at ticket boxes on Kirby Lane. Although there were some grandstands, most spectators who came by car were expected to watch the flying displays from their vehicles. Loudspeakers gave a commentary on what was happening in the air.[307]

---

307 *Leicester Evening Mail*, 12 July 1935

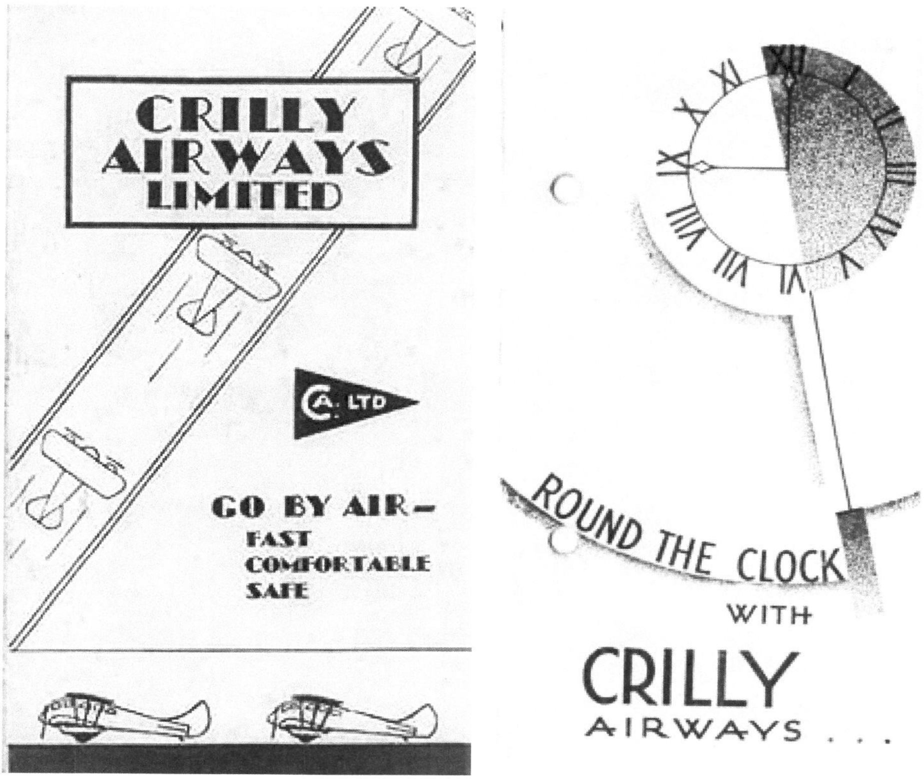

Crilly Airways pamphlet.

The event included an aerobatic and inverted flying display, a fly past of the latest planes, a parachute descent, a landing by keen aviatrice the Duchess of Bedford who was known as the 'Flying Duchess', and an air race, the Grosvenor Challenge Trophy, to Old John and Ratcliffe, won by Lindsay Everard's pilot, who of course would have been familiar with the route. Spectators even had a chance to experience flying for themselves in the evening, as Crilly Airways gave five hundred of them a ride in one of its eight-seater aircraft for five shillings and sixpence each.

Crilly Airways and Provincial Airways operated passenger services from the new Airport of Leicester at Braunstone Aerodrome. Crilly Airways was founded by Frederick Leo Crilly with Leicester airport as its headquarters. He started off by running two eight-seater de Havilland Dragons, one of which was named Spirit of Doncaster. A fleet of three Crilly planes, full of passengers, inaugurated a planned six flight daily air service to Skegness in early June 1935.

An important first for Leicester was the first New Year plane tour, an excursion to Lisbon and Madrid on a 14-seater, three-engined Fokker that took off from Braunstone on the afternoon of 27 December, following a civic reception. The plane stopped at Croydon, from where the flight took off again at 6am. The small group of passengers stayed at the Avenida Palace Hotel in Lisbon where they saw in the New Year of 1936 and did some sightseeing.[308] This was possible as Crilly's had secured an airmail contract with the Portuguese that allowed them to fly to Lisbon.

Crilly Airways's timetable leaflet advertised free conveyance to and from the airport, with cars leaving the Grand Hotel in Leicester city centre for the airport just 25 minutes before scheduled take-off times.[309] There was a free luggage allowance of up to 30lb per passenger. On the leaflets routes were shown from Leicester to Liverpool, Nottingham, Norwich, Northampton and Bristol with links to London. Crilly Airways was the first to offer a kind of frequent flyer scheme: regular travellers were offered special terms of 1,000 miles for ten guineas. Crilly also flew a de Havilland Fox Moth, two General Aircraft Monospars and four Fokker F.XIIs which ran the mail service to Lisbon in Portugal, which would speed up communication across the British Empire. Government approval for

308 *Leicester Evening Mail*, 21 December 1935
309 Crilly Airways Limited, Timetable Details from 6 October 1935

Provincial Airways pamphlet.

Provincial Airways timetable.

Crilly to run a service between Britain and Ireland was turned down. Crilly also failed in his ambition to operate to Gibraltar and West Africa as the Spanish government refused permission to fly over its territory during the Spanish Civil War. As a result of these set backs, Crilly ceased trading in September 1936. His aircraft were bought by British Airways Limited who started the company British Airways Iberia Limited with Crilly as managing director but this company soon went bankrupt too. The planes were then sold again to the fascist Spanish nationalists in the Civil War.

Another airline flying from Braunstone was Provincial Airways Limited, formed in 1933 to operate between Croydon and the South West of England. Provincial advertised flights from Leicester to Torquay taking two hours and 40 minutes. It was promoted as a door-to-door service with the fare inclusive of service charges which, it claimed, would save money as there were no tips, taxi or car fares, or meals to pay for.[310] Like Crilly's, this company soon proved to be commercially unviable and was forced to close in December 1935.

Despite the failure of the commercial airlines, the airport continued in operation, with pilots arriving and landing from all over Europe. An air display marked Coronation Day in 1937. Sometimes the RAF would fly in formation but this came to an end, supposedly because of lobbying by Leicester's pacifist movement. However, the RAF Volunteer Reserve recruited some members of the Leicester Aero Club who were among the first called up when broke out. The aerodrome was also used by the local Civil Air Guard and the Air Cadets for training. This led to a tragedy in July 1939 when Percy Kerfoot of 33 Dunstall Avenue in Braunstone, a 33-year-old engineer's tool maker, was fatally injured when his Hawker Tomtit bi-plane crashed at Kirby Muxloe. He was a member of the Civil Defence Air Guard, aiming for his pilot's A Licence, on what was only his second solo flight. He had been sent up solo

310 Provincial Airways Limited, advertising poster, c.1935

Morgan Squires advertisement, Leicester Daily News, November 1935.

after 30 minutes' dual instruction on the day, although he had had 18 hours total dual instruction before that. Kerfoot was just 300 feet up in the air when two plugs in the engine failed to fire, despite the plane having been overhauled every ten hours of flying time. It was only three hours since it was last inspected.[311]

Accidents were relatively common in those days: in 1938 a Gypsy Moth plane was overturned by a gust of wind as it taxied around the buildings in a Midlands air race. The pilot, J.L. Cave of Redditch, and Miss Mitchell of Portsmouth scrambled out of the cockpit unharmed but the plane had a broken propeller and its starboard wings

311 *Leicester Mercury*, 18 July 1939

were crushed.[312] In another accident at Braunstone, on 22 August 1941, a de Haviland DH.82 Tiger Moth plane that had taken off at Desford went out of control and spun down to the ground. The trainee pilot, Corporal S. Foden, and his instructor had a lucky escape, without injuries, but the aircraft was damaged beyond repair.[313]

Leicester Airport was used by important visitors to the county, such as the Duke of Kent, the King's brother, who landed at Braunstone on the way to compete in a motor race at Donington Park in October 1938. The Duke met his death in an air crash just four years later.[314] Another important visitor was Father Christmas, who flew in to Braunstone from where he paraded to town to begin his Christmas 1938 stint as Santa in Morgan Squires.[315] School children were brought to visit the airport to celebrate Empire Air Day in 1936 by viewing air displays and being shown the facilities.[316] By 1938, war clouds were on the horizon and part of that year's Empire Day's display was devoted to a demonstration by the emergency services of the impact on a house of bombing. Thermite bombs were dropped on the mock house and firemen behind the scenes set off incendiary bombs. The fire fighters and ambulance crew rescued a dummy person from the flames, to raise awareness of the risks of being in a possible air raid and the work being done in preparation.[317]

Not everyone saw the new airport as having a positive impact on the community. Complaints were made to the Council by North Braunstone Labour Party, about the disturbing effect on residents caused by low flying aircraft. For Lewis Cockerill of Braunstone Frith Farm, the impact was disastrous. He complained to the Council that he had lost 33 ewes and 100 lambs as a result of them being frightened by people with dogs, using a footpath through the farm on the way to look at the aerodrome and watch planes. His best fields for grazing his cattle were next to the airport. The cows were startled by the roar of engines ten to 15 feet above them resulting in the loss of calves. He had been forced to buy fresh cattle as the milk supply had been curtailed. Mr Cockerill asked the Council for £200 in compensation for his losses.[318]

The life of the airport was cut short when all civil aviation was banned in August 1939 because of World War Two. The Aero Club continued to use the buildings but for social activities only. During the war the aerodrome functioned as a satellite field for RAF Training Command 51 Group 7 EFTS based at nearby Desford. An obvious military target for the Nazis, the airfield had been identified as a potential location for bombing by the Luftwaffe before the war in a marked up aerial photograph of 24

312 *Leicester Evening Mail,* 22 July 1938
313 Aviation Safety Network website, www.aviation-safety.net, accessed 31 January 2021
314 *Leicester Evening Mail,* 29 August 1942
315 *Leicester Evening Mail,* 10 November 1938
316 *Leicester Evening Mail, 23 May 1936*
317 *Leicester Evening Mail,* 30 May 1938
318 *Leicester Evening Mail,* 14 February 1936

May 1939, showing how far Hitler's preparations for war had already gone.[319] The size of the airfield proved to be quite restrictive and, as the war progressed, planes often crashed through its boundary hedge, a cause of much local concern.

Braunstone Aerodrome operated first as a civil and then a military airfield, from 27 March 1935 until 1946 when it closed. As part of a developing strategy for post war economic recovery and the improvement of transport links for the East Midlands, Councillor Harry Bowerman, chairman of the Leicester Publicity Department, and City Engineer John Beckett met with representatives of the Air Ministry at Birmingham's Elmdon Airport. They discussed the potential for charter air facilities between Braunstone and Elmdon, to connect with the service between Birmingham and Paris although this idea never came to fruition.[320] The small size of the airfield, demonstrated as problematic during the war, and the proximity of civilian housing estates for the expanding Leicester population were important factors in the decision to close.

Technological advances during the War also changed the need for flight infrastructure as planes could now fly much further without breaking their journeys to refuel. Aircraft were also larger and more powerful, requiring longer runways. In October 1949, it was decided that there would be no more flights from Braunstone and the aerodrome was taken over by the Council.[321] It wasn't officially released by the RAF until 1950 when Leicester Corporation refused to allow the Leicestershire Aero Club to use it. The airport facilities had fallen into disrepair, due to vandalism in the intervening years. Of the buildings, the local press reported that at Braunstone there was 'a soundly built club house, put up in the days of the Aero Club, its windows broken and damage done due to wanton destruction'.[322] A group of four men, one of them an ex-paratrooper, were tried for breaking in and stealing brass fittings from the aerodrome, the property of Reid and Sigrist Limited and were sent to prison.[323]

The Parks Committee of the Corporation took over the aerodrome site for sport and playing fields in 1948, which relieved some of the pressure on overcrowded parks.[324] It was the scene of local football matches, for instance Blaby Athletic played against East Leicester there in November 1950.[325] This was not a permanent solution to the use of the site that was later transformed into an industrial estate.

---

319 Terence C. Cartwright: *Bird's Eye Wartime Leicestershire 1939–1945*, Wigston, 2002

320 Ben Beazley: *Post War Leicester*, Alan Sutton Publishing, Avon, 2006, p.25

321 Beazley, p.18

322 *Leicester Mercury*, 13 March 1950

323 *Leicester Mercury*, 19 May 1950, 2 August 1950

324 *Leicester Mercury*, 3 November 1950

325 *Leicester Mercury*, 8 November 1950

5

A PARK FOR THE WEST END

Leicester Corporation began to show an interest in the New Parks area of the Mellor Estate, administered by trustees, from about 1893 when it earmarked some of this land for a public park for the growing population of the West End, an area expanding rapidly following the major works of the River Soar's flood prevention scheme that created the canalised Mile Straight. Soon the need for public open space for residents' leisure became more urgent. The Midland Sheffield and Lincolnshire Railway, later renamed the Great Central, bought land in Bedehouse Meadows from the council, what is now Bede Island and Park, depriving residents of space used for recreation. This area had been waste land since the time of Elizabeth I but children had used it to play since it was drained with the widening of the canal in the 1880s. West End residents felt entitled to have the sum received by the council for its sale spent on other recreational space. In 1897 the council decided to create a new park out of part of the New Parks and set about raising the funds to pay for the project.

Town clerk Mr Bell, with representatives of the council, met with the Local Government Board (LGB) inspector Colonel W.L. Coke on 28 September 1897 to

View of Western Park, postcard, c.1905.

discuss a loan for £30,00 to buy a public park. Mr Bell asked the LGB to approve the loan as the council had made a provisional agreement with the Mellor Estate trustees to buy a portion of the New Parks Estate. This contained 183 acres, two roods and 21 perches off Hinckley Road at the price of £30,000 plus £200 stamp duty, a total cost of £163 an acre. It was a mile and three quarters from the town centre and within easy reach of the expanding West End. Local authorities were forbidden to speculate in land but, because the loan was to buy a park rather than land, the Local Government Board approved it. The land had a frontage of 330 yards to Hinckley Road, from where there could be easy access. There were no immediate plans to do anything with the land as it was well-timbered and would be left in a natural state. The council approved the purchase as it was keen to obtain it at the current price, before it became valuable building land. There were no objections to the purchase of this land, 'beautifully situated on the side of the town where the population was growing, beautiful in itself and enough to meet the town's needs for 80 to 100 years'.[326] The council's Parks and Recreation Grounds Committee gave the scheme the go-ahead after discussing a report on the New Parks Estate and the creation of a park in February 1899.

The cost of work on the New Parks Estate to create the new park was estimated at £4,590, to be spent on building a pavilion big enough to accommodate 400 to 500 people for tea, plus other alterations and buildings. There were no plans to spend money on the fields adjoining the Glenfield footpath but the public would have access. In discussions within the Council at a special meeting in January 1899, a compromise was reached as some councillors thought more should be spent while others less.[327] Cllr Marshall thought the park should have a lake at a cost of around £750. Only the road should be built and the building of the pavilion deferred for a year to see if it was needed, argued Cllr Biggs. Cllr Mann responded to this by commenting, 'There were always some who opposed schemes for the poor.' The debate focussed on whether there should be a lake or a pavilion. Cllr Booth was opposed to both unless there was also a recreation ground for Aylestone. A site visit was proposed and the idea of the lake was dropped as it was thought it would be a danger in winter and too small for boating in summer.[328]

A further loan of £2,600 from the Local Government Board in July 1899 was used to pay for the layout of what was named Western Park, which included the construction of the driveway, alteration of the fences and building a band stand. Much of this work had already been completed as the new park had already opened a few days before the loan was approved. A loan of £31,926 was also received for the improvement of High Street at the same time.[329] The work preparing the park was

326 *Leicester Chronicle and Leicestershire Mercury*, 2 October 1897
327 *Leicester Chronicle and Leicestershire Mercury*, 7 January 1899
328 *Leicester Chronicle and Leicestershire Mercury*, 7 January 1899
329 *Leicester Chronicle and Leicestershire Mercury*, 22 July 1899

Western Park Gates, postcard, c.1910. (Records Office of Leicester, Leicestershire and Rutland)

carried out by the borough surveyor, E.G. Mawbey, and Mr Burn, the superintendent of parks.

The public was invited to the opening ceremony and at 3pm on Thursday 13 July 1899 the new public park for the West End was opened as Western Park by Alderman Clifton, the mayor, Sir Thomas White, and Cllr Flint.[330] At nearly 185 acres it was three times the size of Victoria Park and stood on ground 100 feet higher than the Clock Tower. Its addition increased the total area of Leicester's parks to 407 acres. To improve access and bring in visitors, the Council hoped to negotiate with the Midland Railway to open a station at Shoulder of Mutton Hill. At the opening ceremony Sir Thomas White planted an oak tree and a California pine to mark the long reign of Queen Victoria. Other trees, including limes, formed a wide avenue along the main drive.

The celebrations continued into the evening with tea in a marquee and entertainment from the Borough Police Band. Glees and part songs followed in a concert by Leicester Philharmonic Society and St Mary's Church Choir.[331] A great future for the park was forecast. 'It might become the central park of England, just like Leicester was the central town,' extolled Sir Thomas. 'The Western Park would be able to host gatherings of friendly societies and other bodies, militia and volunteers' camps.'[332] Cllr Flint was presented with a golden key. Not all the land was open to the public immediately; 80 acres were given to the Farms Committee with the intention

330 *Leicestershire Mercury*, 15 July 1899
331 *Leicester Daily Post*, 10 July 1899
332 *Leicester Chronicle and Leicestershire Mercury*, 15 July 1899

Horse working on Western Park.

it would be handed back to the Parks Committee in five years' time, after the land had been developed. To start with the public had the run of 100 acres, with a portion of the land reserved for cricket and other sports. Western Park in the 21st century contains about 178 acres. New bye-laws for Western Park were discussed and adopted by the Council a couple of weeks after the opening, including one which prohibited making speeches. This could have affected gatherings of Friendly Societies when their presidents gave an address, although the Town Clerk promised that a great deal of discrimination and latitude would be given.[333]

A description in the *Leicester Daily Post* in 1913 sums up the natural attraction of Western Park in words that are still applicable in the present, 'Here the undulating ground, studded with old trees and the well-grown spinneys, are very little altered from what they would have been like 100 years ago. The park is still far enough away from the town for it to retain its country aspect. There are no factory chimneys or other industrial eyesores visible to remind one of such a thing as work, and the open space available for games make it 'par excellence' the favourite park for juvenile athletes.'[334]

Entertainment on the park was advertised in local newspapers as 'Music in the Parks'; for instance in July 1902 the Borough Workmen's Band performed. Brass

333 *Leicester Chronicle and Leicestershire Mercury*, 29 July 1899
334 *Leicester Daily Post*, 27 August 1913

Western Park bandstand, taken in 2021.

bands were ideal for outdoor performances because the loudness of the instruments meant they did not need artificial amplification. These concerts were popular and a bandstand was erected soon after the park opened. It is still in use for Sunday concerts during the summer months over a century later.

The cottage in Shoulder of Mutton Close, on the Hinckley Road side of the park, was bought by the Corporation from the Mellor Trustees after modernisation in 1902. The property became the home of the resident park attendant, William Ashton who was living there by 1912. During the 1930s, the cottage was demolished and replaced by another house nearby on the same plot. This was occupied by the next resident park attendant, Sidney Alfred Barton, his wife, and sister-in-law by 1939.[335] By the 1980s the house was no longer occupied by a member of park staff and was empty until it was repurposed as the EcoHouse, a show home demonstrating sustainable living. The EcoHouse closed and was left empty from around 2014. At the time of writing, in 2021, there were plans by Western Ward Community Enterprise, a small group of volunteers, to reconfigure and repurpose the building for use by the community in an initiative called Project Hive. This has involved many events and initiatives towards raising the funds to carry out the scheme, such as a Scarecrow Trail which began in September 2019.

Within Western Park are several interesting structures, two of which are Grade II-listed. Situated within the park at the end of the drive is the early-19th century house built around the 1820s as a farmhouse for New Parks Farm, perhaps by John Clarke who took out a mortgage for £33,000 in 1826. This late-Georgian residence has a stuccoed front and now has a hipped roof of slate which replaced an upper floor

335 *Kelly's Directory of Leicester*, 1912 and 1941. 1939 Register

Headley's Tea Rooms. (Records Office of Leicester, Leicestershire and Rutland)

with gable roof and dormer windows on an adjoining wing sometime during the 20th century, reducing it from three to two storeys. This work may have been done between 1948 when the caterer renting the café left and March 1950 when it was reopened and run by the council. The restored sash windows have distinctive gothic glazing bars and there is a patterned iron balcony to the front first floor windows, overlooking the bandstand.

For most of the 20th century the Grade II-listed house and its outbuildings were used by parks staff and as a café. The house was renamed The Pavilion and used as accommodation for a caretaker and refreshment rooms, run by Polly Headley, assisted by her daughter Anne who was manageress. The Headleys also had a family business, a confectioner's and bakery on Andrewes Street run by husband John, who died in 1903.[336] The cafe in Western Park, after a spell between 1935 and 1938 when it was run by a Miss Burgess, passed on to the youngest son of John and Polly, Fred and his wife Estella, who were still there running the family business at the Pavilion in 1939. The names of master caterer and voluntary minister of the Gospel, Fred Headley, a Jehovah's Witness, and his wife Estella appear on the 1939 Register which recorded everyone ready for wartime measures.

Another resident within Western Park was the head groundsman for the park and adjacent golf links who lived in a building next to the Pavilion called The Lodge. In 1939 this was Frederick Cherrill with his wife Emily. The outbuildings became known as the Depot and stored equipment used to maintain the park. A later resident, head gardener Albert Bullers, fell down a well he accidentally discovered in the garden

336 *Wright's Directory of Leicester*, 1911. Census of England and Wales, 1911

Western Park House, taken in 2020.

of the property. Towards the end of the 20th century the cafe closed, leaving the house and outbuildings empty for a while but in the early 21st century the former farmhouse and Pavilion was bought by Naresh and Sharon Parmar who began its restoration, together with the adjoining Lodge, in 2002. The family homes created were ready to move into in 2003. The Parmars later bought the Depot building and converted it into residential homes. These were completed in 2021.

To the right of the top of the drive, between the Park, the former Open Air School, Christ the King School, and some of the gardens of Letchworth Road is a spinney. This spinney is of special interest as it has survived from before the park was laid out. It appeared in a map dated 1828 and in the first Ordnance Survey of around 1887 and may be much older, perhaps dating back to the time of enclosure or before.[337] It has been closed off to the public for many years and has become a haven for flora and wildlife. To the left of the drive bowling greens and pavilions and some public tennis courts. One is typically early 20th century in design and the other, belonging to the Western Park Ladies' Bowls Club, has the clean, striking 'moderne' lines associated with the 1930s. After more than 105 years, the Western Park Bowls Club united with the ladies' club. In June 2021 Leicester Pétanque Club moved into the traditional pavilion and one of the former greens changed into 'pistes' to accommodate the French sport. A baseball field was laid out in 2008, near the Park Rise entrance, the home of the Leicester Blue Sox Baseball Club, national champions of the British Baseball Federation in 2009 and 2012.

337 A plan of Leicester shewing the limits of the borough, boundaries of parishes and extra parochial liberties, made from actual survey in the year 1828, published by A. Cockshaw, Leicester

Tennis court, Western Park, c.1920s. (Records Office of Leicester, Leicestershire and Rutland)

The pond in the park used for paddling was a survival from when it was a watering hole for farm animals or a fish pond. There was an idea for it to be enlarged as part of a job-creation scheme proposed by Cllr Amos Sherriff in 1911, but it is not clear whether this scheme was actually carried out. At a special meeting at the Town Hall on work for the unemployed, Cllr Sherriff said 'he believed everybody recognised they could not allow a man to decay in the street, without some effort being made to try and save him from degradation.[338] There was only one way a poor man could get a living and that was by working. 'It was worse for the older men, aged 45 and over,' he said, 'as manufacturers wanted the quick and nimble.' Apart from the scheme to improve the paddling pond, among the suggestions for things the unemployed could do to keep away from the dreaded Poor Law was the creation of allotments, or repainting and rewriting the signs over the doors of policemen's houses, or else to transform the piece of land that ran from West Bridge to the Boulevard road into an attractive promenade, possibly the future Castle Gardens.

The Western Park pond extended year by year until the West Enders began to call it a lake. Cllr Collier moving a report from the Parks and Recreation Committee said in 1914, 'It was very interesting in the summer months to see going on not only mixed bathing but the various other enjoyments of youngsters in the district.' He said the

338 *Leicester Chronicle and Leicestershire Mercury*, 25 November 1911

Western Park pond, 1900s. (Records Office of Leicester, Leicestershire and Rutland)

paddling pool the council proposed to provide would nowhere be more than a foot deep, and in it the children could paddle and splash to their heart's content. 'The children were also in the habit of preparing for his Majesty's Navy by floating miniature torpedo boats and yachts thereon.'[339] Although there was other play equipment on the

339 *Leicester Chronicle and Leicestershire Mercury*, 31 October 1914

Western Park paddling pool and playground, 1930s. (Records Office of Leicester, Leicestershire and Rutland)

park, the pond was not concreted and converted into a more formal paddling pool and model boating lake until 1938.

Play equipment was an early introduction to the park, providing facilities that have given pleasure to generations of children, particularly important for those whose own homes have no or little outdoor space in which to play. Margaret Ryan, a little girl living on Wheat Street in the poor Wharf Street area of the city, won a fountain pen for her letter to 'Auntie Mollie', editor of 'Children's Corner' in the *Leicester Evening Mail* in 1931, before the transformation of the pond into a concreted paddling pool,

> 'I did not go to the seaside this year, but on August Monday I went to Western Park for the day. When I arrived there, my two friends and I sat down by the paddling pond. Afterwards, we had a slide on the shoot. Then at one o'clock, we sat in a quiet place to eat our dinner before going for another paddle. We had a very amusing game in the paddling pond, throwing the ball to each other. Another game we played was hot rice. Before we went home, there was just time to play on the swings. It was a very happy day, and the next best thing to going to the seaside.'[340]

The large open space of Western Park provided space for mass gatherings and community celebrations. Leicester's celebrations for the Coronation of King George V in June 1911 went on over a couple of days, and included the spectacles of a procession and a historical pageant. As well as events on Victoria Park and the Mayor's Garden Party in Abbey Park, Western Park also provided an ideal location. An estimated 10,000 people went there to celebrate the royal occasion with amusements, including

340 *Leicester Evening Mail*, 22 August 1931

Climbing the slippery pole, King George V Coronation celebrations, June 1911. (Image Leicestershire)

heartily applauded comedy turns. The Borough Workmen's Band, conducted by Mr J. Chapman, 'discoursed sweet music' to the gathered crowd. As well as music from the band, they enjoyed rustic games like climbing the greasy pole, which was covered with soft soap, a source of amusement that kept hundreds roaring with laughter for hours. After two failed attempts, a boy called Green managed to climb it three times.

Among other entertainments, Mr Freer of the Cossington Street Gymnasium led a display of boys' physical drill. There was may pole dancing, 'perhaps the prettiest scene of the afternoon', by children of Mantle Road Council School, taught by Miss Davy, assisted by Miss Wilford and Miss Harris. Another feature of the afternoon was a floral display on decorated mail carts and cycles. These arrived in a procession from Western Boulevard to be judged by Mrs Biggs, Mrs Wakerley and Mrs Russell. Rain in the afternoon doesn't seem to have spoilt the party and in the evening, at 10pm, the first rocket of a firework display went up, drawing the crowds to the park's southern corner. 'The effect was sublime as the many coloured lights were thrown up into the immense dome of heaven.'[341] The display included set pieces, such as emblematic devices and the Sovereign's initials – 'an exquisite tableau of beauty'. The day ended with a bonfire and, of course, by everyone standing for the National Anthem.[342]

Western Park was extended following the corporation's purchase of the former farmland of Western Park Dairy and New Parks Farm in 1936.

Western Park Open Air School

Adjacent to the driveway is the former Western Park Open Air School, designed by Leicester Education Committee architect and surveyor James Osbert Thompson. It was built between 1928 and 1930 by contractors E. Orton and Dalby Ltd, of Hugglescote at a cost of £10,837, on land which at that time was in Blaby Rural District. As an outstanding example of progressive design in education, the school was chosen by the Royal Institute of British Architects to illustrate its Modern Schools exhibition in 1937.[343]

Leicester had a reputation for being progressive in the field of health and appointed a school medical officer of health in 1905, making links between citizenship and health, nowadays recognised as an important factor in social inclusion. This was two years before being required to do so by the Education Administration Provisions Act. A school medical service, with medical inspections of school children, brought some health care to families before the post-war National Health Service introduced universal and free provision for all, as from 1912 treatment in schools was free.

Western Park Open Air School opened on 7 November 1930, under the leadership of headmistress Nora Maltby (who lived on Westhill Road), with 180 boys and girls on role and a waiting list. The arts and crafts-style building, with its separate chalet-style classrooms, was described by contemporaries as 'domestic – quite unlike any ordinary school and a distinct addition to the amenities of the park, as well as being eminently suitable for its purpose which at the same time harmonises admirably with its rural surroundings'. The domestic style of the main school building is typical of the

341 *Leicester Daily Post*, 9 May 1911, 22 June 1911, 24 June 1911
342 *Leicester Chronicle and Leicestershire Mercury*, 1 July 1911
343 Tom Hulme: *'A Nation Depends on Its Children': School Buildings and Citizenship in England and Wales, 1900–1939*, Journal of British Studies 54, April 2015, pp.406-432, p.426

Western Park Open Air School, taken 2014.

arts and crafts design in Western Park Garden Suburb and reminiscent of the work of Norman Shaw and local architect Ralph Waldo Bedingfield, whose work would have been very familiar to Thompson.

Children selected to attend the school were recovering from debilitating illnesses, particularly respiratory diseases. In the absence of antibiotics and other modern pharmacological therapeutic methods, the school offered an important chance of recovery, and an opportunity to regain strength for children who might otherwise have been unable to gain an education. Before this specialist facility opened, frail and convalescent children had been sent to the Leicester Poor Boys' and Girls' Holiday Home in the dunes at Mablethorpe, outside the holiday season in spring and autumn.

Positive results for the children led to a replication of outdoor facilities near home. Playground Schools, where desks were placed outdoors at the existing Leicester schools, St John's in Clarendon Park and Hinckley Road School (now Dovelands), were used until the purpose-built Open Air School was built in Western Park. At the new school, considerable time was given to subjects suitable for outdoor instruction, such as nature study, horticulture and various forms of manual work. Pupils received three meals a day at the school and every afternoon had an outdoor nap of an hour and a quarter, lying on folding beds in the playground, 'delightfully situated with wide prospects of green fields and forest trees'. The school's situation on parkland on

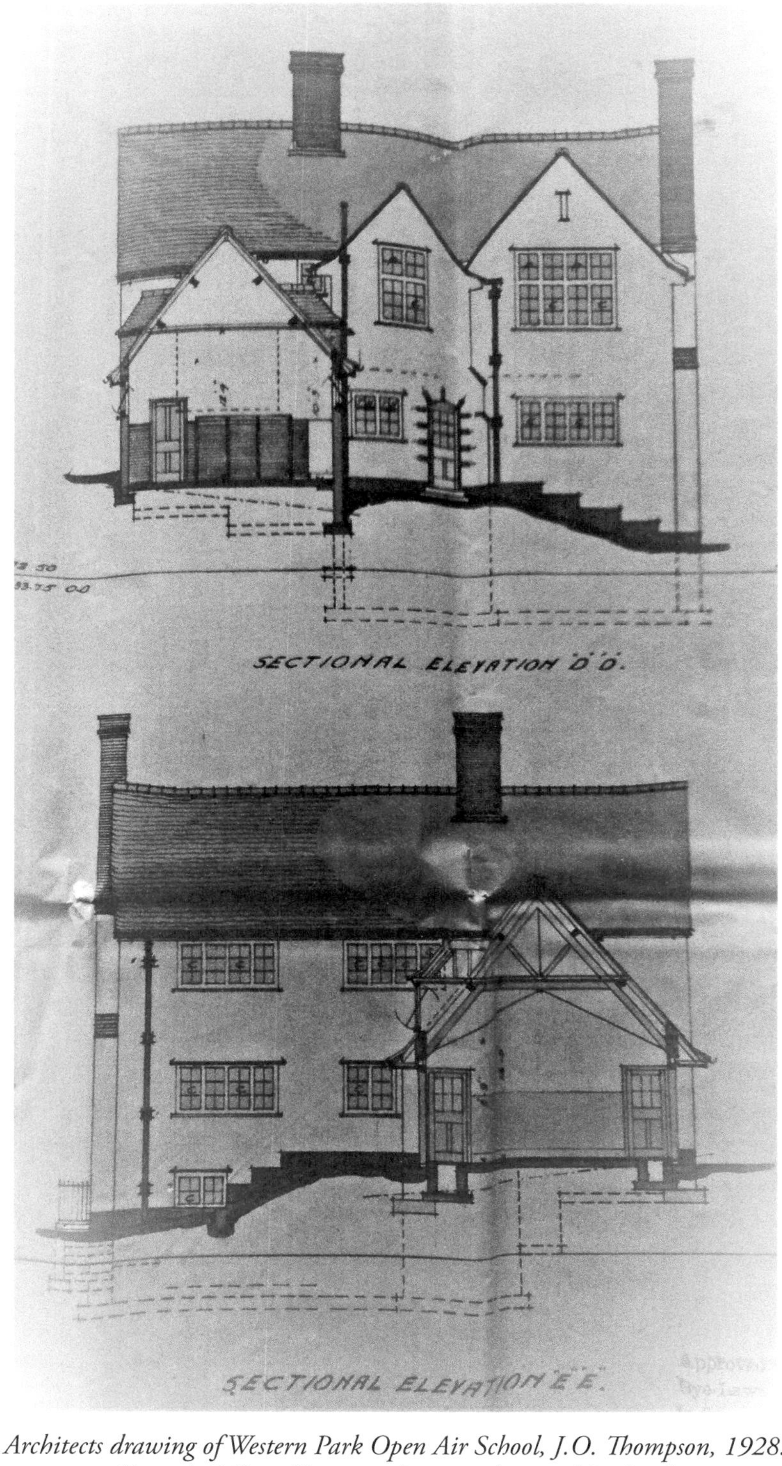

Architects drawing of Western Park Open Air School, J.O. Thompson, 1928.
(Records Office of Leicester, Leicestershire and Rutland)

The playground, Western Park Open Air School. (Postcard)

the edge of the city, facing open countryside and the building's design were chosen to facilitate the medically devised regime.

The site for the Open Air School was selected because it was south facing, screened and sheltered to the rear by a hill and the spinney, giving stimulating views across the countryside, and allowing pupils to take rural walks. Before the school's construction, the area of land it occupied was used for grazing by the park's work horses. By 1930 powered vehicles were making the horses redundant and so less grass for their grazing was required. Taking advantage of the slope, the land was laid out in three terraces connected by concrete steps and broad, inclined pathways. The playground had a low retaining wall built of stone, which also doubled as a rock garden. There was a vegetable garden for lessons in gardening and access to the park for games.

Classrooms were in three separate, south-facing, chalet-style blocks of twin rooms, each accommodating 30 pupils. These classrooms were glazed on three sides by opening casement windows with cills 18 inches above the floor and pivot fanlights in the upper casements. The fourth side was a wooden folding partition dividing the structure into two rooms. Heating was by stove and the floor made of wood blocks. The purpose of the design was that the three sides could be completely open or closed according to the weather and fanlights could be open in all weathers giving excellent ventilation. The partition was painted in a low-tone colour and children worked facing it so there was no glare in their eyes. It was easily folded back to create one larger room, open on all four sides. The stove was mainly for drying and warming the building and furniture, not for heating the air, which under open air conditions

Open chalet classroom windows, Western Park Open Air School. (Postcard)

was constantly being circulated and removed. A fourth block contained cloakrooms and lavatories. A short time after the school opened, an additional small building was erected in which to store the folding beds.

Classrooms were arranged so that cool air came in at the top through fanlights and floor-level draughts were prevented by the 18-inch cills so as to keep the head cool and the feet warm. According to reports, every half hour the pupils had a good run or game in the park to keep warm. The chief school medical officer of health, Dr Allan Warner's report for the Education Committee referred to the confined, sunless homes in narrow streets where many of the children who came to the school lived, 'The children who come daily to this spot from close and crowded houses must find pleasure in the beauty of the natural objects that surround them. These pleasures are really medicinal, they have a soothing effect which should help to heal the unstable, nervous child and prevent mental degeneracy.'[344]

A writer for the *Leicester Daily Post* visited the Open Air School shortly after its opening. Delighted by its rural location and impressed by the regime followed by the children in their quest for health, the following insight into the routines of the pupils was shared with readers,

344 Annual Report of the Medical Officer for the year ended 31 December 1929, Leicester Education Committee Minutes, 1929–1930, ROLLR

Chalet classrooms, Western Park Open Air School. (Records Office of Leicester, Leicestershire and Rutland)

> 'Situated as it is, in the most rural and ideal surroundings, with plenty of space, the children are allowed the utmost freedom. The classrooms, very spacious buildings, are built to open on three sides, and in summer and winter there is always one side open unless the weather is really treacherous. Children are sent to the school, if certified delicate, from all the other schools in the city and the time given them to regain their health is one year. If by the end of that time they are still unfit, then they are allowed to remain for a longer period.'[345]

When the pupils entered the school, they were allocated a number which identified the things they were given for their personal use to promote hygiene: two suits, a blanket, towels, toothbrush, hairbrush, comb, and bags. In addition, the boys were supplied with a jersey. Each morning, on their arrival at school, the children changed into sun suits. The girls were provided with blue cotton knickers and almost backless jumpers to wear, and the boys wore khaki trousers. This shows that the regime followed was influenced by heliotherapy devised by Swiss physician August Rollier for his *Ecole du Soleil* in alpine Leysin.[346] As in Switzerland, the children's bodies were described as 'beautifully bronzed', demonstrating the emerging fashion for a suntan in the 1930s and the mistaken association of tanned skin with health.

For their lessons, they were grouped not by age but by how far advanced in their learning they were, as some of them had little previous education. Regular showers were part of the school routine. Boys showered twice a week but girls only once. While

345 *Leicester Evening Mail*, 14 July 1932

346 Susan Barton: *Healthy Living in the Alps: the origins of winter tourism in Switzerland, 1860–1914*, Manchester University Press, 2008

they were in the shower, the nurse in charge gave them drill and exercises while their bodies were being douched with water, a form of hydrotherapy.

Just like their more robust contemporaries in mainstream schools, the children at Western Park Open Air School enjoyed many fun activities. Gardening was part of their curriculum, and their produce was entered into shows and competitions. In 1939, the school won the Jonathan North Shield for its collection of flowers and vegetables exhibited at the Leicester and Leicestershire Horticultural Society flower show.[347] Arts and drama were important aspects of their education and in July 1950 pupils performed a costumed play, *Don Quixote*. For armour, they attached milk bottle tops to waistcoats. Black out curtains, used in the war, were repurposed to make slim trousers or hose. Other curtains were dyed to make mantillas. Other props created were a windmill and dragons. Among the characters was a girl dressed as a lion.[348]

Following medical advances, especially the development of antibiotics such as streptomycin for the treatment of tuberculosis, which meant open-air education was no longer used as a therapy, Western Park Open Air School became a school for children with health problems and special educational needs. It finally closed down in 2005 and was abandoned. Many of the original features of the buildings have survived as evidence of its former use. The school buildings are attractive and of architectural as well as social and historical interest, demonstrating the practical

347 *Leicester Mercury*, 14 July 1939
348 *Leicester Mercury*, 21 July 1950

Cast of a performance of Don Quixote, pupils of Western Park Open Air School July 1950. (Records Office of Leicester, Leicestershire and Rutland)

application of medical theories of the early 20th century, and also the involvement of local authorities and education committees in health initiatives, before the creation of the NHS. In recognition of Western Park Open Air School's heritage value and rarity, the buildings are listed at Grade II by Historic England.

From 2020 proposals by Naresh Parmar with plans to restore and repurpose the school buildings by architect Muthar Al-Salloum of MAS Architecture were under way but delayed by the Covid-19 pandemic. Planning permission was applied for in 2021.

Western Park Golf Course

More land from the New Parks Estate was approved for use as a municipal golf course in 1909. The prime mover for this project, Cllr Loseby intended the course to be for those who could not afford to pay a large subscription to play golf at a private club. He was convinced the game would increase in popularity and that those who were golfers were eager to extend the pleasures of the game to the working class. The site for this, in 'picturesque and healthy surroundings', was adjacent to the north-west side of Western Park, not yet divided from it by Glenfield Road which, until it was extended in the 1930s, was just a footpath across the fields to Glenfield. The new 43-acre, nine-hole Western Park Golf Course was opened in the rain, by the mayor, Cllr Chitham, in May 1910, with a fair number of spectators and players there to see the first ball struck. The opening game was between the mayor and Cllr Loseby. Cllr Chitham led with a clean, pretty drive but Cllr Loseby sent the ball out of bounds.

Apart from Nottingham, as yet no other town had municipal golf links. Characteristic of class distinctions and segregation at the time, there were two clubs associated with the course. As well as a regular club, Western Park Golf Club which opened with 180 members, there was a separate club for working men, the Artisans' Golf Club formed by the Council with a membership fee of seven shillings a year or thruppence ha'penny a week. The Council hoped that this would 'bring recreative sport within reach of the humblest purse'. 'True, it is not as exciting as a football or cricket match. The typical operative, however, has merely to play golf, instead of being a mere spectator on the football or cricket field, to realise it is ideally healthy and invigorating.'[349] Now there was an opportunity for 'the humble worker to indulge in a game hitherto associated in the popular mind with the rich and leisured members of the community only'.[350] When the course first opened it had only nine holes and was crowded most afternoons and evenings. Because of this, there were fears that some of the 250 members of Western Park Golf Club and the 50 in the Artisans Golf Club might resign.

The Western Park Golf Club had a successful first year and by the time of its first AGM in 1911, chaired by Cllr Chitham as president, there were 264 members,

349 *Leicester Daily Post*, 15 April 1910
350 *Leicester Chronicle*, 7 May 1910

The site of Glenfield Road golf links, Western Park Estate Brochure, c. 1909. (Records Office of Leicester, Leicestershire and Rutland)

including 63 women.[351] Because of the inadequacy of the unpleasantly crowded nine-hole course, following a petition signed by 213 members it was enlarged and extended to 18 holes in 1912 at a cost of £200 plus annual maintenance costs of £426. The local newspaper commented on the remarkable popularity of the game, particularly among the middle and professional classes; only 40 artisans had taken an annual ticket but 267 had paid a guinea for the regular Western Park Golf Club.[352] The Club was affiliated to the newly formed Leicestershire and Rutland Golf Union. There were monthly medal competitions and Alfred Corah presented a silver cup as a competition prize.[353] The Club's AGM in 1912, held at the Turkey Cafe on Granby Street, called for a pavilion to be built which might attract more members or help retain existing ones.

The lack of a pavilion and also alleged poor maintenance of the course remained grievances. A frequent complaint to the Parks Committee was the poor condition of the Western Park course, as well as the lack of a pavilion with changing facilities, which cost the Club members and prevented them getting matches against visiting clubs. This was alluded to at the Club dinner in 1913 at the Saracen's Head. In his toast to the Western Park Club and its Officers, Mr Rogers joked that a number

---

351 *Leicester Daily Post*, 16 May 1911
352 *Leicester Daily Post*, 30 January 1911
353 *Leicester Daily Post*, 16 May 1911

of Suffragettes intended to cut up the greens on the Western Park course, but their designs could not be carried out because they could not find any greens.[354] This was a reference to recent attacks by suffragettes with knives and trowels on golf courses. Slogans such as 'No Votes, No Golf' were carved during the following night on the greens of the Leicestershire Golf Club at Evington.[355] In 1913 the Western Park Golf Club AGM was again held in the Turkey Cafe. Ernest Hancock, who lived at Summer Hill on Letchworth Road, was the honorary treasurer. The club now had 241 members. There were tournaments for lady members and two matches during the year with the Artisans' Club. It was mentioned that the Corporation Omnibus Bill of that year included a clause asking the Local Government Board to give power to councils to make golf links, four years after Leicester Corporation had taken the decision to do so.

The area surrounding the golf course remained farm land: St Catherine's Home for Incurables, established in 1902 and run by nuns of the Dominican order, which later became a nursing home, did some farming and kept pigs, and Bird's Nest Farm continued as an agricultural concern. Golf balls being hit into the fields caused problems with trespassers and damage to crops by golfers and boys searching for balls, some of whom were arrested and faced court appearances. Two boys, 14-year-old Harry Holloway of Ruby Street and Carl Harrison, aged 15, of Pool Road, both working as leather sisers, were in the juvenile court in 1910 for damaging wheat in a field belonging to John Howkins at New Parks. They had walked in a zigzag fashion through the field, claiming to the court they were finding a 'near way' short cut to Western Park. A witness said they seemed to be looking for something among the wheat. The boys were each ordered to pay 3s 6d towards the costs and damage or three days imprisonment. In another case on the same day in the adult court, a policeman said he had seen Reginald Kirby, a 32-year-old clerk, climb a hedge into the wheat field to look for a golf ball but he returned to the golf course when he saw the policeman. When P.C. Stapleton spoke to him, Kirby said he was very sorry, but 'it is very annoying to lose these golf balls'. Kirby was ordered to pay ten shillings towards the costs or three days in prison. 'Similar cases would in future be more sternly dealt with', added the chairman of the magistrates.[356]

Golf continued to be played on the course through World War One until 1917, when food shortages were becoming critical. The Parks and Recreation Committee recommended that the land be laid down for mowing to produce hay, to the objections

354 *Leicester Daily Post*, 15 February 1913

355 Jess Jenkins: *The Burning Question, The Struggle for Women's Suffrage in Leicestershire*, Friends of the Records Office for Leicestershire, Leicester and Rutland, Occasional Papers 5, nd, p.141

356 *Leicester Daily Post*, 25 July 1910

Former golf course pavilion, Glenfield Road, taken in 2021.

of golfers and some councillors, several of whom played golf.[357] This would release the groundsmen for other work, such as tending the allotments and potato plots on Abbey and Victoria Park. Vegetables instead of flowers were planted in flower beds, although this would not have affected Western Park much, with its more natural landscape.[358]

After the War, in October 1920, the Council agreed that the course should be relaid and reseeded.[359] It reopened in 1921, initially as a nine-hole course with the remainder of the 18 holes reopening later that year. Facilities were also improved by the addition of the longed-for pavilion in 1921 an old army hut replaced by the present structure in 1927, which still stands next to Westgate School on Glenfield Road, although lockers had been installed and a drinking fountain provided by early 1915.[360] During World War Two, the course was not dug up again but its 80 acres were rented out as grazing for sheep, for 360 days at a time.

After World War Two, from 1950, Western Park Golf Course was relocated to 125 acres of land surrounding the site of Kirby Frith Hall, an area added to Leicester by the extension of the city's boundaries in 1935. An additional part of the course lay across the city boundary on the Glenfield side, in the area administered by Blaby District Council, which objected to there being nine holes over the border. The objection was over-ruled by the Minister of Town and Country Planning and the nine new holes on the county side were added to those already laid out within the city, making a full 18-hole course. The cost of the new course was £14,642 and took about 18 months to complete. Until

357 *Leicester Daily Post*, 25 April 1917
358 *Leicester Daily Post*, 24 April 1917
359 *Leicester Daily Post*, 20 October 1920
360 *Leicester Chronicle*, 9 January 1915

Western Golf Course, publicity pamphlet, c.1990s.

it was ready, the existing Western Park course off Glenfield Road, reduced to 14 holes since the war, remained open. Jack Loach, the Western Park professional golfer at the time, said that on paper 'the new course looks exceptionally good'.[361]

The new Kirby Frith site became an important wildlife habitat; the City Wildlife Project which ran from 1983 to 1987, identified that the 52.1-hectare golf course retained the remnants of an ancient hay meadow.[362] Western Park Golf Course remained at Kirby Frith until the austerity imposed by the national Government on local councils forced its closure in 2015, with the Council focussing provision on what had been its second course at Humberstone Heights.

Despite the creation of Western Park and the golf course, the area around them remained countryside until almost the middle of the 20th century and continued to be used for country walks as recreation.

A small book produced by the *Leicester Mercury,* in around 1930, *Footpath Rambles Up-To-Date,* a title that perhaps acknowledges the changes going on around Leicestershire at the time, details about 20 country walks mostly along footpaths that could be reached by public transport. There is one for Western Park, Glenfield and New Parks that starts about 100 yards from the tram terminus at the park gates, up Shoulder of Mutton Hill. The footpath to the right, crosses Western Park and then continues over stiles, crossing fields, across the Glenfield path, through farms, a

361 *Leicester Mercury*, 5 October 1950
362 David Nash and David Reeder (eds): *Leicester in the Twentieth Century*, Alan Sutton, Avon, 1993, p.37

Western Park Golf Course, taken 2014.

stack yard and over the Swannington railway, without ever encountering a main road. Another hike to Glenfield and Kirby Muxloe begins on Glenfield Road.

Great changes have come to the Glenfield footpath in recent years. It used to start at the top of Watt's Causeway (King Richard's-road) and lead past the Dane Hills, where an Easter Monday fair was an attraction for thousands of Leicester people.

The path has become Glenfield-road, and there is little of the footpath left until the Western Park is reached. Even when the other side of the Park is arrived at the footpath soon degenerates into a road

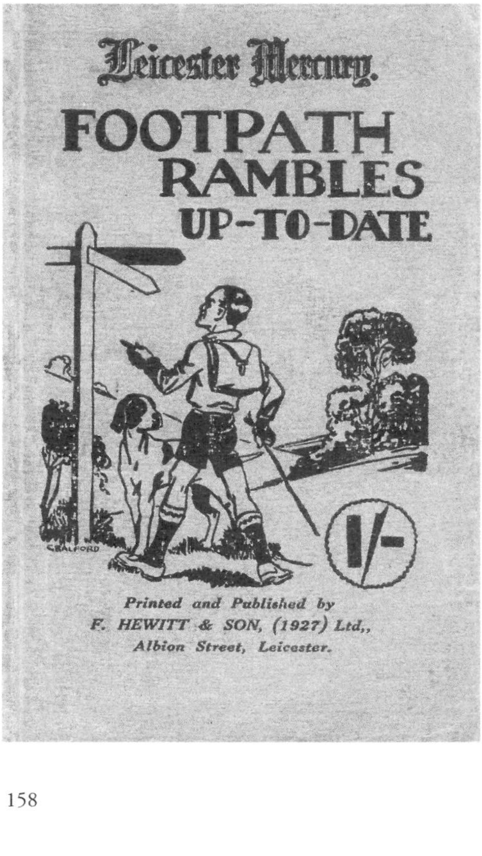

Footpath Rambles booklet cover, Leicester Mercury c.1930.

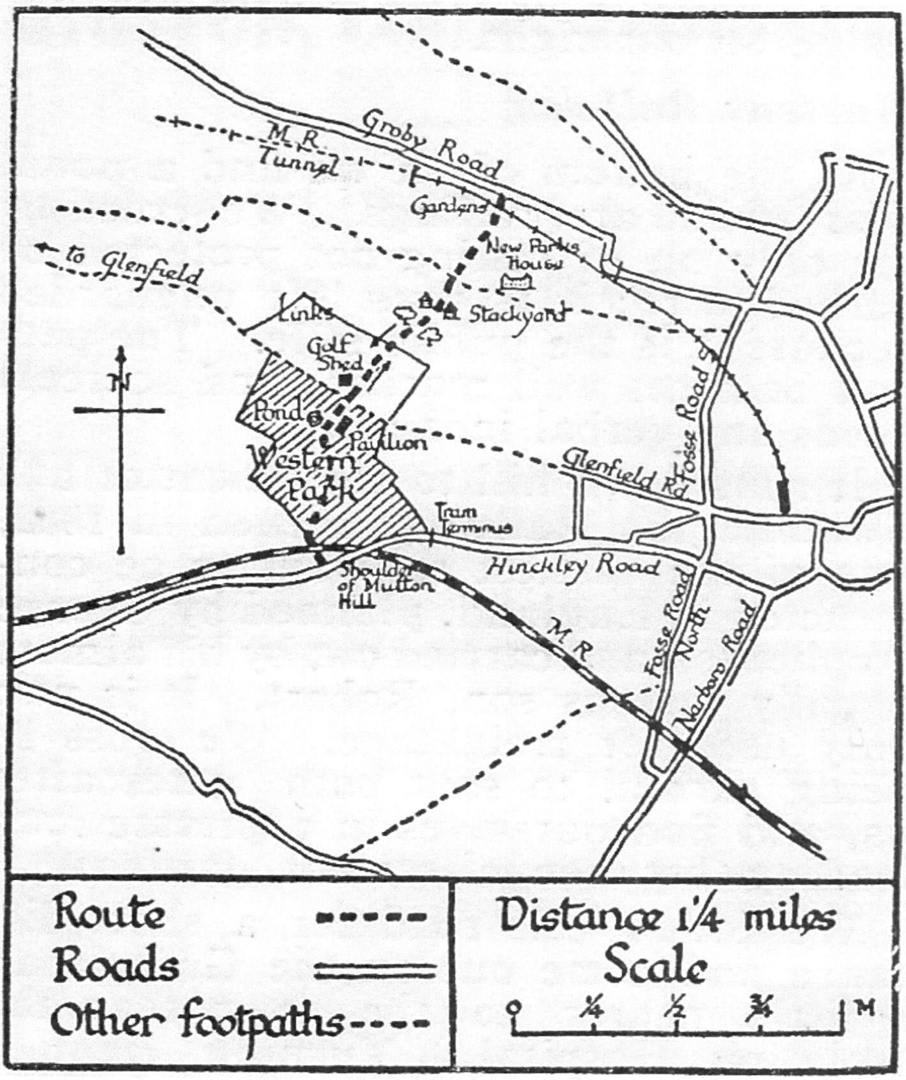

Footpath Rambles, walk map, c.1930.

again – part of the Dominion Estate. Proceed along this road until nearly at Glenfield, when a right must be taken to follow the path to the village. Here we pass on the left the entrance to the drive leading to Kirby Frith, a house which Elizabeth I is said to have visited.[363]

The role of Western Park in wartime

A peaceful place of beauty such as Western Park can seem hard to imagine as having played a role in both world wars. During World War One, following the recruitment

363 *Footpath Rambles Up-To-Date, Leicester Mercury*, nd, c.1930

drive of 1914, 1,000 men were drilled on the park before being despatched to the Front.[364] As part of their training, the signallers section of the Leicester Volunteer Corps held their parades in Western Park and the St John Ambulance Brigade members met there weekly.[365] Volunteers of the Leicester Motor Corps were ordered to meet in uniform, without their motor cycles, in the Magazine Drill Hall on Thursday summer evenings from where they would proceed to Western Park for bayonet fighting exercises.[366] The Junior Training Corps members were also required to march to the Park, with band and drums for battalion drill on Monday evenings.[367]

An astonishing estimate of 40,000 spectators went to the Western Park in early June 1916 to witness the presentation of a BE1 Sopwith Snipe bi-plane, named 'The City of Leicester', to a representative of the colony of Canada. Money to pay for the plane was raised by the local Chamber of Commerce, as part of the Aircraft for the Dominions initiative. A special tram service arranged to bring crowds of spectators to the park proved to be inadequate. Western Park was thronged. The plane stood in front of the small building next to the cricket ground, in a roped off area, where it was guarded by four men of the National Reserve carrying loaded rifles. Bands played martial and patriotic music from behind the Pavilion where there was a large contingent of the Junior Training Corps. The Leicester Citizen's Volunteer Corps helped with crowd control and provided a guard of honour for the dignitaries.

The High Commissioner for Canada, Sir George Perley, K.C.M.G., M.P., Lady Perley and Lord Desborough, president of the Imperial Air Fleet Committee attended the ceremony. The sum of 2,000 guineas had been raised towards the cost of providing the plane for the Canadian Forces to use during the war. Within ten days of the launch of the appeal this amount had been raised by 154 subscribers. The idea of inviting the larger towns and cities to raise funds for aeroplanes for the colonial units co-operating with the British Expeditionary Forces had come from Lord Desborough. These planes would form the nucleus of a new air fleet, while at the same time embodying an expression of cordial feeling between the Mother Country and the Colonies.

The high ground of Western Park was chosen for the event as the original location, Victoria Park, was unsuitable for landing an aircraft. The bi-plane flew over Leicester before turning and landing on the park. In the speeches, listeners were told by Alec Lorrimer of the Chamber of Commerce, that if the plane met with misfortune during its wartime operations, the War Office would replace it with another machine which would accompany Canadian troops back to Canada. Addressing the crowd, Lord Desborough said that the plane would show not only the patriotism and the love of

364 Jack Simmons: *Leicester Past and Present, Vol. 2, Modern City*, London, 1974, p.62
365 *Leicester Daily Post*, 4 March 1916
366 *Leicester Daily Post*, 3 July 1915
367 *Leicester Daily Post*, 12 July 1915

Dedication of aeroplane to Canada. (Records Office of Leicester, Leicestershire and Rutland)

Leicester for Canada, but the thanks of the War Office for the splendid work Canada had done in this dreadful war.

Hanging from the propeller, in a silk bag, was a bottle of champagne adorned with red, white and blue ribbons, ready for Lady Perley to christen the plane. Smashing it with a hammer, she said, 'I name thee Leicester and wish thee good luck.' The cloths covering the name 'Leicester' were drawn aside and Mr Lorrimer presented the aircraft to Sir George Perley representing the Canadian Government. The pilot started the engine, warning those behind to get out of the way. Before it became airborne, a great wind caused by the propeller blew the hair of those near. Flying round the park, the pilot waved over the side of the plane, while the crowd cheered until the aircraft disappeared to the south. The size of the crowd on a hot day meant the services of nursing sisters and first aiders were required to treat 38 people, mostly for cases of fainting. The only serious injury was to the Army lorry driver assisting with the plane, who sprained his wrist starting a lorry, no doubt by turning the starting handle too vigorously.[368]

Another World War One event in July 1916, not on the park but on Westhill Road where a marquee was erected, was organised by the Western Park Estate Wounded Soldiers' Committee, for 200 wounded soldiers from the Base Hospital. As they arrived after a car ride round Groby, Ratby and Kirby Muxloe, the soldiers were given

368 *Leicester Daily Post*, 5 June 1916

'smokes' before a programme of sports such as apple bobbing, tug-of-war, blindfold and obstacle races. This was followed by a concert with performances by Madame Ada White, the Misses Barfield, Miss Elsa Groocock, Misters Goddard, McKenzie, Wells, Arnold, Sutcliffe and Tory.[369]

On Easter Monday 1917, the Leicester New Military Band gave a concert in Western Park for wounded soldiers followed by a tea provided by the West End Association for Wounded Soldiers.[370] This band attracted large audiences to its regular concerts on the Park. Programmes and flags (paper badges or tokens attached with a single pin) were sold in aid of the Prisoner of War Fund.[371]

World War Two brought new dangers from above as the Luftwaffe flew overhead, dropping bombs on military and civilian targets alike. As part of the defences against these aerial attacks, a searchlight battery was positioned on the hill of the Park.[372] The footprint it left behind in the form of marks on the ground has been mistaken for earthworks associated with a pre-historic henge. All young people were expected to help out in the war effort as soon as they were old enough and to join one of the voluntary service organisations, such as air, navy or army cadets.

Iris Whiles, who lived on Winstanley Drive, joined the Air Raid Precaution (ARP) organisation as a messenger when she was 16. As the air raid sirens went off, warning of an air raid, Iris had to cycle to the ARP Depot in Western Park. If other communications failed, she had to ride round on her bike to deliver messages by hand, even during a raid. One night, she recalled, she had to go to the top of the park where the searchlight was. The searchlight had an enemy aircraft in its beam. The plane swooped down and started machine gunning the searchlight position and Iris had to cycle furiously to dodge the machine gun bullets.[373] Despite her hair raising adventure, Iris went to work the next day without a hair out of place, as she had had her curlers in under her helmet. Another young person, a pupil of Wyggeston Boy's School during the war, John Eley, quoted in Vincent Holyoak's book on wartime Leicester, *But For These Things*, remembered, 'A lot of the schoolboys used to do fire watching up to about 10pm on school premises.' Eley used to go to the school in Western Park for his watch, where an adult would take over after him for the rest of the night.[374]

Western Park Open Air School was designated as a place of safety for children. At the start of the war, schools were closed for two weeks or until they had been made

369 *Leicester Daily Post*, 24 July 1916

370 *Leicester Journal*, 13 April 1917

371 *Leicester Journal*, 9 August 1918

372 Terence C. Cartwright: *Bird's Eye Wartime Leicestershire 1939–1945*, p.10

373 Iris Whiles, WW2 People's War, contributed by CSV Action Desk, Leicester to BBC.co.uk, httpss://www.bbc.co.uk/history/ww2peopleswar/stories/57/a4373057.html, accessed 1 May 2020

374 Holyoak, p.99

safer, in case they came under attack. Altogether air raid precaution schemes cost the Education Committee £78,000, spent on providing steel shoring for 350 classrooms and three miles of concrete lined, covered trenches to protect the city's 27,000 school children.[375] Western Park Open Air School was one of those that had its own air raid shelter in the grounds. Parents were warned against going to schools to collect their children if an air raid siren was sounding. All children were to be kept in the covered trenches that formed the air raid shelters in school grounds or to stay in sandbagged rooms in the school buildings. If the homes of children were bombed during the day, they could be taken to Western Park Open Air School or to Haddenham Road (now Manor House) overnight until other arrangements could be made.

Out of school hours, children not near their homes in the streets or parks which were patrolled, would be directed to the nearest shelter by ARP volunteers. They were warned never to move away from home without their gas mask. ARP Depots were open 24 hours a day and served as bases for volunteer wardens, civil defence and first aid posts for the St John's Ambulance Brigade. For children playing on Western Park, there was an ARP depot close by, near the gates from Hinckley Road, which after the war became part of King Richard III Boys' Intermediate School and later MENCAP's Constance Jackson Centre. This building was demolished in 2018 when vandalism and arson attacks on the empty structure left it in an unsafe condition.

Another volunteer organisation, the Home Guard's 'B' Company, West City, had its company headquarters in the Pavilion in Western Park. Five platoons made up the West City Company: New Parks under the leadership of platoon commander R.A. Knight; Aero Club Braunstone led by J. Horne; Braunstone Park commanded by E.N. Evison; Braunstone Village under M.G. Allen; and Western Park whose platoon commander was W.H. Smedley DCM.[376] The Home Guard worked in their day jobs for the war effort and trained to be the country's last line of defence in case of invasion at weekends and after work.

Born in 1892, William Smedley, platoon commander for Western Park, in his day job was managing director of an advertising and publisher agency, assisted by his wife, Claris. They lived on Hilders Road where they had a live-in housekeeper, Olive Sherratt. Ralph Knight, commander of the New Parks platoon and born in 1895, lived on Fosse Road North. In his civilian life he had been a buyer in a boot and shoe warehouse. In 1939 Ralph had volunteered as an ARP warden. John Horne of Hand Avenue, born in 1889, was a shoe finisher in his day job. Too old to be eligible for service and combat in the military, these men no doubt had experience of battle in World War One. As well as those over the maximum age to enlist, the Home Guard had younger members, teenage boys waiting until they reached an age to be recruited to full time service.

375 Work Projects Administration Bibliography of Air Raid Precautions and Civil Defence, Washington DC, 1942

376 Austin J. Ruddy: *To the Last Round*, Leicester Mercury, 2007

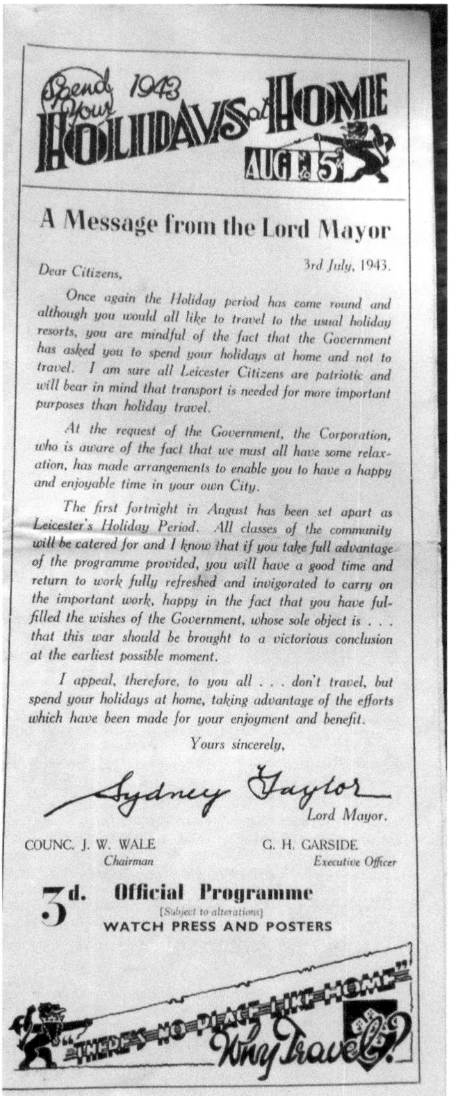
Spend Your 1943 HOLIDAYS at HOME AUG 1–15

A Message from the Lord Mayor

Dear Citizens, 3rd July, 1943.

Once again the Holiday period has come round and although you would all like to travel to the usual holiday resorts, you are mindful of the fact that the Government has asked you to spend your holidays at home and not to travel. I am sure all Leicester Citizens are patriotic and will bear in mind that transport is needed for more important purposes than holiday travel.

At the request of the Government, the Corporation, who is aware of the fact that we must all have some relaxation, has made arrangements to enable you to have a happy and enjoyable time in your own City.

The first fortnight in August has been set apart as Leicester's Holiday Period. All classes of the community will be catered for and I know that if you take full advantage of the programme provided, you will have a good time and return to work fully refreshed and invigorated to carry on the important work, happy in the fact that you have fulfilled the wishes of the Government, whose sole object is . . . that this war should be brought to a victorious conclusion at the earliest possible moment.

I appeal, therefore, to you all . . . don't travel, but spend your holidays at home, taking advantage of the efforts which have been made for your enjoyment and benefit.

Yours sincerely,

Sydney Taylor
Lord Mayor.

COUNC. J. W. WALE, *Chairman* — G. H. GARSIDE, *Executive Officer*

3d. **Official Programme** [Subject to alterations] WATCH PRESS AND POSTERS

"THERE'S NO PLACE LIKE HOME" Why Travel?

Holidays at Home pamphlet, 1943.

Despite the threat of attack from the air, Western Park played an important role in the leisure of Leicester people during the war, a time when many families were separated and seaside holidays out of the question. Recognising that a break from routine could help morale, as well as giving much needed rest from the intensity of war work, in 1943 the government asked Billy Butlin, of holiday camp fame, to assist towns around the country, including Leicester, to organise special weeks to encourage people to take 'holidays at home'. This was an important acknowledgement that, even in wartime, people needed a break. Butlin had purchased the main travelling fairs that were brought back into use to tour from town to town during their respective holiday weeks.[377]

Butlin recruited his fairground friends, Charlie and Billy Manning. They formed three travelling fairs sharing 44 rides between them. Among them were galloping horses and switchback roundabouts – the latter decorated with cars in the shape of animals and sometimes known as 'Noah's Arks'. This kind of ride had originally cost £12,000 but Butlin was able to buy every one of the ten or so in the country for between £200 and £500.[378] In Leicester in 1943 the fun fair, run by Henry P. Studt & Son of South Wales, was erected on Lee Street Car Park, at that time a surface-level open space. The fair had a different location in 1944 when it was on St Margaret's Pasture.

377 Susan Barton: *Working-class organisations and popular tourism, 1840–1970*, Manchester University Press, 2005, p184; Colin Ward and Dennis Hardy, *Goodnight Campers! The history of the British holiday camp*, Mansell, London, 1986, p.72

378 *The Billy Butlin Story*, London, Robson Books, 1982

In 1943, Leicester's designated 'Holidays at Home' period was between 1 and 15 August, at that time the usual holiday period for the city before the establishment of the July Fortnight. In a message in the official programme leaflet promoting the attractions and activities, Lord Mayor Sydney Taylor wrote, 'Once again the holiday period has come round and although you would like to travel to the usual holiday resorts, you are mindful of the fact that the Government has asked you to spend your holidays at home and not to travel. I am sure all Leicester citizens are patriotic and will bear in mind that transport is needed for more important purposes than holiday travel.

'At the request of the Government, the Corporation, who is aware of the fact that we must all have some relaxation, has made arrangements to enable you to have a happy and enjoyable time in your own city.'[379]

The main venues, apart from the fair, were the museum on New Walk where as well as special art exhibitions, there were concerts and where Ninette de Valois gave a lecture on 'The Ballet'. At De Montfort Hall, shows included Russian ballet, and orchestral and other concerts. At the Tigers' rugby ground there was wrestling and the football ground on Filbert Street hosted a horse show. Other amusements, games and entertainments rotated around the city's main parks, the ones that had not been dug up to grow food because of their value for recreation. This gave everyone an opportunity to join in the amusements in their own neighbourhood.

Western Park played its part. In 1943 there were concerts in the band stand where 6d was charged to sit on a chair. Different groups of musicians and performers provided the music each day: there was the Imperial Band; the Royal Artillery Mounted Band; the Band of His Majesty's Cold Stream Guards; the Scots Guards; the City of Leicester Club and Institute Band; the Frontline Concert Party; 'Bombers' Concert Party; 'S' Park 'S' Concert Party; and the Vaudeville Concert Party. Children weren't forgotten and shows for a young audience were Elliott's Marionettes from Market Harborough, an Arena Show with puppets and Clown Lez, Lolly and Pop Marionettes, Punch and Judy and a children's day with a fancy dress parade and sports. The band of the 1st Battalion of the Home Guard provided the accompaniment for Dancing on the Lawn. Western Park Golf Course also featured special novelty competitions, such as Four Ball v Bogey, and Mixed Foursomes. There was catering on the parks from mobile canteens, although refreshments were inevitably restricted due to rationing and were only provided where no other facility existed. Customers had to bring their own cups. Hot water was provided free of charge for people to make their own cups of tea.

For 1944 the Holidays at Home programme was similar to that of the previous year. The Barber of Seville and Madame Butterfly were performed at De Montfort Hall, where there was also dancing and a visit from the popular touring wireless show

379 Holidays at Home, Official Programme, leaflet, Leicester, 1943

Holidays at Home pamphlet, 1944.

Brains Trust. This time the concert parties appearing on Western Park and around the city had been replaced by groups calling themselves 'follies'. There were the Jollity Follies, the North Regional Follies and the Dawlish Follies. Other entertainments were billed as the Corvettes, Jolly Good Company, Broadway Entertainers and the Jolly Revelles. Dennis Beere performed as Jingles the Jester.

In the years since the end of World War Two, Western Park has been an important location for many public events, sports and entertainment. Beginning in 2011, the Western Park Festival, organised by the Friends of Western Park group of volunteers led by the herculean efforts of Adrian Alexander, provided fun for families and musical entertainment from Leicester musicians and bands. The Friends of Western Park has also raised funds to improve facilities, such as play equipment, and volunteering to plant bulbs, trees and clearing litter. Their efforts contributed to the award of the park's Green Flag status in 2015.

In June 2021 came the heartbreaking news that 35 of the beautiful, mature lime trees lining the drive, over 120 years old, were infected by the highly infectious and terminal disease phytophthora. To protect the rest of the park's 10,000 trees, as well as the public from falling branches, these and other diseased trees – including scots pine near the entrance, infected by red ring – more than 100 in total, were scheduled to be removed and replaced with healthy specimens in the autumn of 2021.

The Covid-19 pandemic of 2020 and 2021 saw Western Park play an important role as a place where local people, confined to their homes by lockdown for most of the day, could enjoy outdoor exercise.

6

WESTERN PARK ESTATES – THE RISE OF SUBURBIA

Western Park Estate and Garden Suburb

As the 19th century turned into the 20th, Sir John Mellor's sons, the Trustees of the Mellor Estate, planned to sell the land overlooking the newly opened Western Park for high-quality house building, in accordance with the probate terms of their late father's will of 1887. Plots of land on the New Parks Estate for house building were offered for sale from July 1887. There were several splendid sites on the estate for villa residences, the fields having a frontage on to Hinckley Road, within the boundary of the borough. Potential purchasers could see the plan of the estate at the offices of surveyors R.J. and J. Goodman on Friar Lane.[380] However, no overarching scheme for a planned residential development came to fruition until the Edwardian years.

The first roads in the neighbourhood that was to take its name from the nearby park were beginning to be laid out from 1905 when Sir John Tudor Walters paid the Mellor Trustees £2,000 for six acres of freehold land on 17 July 1905. The south side of this land fronted Hinckley Road by 380 feet. It bordered Western Park by 731 feet on the west and 180 feet six inches on the north west. On the north it was 743 feet wide and on the east 451 feet, a small beginning for the neighbourhood. Tudor Walters agreed to install sewers within two years, along Road No. 1 or Western Park Road and Road No. 2, the future Mellor Road. The map included with the conveyancing indenture shows that plans for the first roads were already drawn up at the time of the sale to Tudor Walters. The same plan shows that a third, as yet unnamed road, was proposed to the east, what was to become Westfield Road. A covenant stipulated that only private dwelling houses and stabling should be built in the development. Houses fronting on to Hinckley Road were to have a repair lease value of £25 a year, on Western Park Road £22 a year, and on Mellor Road £18 annually, evidence perhaps that the Mellors wanted this to be a quality development.[381]

380 *Leicester Journal*, 22 July 1887

381 Supplemental Abstract of the Title of Sir John Tudor Walters Kt, MP, to a piece of Freehold Land situate on the Hinckley Road, Leicester, 17 July 1905, loaned by Lucy Eddowes

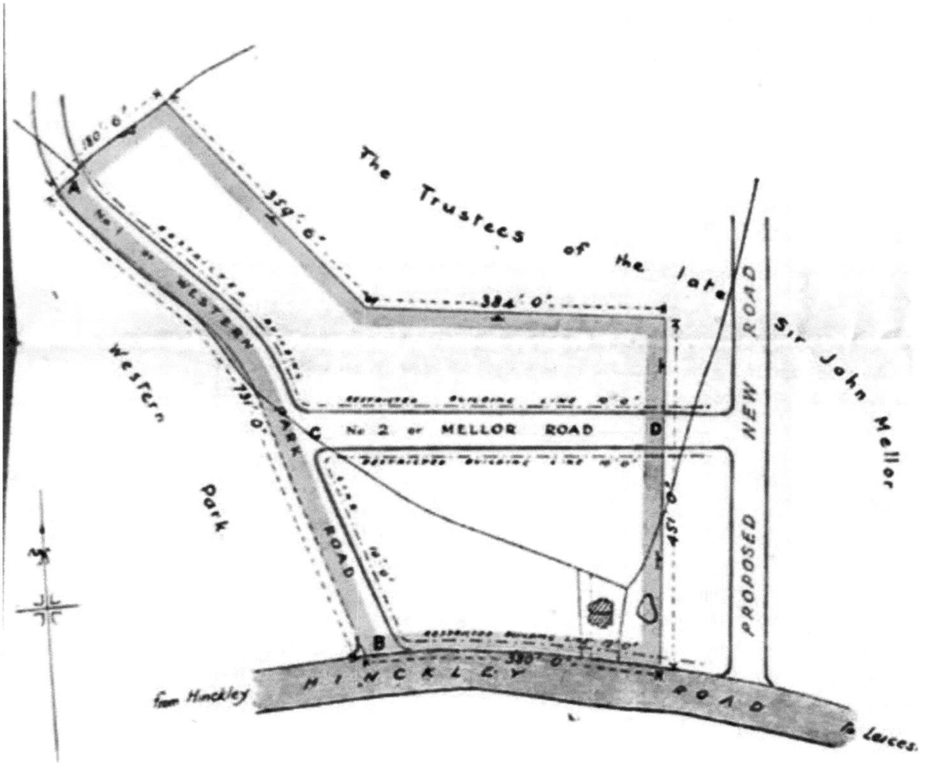

Plan of Road 1 and Road 2 Western Park Estate, house deeds, 1905.

John Tudor Walters soon resold part of the land to builders Bradshaw Brothers of Tudor Road on 15 December 1905 and more in a further transaction on 10 September 1906.[382] The Bradshaws had already applied for planning permission from Leicester Borough to construct 19 houses facing Western Park. Solid Edwardian semi-detached houses began to appear on Western Park Road, mostly beyond Mellor Road. In 1908 Bradshaw Brothers had permission to build four more, followed by a further six in 1911 and finally a single property in 1912. Another early developer building on Western Park Road was W.G. Simons who received permission for five houses there in 1908. Plans may have been amended as not all the houses with planning permission were built. There are fewer properties on the road than the total approved.

Built speculatively, not all houses were sold immediately: a house called Felbrigg was occupied by a tenant, Joseph Cornick, when it was sold for £870 by the Bradshaws to John Herbert Smith in March 1918.[383] Smith took out a mortgage for £600 with the Leicester Permanent Building Society, with repayments of £3 18s 0d a month.

382 Conveyancing indenture, 26 March 1918, loaned by Mr Tony Booth
383 Abstract of Title of Mr J.H. Smith to a messuage at 37 Western Park Road, Leicester, 26 March 1918, loaned by Mr Tony Booth

Perhaps Smith, a hosiery manufacturer in business at J. Haines and Company, raised some of his £270 deposit with the equity from his previous home on Meadhurst Road.

For a while, Mellor Road had houses on the north side only: three near the junction with Western Park Road and eight at the Westfield Road end. Planning permission for six houses on Mellor Road was granted to a developer called Hutchinson in February 1905. Most of the houses on this road were built between 1905 and 1915. The road has a mysterious house numbering system, jumping from 25 to 55 which are next door to each other. Perhaps the lower numbered homes were built on double plots. One of the early inhabitants was a Labour councillor, Walter Oram, who lived on Mellor Road. By 1939, Walter Oram, in business as a cardboard box manufacturer, had moved to Letchworth Road, a house almost opposite Sunnycroft Road, with his wife Agnes and daughter Edith, who was the paid secretary of the British Red Cross.

Ready for the next phase of development, the Mellor Trustees agreed to install a water supply to part of what was to be Letchworth Road and Westfield Road in September 1906.[384] A separate agreement was reached between the Borough of Leicester and Blaby Rural District Council in April 1910, allowing sewage to flow into the Corporation's system and another between the Mellor Trustees and Blaby RDC to create the sewers and drains in the part of the new estate where it extended across the boundary.[385] The construction of main drains and sewers was assured before John Tudor Walters purchased land for development. By 1908 Westfield Road had a row of semi-detached houses at the Hinckley Road end, designed by Ralph W. Bedingfield, built along the eastern side only. These will be discussed in more detail later. Bedingfield may have been the architect for Western Park Road as there are similarities between the properties and there is evidence that he was working with Bradshaw Brothers on Westfield Road.

This original block of streets of large, single fronted, solid, semi-detached villas of a similar design, were mostly developed speculatively by local firm Bradshaw Brothers. The Bradshaw brothers themselves, Arthur and Henry, lived in a house they had built on Western Park Road before it was sold. They continued to make their own homes in the area. Henry and Arthur later moved into Mellor Road. Their father Charles Bradshaw, also in the construction industry, moved from 173 Fosse Road North into a Westfield Road house on the corner with Letchworth Road. By 1925 Charles had made his home at Silverstone on Letchworth Road. This typically Edwardian first section of the development predates the area's forthcoming Garden City suburb

384 *Leicester Daily Post*, 22 September 1906

385 Agreement between Mayor, Aldermen and Burgesses of Leicester and the Rural District Council of Blaby, 18 April 1910; Agreement between the Trustees of the Right Honourable Sir John Tudor Mellor deceased and Blaby RDC, 12 April 1910; Agreement between right Honourable John William Mellor, James Robert Mellor and Francis Hamilton Mellor and Blaby Rural District Council, Indentures loaned by Su Bird

concept in its design, the houses are still within the context of late Victorian domestic architecture. On Hinckley Road, the stretch opposite Western Park, Victorian villa style properties predominate, typical of ribbon development along main roads in that period, displaying names such as Ladysmith and Mafeking placing their construction firmly in the period of the Boer War.

The Arts and Crafts Garden Suburb and Sir John Tudor Walters

The next phase in the development of the new suburb of Western Park in part of what was the New Parks was inspired by two major early-20th century social and aesthetic trends, the Garden City and the Arts and Crafts movements. The road that forms the spinal column of the new estate is Letchworth Road, named after the first garden city created in Hertfordshire with building from 1899, the vision of Ebenezer Howard. Garden cities or suburbs were a reaction against the over-density of urban development that followed industrialisation. Terraced streets of small, dark houses without gardens housed the working classes, with larger villa properties for those who were better off.

The garden suburb concept was intended as a compromise between urban and rural lifestyles. House building design broke from the monotony of identical terraces for a more individual approach, reflecting an idealised, vernacular, country cottage design with light, airy, healthy homes, each surrounded by its own garden, an alternative to perceived urban ugliness. Unlike in Howard's vision though, Western Park was to be out of the price range of most workers and the preserve of affluent professionals and industrialists with a few exceptions, such as the railway shunter Ambrose Underwood who lived at the house named The Cedars with his family plus four boarders.

The sales brochure advertising land on the estate, as well as cash payments, offered plots for sale by instalments to help purchasers acquire freehold sites on which to build their houses. The prices quoted for plots were promoted as being 'at an exceedingly low figure to secure rapid development' and were supposedly within reach of those of moderate means. Plots of land were sold separately from the houses and could be purchased in instalments over a period of up to seven years. House building could not begin until the land was paid for in full. While paying off the debt for the plot of land, purchasers could begin laying out their garden, plant fruit trees, lay down a lawn and make use of the land which would be part of their future homes, 'while it would yield an immediate profit by its produce'.[386]

Those buyers able to pay for their land immediately could begin building straight away. The price of plots was advertised in the brochure at four shillings a square yard, including the cost of sewering and road making. The size of plots varied from

386 Brochure advertising new housing development, Western Park, ROLLR 8D62/Box76/9

Western Park Road, taken in 2021.

300 to 2,000 square yards, although most demand was expected for those with an area of 500 or 600 square yards. For a plot of 500 square yards, the cost would be £100. A buyer who opted to pay over seven years, would be responsible for monthly payments of £1 6s 9d a month, or £16 1s 0d a year. A five year repayment plan would need a commitment to pay £1 16s 5d monthly or £21 17s 0d a year. The balance could be paid at any time. Plot owners were also free to sell their plots if they changed their mind and might make a profit if the value of the land had increased. The sales brochure further tempted buyers with the promise of no conveyancing, survey, land tax, or legal fees. No deposit was required and interest was a low rate for the time of three per cent. In some ways, the scheme resembled the future plotland developments popular with those seeking to build their own low-cost housing, perhaps starting with a tent or hut, popular in the 1920s and 1930s.[387]

On completion of the payment for the land, the estate owners could advance the cost of building the house according to approved plans, with repayments over several years. If a plot owner wanted to build a house costing £300, for example, with a loan over 20 years, the amount paid including principal and interest would be £1 16s 0d a month or £21 2s 0d annually. Life assurance could also be arranged and added to the repayments. Expert advice on planning the house and the supervision of building was available if required. The 12-page sales brochure was illustrated by Ralph Bedingfield's charming drawings of examples of houses and sample plans of floor layouts. There were also photos of some of his completed houses. This illustrates Bedingfield's close involvement with the development of Western Park

387 Colin Ward and Dennis Hardy, *Arcadia for All*, London, 1986

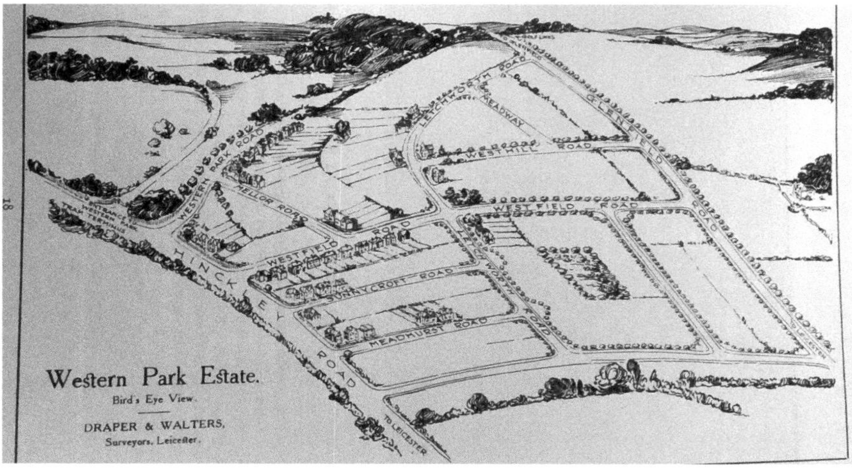

Plan of Western Park Estate from sales brochure, c.1909. (Records Office of Leicester, Leicestershire and Rutland)

and is perhaps evidence that he was the adviser on the design and construction of the properties that led to him being the most popular architect in the area.

The estate owners' aim was that 'charm and individuality shall be imparted to each house, though the cost of building may not be more than £300 or £400 ... and which could be part of the special arrangements proposed'. On offer was,

> 'A choice from a great variety of plans, showing picturesque exteriors and well-considered internal comforts and conveniences that make for economy in up-keep, and lessen domestic labour. Narrow entrances are avoided; dark, steep staircases, having "winders"; cramped unlighted passages; semi-obscured sitting rooms, looking out on dull, shabby back yards; cheap looking grates, with gaudy tiles and flash chimney pieces; small kitchens with bad ranges and antiquated dressers. The modern house is the reverse in many ways of that which characterised the typical Victorian dwelling. Its rooms have plenty of air space and light in all parts. Its appointments are refined, unpretentious and good.'[388]

The brochure included photographs of the surrounding rural environment and an impossible promise that the views across the countryside would never be lost to future building as they were on the edge of the town. To complete the new landscape, tree planting, turfing the verges of the roads and other environmental works commissioned by Tudor Walters as owner, created an attractive estate. Potential buyers were directed to the owner's agent, Walter C. Cooper at Draper and Walters, surveyors, the business of John Tudor Walters on Friar Lane, whose phone number was given as Western Park 19 or Central 754. Those who made their homes in Western Park were clearly buying into a particular lifestyle and romantic ideal.

388 Brochure advertising new housing development

Drawing of suggested design for semi-detached houses, by Ralph Bedingfield, from sales brochure, c.1909. (Records Office of Leicester, Leicestershire and Rutland)

Born in Pontypool in Wales, John Tudor Walters's own home was at 1 Granville Road in Leicester but he moved to The Way Side in Oadby during the 1900s. As well as his architect and surveying business, Tudor Walters was councillor for Wycliffe ward for 12 years from 1895 and chair of the Education Committee in Leicester. He championed the creation of the first social housing in Leicester, the Winifred Street Flats, proposed in 1896 and ready for their first residents in 1900. He was elected as member of parliament for Sheffield Brightside between 1906 and 1922 and for Penryn and Falmouth between 1929 and 1931. In 1912 he became Sir John and was made Paymaster General under Lloyd George.

Tudor Walters, an architect himself, had a keen interest in new styles of domestic architecture. Among his other business and philanthropic interests, Walters was director of the Industrial Housing Association, the Legal and General Insurance Society and Markham Main Colliery. He purchased several plots of land in the Western Park Estate from the Mellor Trustees, which allowed him to control development. A covenant in some house deeds shows that all plans for houses had to be approved by Tudor Walters or his surveyor. No building could take place without this approval. On Letchworth Road, houses had to meet the requirement that a repairing lease would be worth £30 a year.[389] Elsewhere on the estate this was lower, for example on

389 Purchase agreement between Sir John Tudor Walters and Henry Hancock, 27 April 1912, indenture loaned by Su Bird.

Westhill Road, this was reduced to £18 a year.[390] Reflecting the earlier industries in the neighbourhood, another covenant forbade clay, sand or gravel digging, brick or tile making, or 'anything to cause a nuisance or annoyance to neighbours'.[391]

At some point Walters formed and became director of the Housing and Town Planning Trust, a vehicle through which he was able to purchase more plots of land in Western Park and perhaps elsewhere.[392] Tudor Walters also held shares in Hampstead Garden Suburb (1907) and was one of the founders of the Romford Garden Suburb, Gidea Park, begun in 1911. Elsewhere in Leicester, Tudor Walters was a supporter of the Anchor Boot and Shoe workers' cooperative initiative at Humberstone Garden Suburb, where he made a speech at the ceremonial laying of a memorial stone commemorating the beginning of work on the first houses there in 1908.

Walters's interest in housing was an important influence on his political career. He chaired a committee set up in 1917 to consider questions relating to the construction of dwellings for the working class. Published in 1918, the committee's report was mostly written by the influential garden city architect Raymond Unwin, who had been involved with the design of the Anchor community at Humberstone. Known as the Tudor Walters Report, the findings promoted garden city principles by recommending a maximum of 12 houses per acre in towns and eight per acre in the country with a minimum of 70 feet between houses. The Committee had been split in opinion with a garden city group that sought a vernacular cottage solution continuing the Arts and Craft movement styles of design. The garden city advocates were to have a major influence on Leicester council housing estate design in the inter-war years, most notably on the Park (Saffron Lane) and Braunstone Estates.

As one of the leading exponents of the Garden City movement, John Tudor Walters was keen that the development adjacent to Western Park should be developed along the lines promoted by that movement. Tudor Walters was able to influence the development of the new Western Park Estate as a Garden City suburb, albeit minus workplaces, by purchasing parcels of land containing several plots from the trustees of the Mellor Estate, and by arranging the layout of roads and utilities such as sewers, water and electricity cables. In 1912, Tudor Walters extended his interest in the Western Park Estate when he paid just over £3,631 for 18 acres and 23 perches of land in what was Blaby Rural District. These were the fields Slater's Hill Close, Johnson's Hill and part of Black Anna's Bower which were laid out as Meadway and extensions to Letchworth, Westhill and Westfield Roads.[393] A minimum value for all houses erected on the individually sold plots was £18 on a repairing lease. Covenants

390 Property deed loaned by Sarah Hughes

391 Purchase agreement between Sir John Tudor Walters and Henry Hancock, 27 April 1912, indenture loaned by Su Bird.

392 *Leicester Mercury*, August 1943

393 Deeds leant by Sarah Hughes

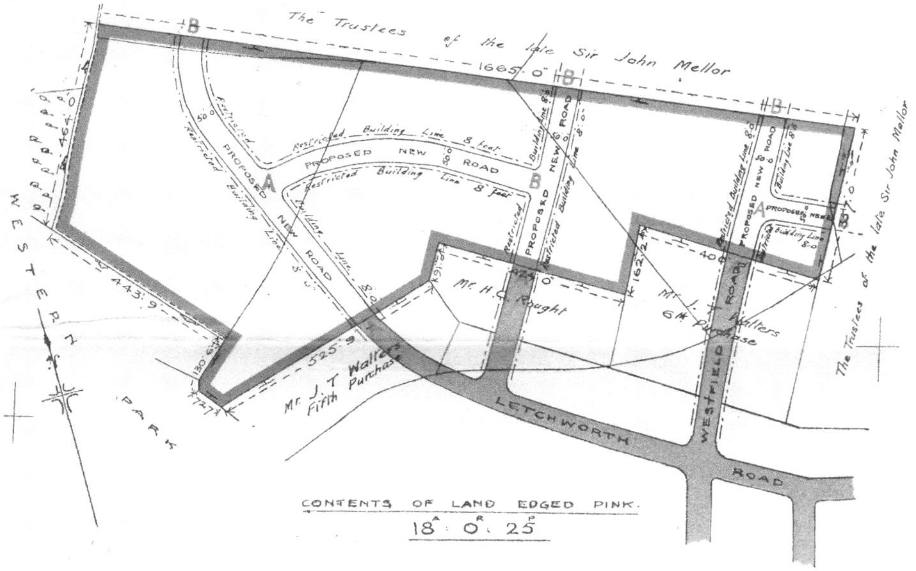

Plan of part of Western Park Estate, house deeds, c.1919.

that maintained the spacious ambience and garden city features of the estate stipulated that roads had to be 50 feet in width with houses set back to a building line of a minimum of ten feet on Letchworth Road and on Westhill Road eight feet from the boundary with the street, providing ample front gardens. All properties erected had to have a live fence or hedge, an iron fence or a palisaded fence with a dwarf wall, no higher than 4ft 6in, along the boundaries. Reflecting the surrounding rural environment, hedges needed to be guarded by iron hurdles strong enough to keep out cattle, or a wall or close-boarded fence not less than five feet or more than 6ft 6in in height around rear gardens. As well as fencing off their building plot, purchasers had to complete the formation of the side causeway (pavement) with materials specified by the local authority and maintain half of the width of the road near their boundary line until the council took it over once half of the plots on the road had been taken up.

In order to purchase the land needed to fulfil his ambition of creating a garden suburb, Tudor Walters needed to raise capital. In January of 1912, he borrowed £10,000 at an annual rate of interest of five per cent from Thomas Wilson Helme of Springfield Hall in Lancaster. This loan was to be repaid by January 1917. As security for the loan, Tudor Walters conveyed several parcels of land to Helme who would receive sales receipts from any plots sold. A minimum sale price of 2s 9d per square yard was stipulated but plots actually sold for 3s 6d a square yard, the price paid by Henry Hancock in 1912.[394] By June 1912, £3,500 had already been paid to Helme in four separate instalments.

394 Purchase agreement between Sir John Tudor Walters and Henry Hancock, 27 April 1912, indenture loaned by Su Bird

Thomas Wilson Helme was the son of Sir Norval Watson Helme MP. Walters would have known Sir Norval as both were Liberal Members of Parliament. For Thomas Wilson Helme, this may have been simply an investment opportunity as he seems to have no other involvement with either Leicester, housing or as a developer. Helme's main interest, outside his business and local politics in his home town of Lancaster, was in the Scouting movement, in which he was a district commissioner. He was also a freemason. Tudor Walters and Helme jointly held at least four plots which were sold to people hoping to build a home. World War One would have disrupted their plans somewhat but any set back was only temporary. In 1918 lots 163 to 166 were sold to Harry Smart, who resold one of them four years later in 1922 to Lizzie Fowkes on which the distinctive bungalow Nestena was built.

Another purchaser of a parcel of land was Henry Cooke Rought of Evington Drive, a manager at the disinfectant manufacturer, Mills and Company. Whether he held the land as security for a loan to Tudor Walters, intended to have a house built for himself, or was investing in land to resell at a profit is unknown, as sadly Rought died in 1919. Evidence that speculation was involved can be seen on the plans of the estate before its development. The lots or parcels of land often crossed the new or proposed road layouts, so would not have been for just one house but subdivided into smaller plots.

The houses on Letchworth Road and the surrounding roads demonstrate the principles of domestic design based on vernacular styles built with the individuality of traditional craft skills. In Western Park, bespoke designs were typically commissioned from local architects by the original purchasers of the plots.[395] If needed, advice on the choice of design and builder was offered by Western Park Estates. The key feature of the Western Park garden suburb was, and remains, the individual. Although encapsulating modern ideas for the time, the designs themselves were often based on nostalgia for a bygone rural ideal. The houses embodied the concept behind the vernacular or domestic revival movement and offered an alternative to the urban, based on the village and countryside.[396] Individuality and high standards of craftsmanship demonstrated a tiredness with industrialisation's mass production. Not just the exteriors of the properties but the interiors too contain Arts and Crafts detail, reflecting the influence of Voysey, Waals, Gimson, Peach and Fletcher, all of whom had local connections through Leicester School of Art. Reflecting garden suburb principles, the space between and around the houses is important too and contributes to the visual appeal of the community. However, the style was not without its derogatory critics, who called the developments pseudo-Tudor or fake rural.[397]

---

395 J.W.R. Whitehead and Christine M.M. Carr: *The Creators of England's Inter-war Suburbs*, Urban History, 28, 2, Cambridge University Press, 2001, pp218-235

396 M. Swenarton: *Homes Fit For Heroes*, 1981, p.7

397 Whitehead and Carr

Built in furniture in Overdale, Letchworth Road.

Houses on Letchworth Road overlooking Western Park or with large gardens often had their principal rooms reversed in layout, with the kitchen and storage areas facing the street, so that living and dining rooms could benefit from the views to the rear. The road layouts have, for the most part, broken with the grid layouts of the straight terraced streets and gently wind in an apparently more natural manner, reminiscent of a village lane in places, in keeping with Garden City planning principles of layout.

The interiors of the properties demonstrate similar aesthetics and retain internal features that depict the best in Arts and Crafts design. Some of the occupants of the houses furnished their homes in a manner demonstrating their ideas of good taste and devotion to quality furnishing. Fire places, stair rails, tiling and built-in furniture reminiscent of Voysey and Waals, all feature highly. Some of the Gimson furniture in Leicester Museum's collection furnished at least one of the houses on Letchworth Road.

The suburb of Western Park demonstrates some the main features of early-20th century domestic architecture in transition from the Victorian to the modern. The earlier Edwardian semi-detached properties still have some of the overshadowing associated with terraced housing. These were soon superseded by the lighter and more airy Arts and Crafts designs, with more surrounding space and large gardens. The Edwardian style of domesticity, like the Victorian, had cooking in the kitchen which housed a coal-fueled range, separate from washing and cleaning in the scullery where the sink was situated, often along with a copper for heating water and washing laundry. The properties were mostly built for large families with possible accommodation for domestic servants. All houses had a coalhouse or coal store in which to keep fuel for heating and cooking. They were all built with a bathroom and indoor and outdoor toilets, showing a modern attitude to cleanliness. The word 'lavatory' was used to describe a washbasin.

Following Garden City principles, large gardens could allow self-sufficiency in vegetables if necessary, although the affluent residents of Western Park might employ a gardener or tend their gardens as a hobby, a growing pastime as families moved to suburbs, rather than to supplement their diet or income. Most of the gardens, though, were ornamental and reflected growing middle-class leisure. Some of them evoked the influence of Gertrude Jekyll in their layout and choice of plants.

Some houses were built with a cycle store for independent transport and some forward-thinking residents had their houses built with that symbol of 20th century modernity, a motor house or soon had one added. 'Motor house' was an adaptation of the existing words 'carriage house' to describe a structure in which to store a vehicle. The word garage as a place to store a motor car was not yet in common use. Others did not anticipate the rate of change in personal transport, for example, in 1910 Ralph W. Bedingfield drew up plans for his client, Mr Carr, for a house on the corner of Western Park Road and Hinckley Road which included a stable with space for a trap.[398] A covenant for the earliest properties on Western Park Road stipulates only a house and associated stabling could be erected. From around 1922 the new word 'garage' had replaced the English term 'motor house' in planning applications, and presumably in spoken language, as the noun meaning a place to store a motor car. One of the earliest mentions of a local house with a garage rather than a motor house

398 Building plans, ROLLR 1910/15606, 13 May 1910

Garden of Ruella, Letchworth Road, 1931. (Courtesy of Su Bird)

was in plans approved on 18 March 1922, designed by A.W. Adcock for Mr T. Bloor's Ashfield on Meadway. A single planning application for two further garages submitted by H. Bland, for clients Mr Benson and Mr Holroyd of Denton (designed by Frank Jones) on the corner with Letchworth Road, was approved on Meadway in November 1922. From this time, the plans for a building in Western Park in which to store a car always used the word garage.

While architecture styles reflect the Arts and Crafts movement, as the Western Park development progressed more art deco and moderne styling began to appear. However it is the Arts and Crafts style, typified by the work of Ralph Waldo Bedingfield that defines the area and makes it a special place within Leicester as well as in the history of art and design locally.

Ralph Waldo Bedingfield

Architect Ralph Waldo Bedingfield (1872–1940), based in Hotel Street and later at The Crescent in Leicester, had a major influence on the appearance and ambiance of the estate. Ralph W. Bedingfield, not to be confused with his older brother Waller King Bedingfield who was also an architect, had a creative involvement with Western Park lasting over a quarter of a century from around 1905 to 1933. A large proportion of the individually designed houses, examples of which are on Glenfield Road, Letchworth Road, Westhill Road, Westfield Road and Meadhurst Road are his work. He also designed some substantial semi-detached properties on the lower end of Westfield Road, nearest to Hinckley Road and possibly several of those on Western Park Road. These semis, though, are not uniform as became almost the norm for the semi-detached genre, as they are a-symmetrical with a different style of windows, either bay or ribbon, within the pairs.

In all his designs in the area, the influence of the Arts and Crafts and Garden City movements is evident. With his white pebble dash walls, rows of mullioned windows, tall chimneys, hipped gables, timber framing, ribbon windows, bays and verandahs and neo-vernacular style, Bedingfield seems to have been influenced especially by contemporaries Richard Norman Shaw (1831–1912), Ernest Newton (1856–1922) and Charles F. A. Voysey (1857–1941), as were other architects commissioned to work in Western Park. Bedingfield's own work in the area was characterised by understated simplicity, characteristic of the Arts and Crafts genre. He was particularly fond of using white roughcast or pebble-dash rendering on his properties, also reflecting the popularity of the style with his clients. Indeed, roughcast renders were a fashionable design staple of the late 19th and early 20th centuries, particularly popular with Richard Norman Shaw. Bedingfield's association with Leicester School of Art would have given him connections with local Arts and Crafts designers such as Ernest Gimson, George Bankart, John Paul Cooper, Peter Waals and Harry Peach of Dryad.

Bedingfield studied at Leicester School of Art, a forerunner of De Montfort University, where he was awarded the Perspective Prize Second Grade in 1889. In 1891 he was graded first class for his studies in Perspective, Theory and Practice. The next year, Bedingfield was graded first class for his work in 'Shading from the Cast' and 'Outline from the Cast' and a second grade for his Models. A talented student, he was awarded the Queen's Prize in 1892 for his design for a bank and a silver medal in 1893 for his measured drawings of a screen at King's College Chapel in Cambridge, plus a bronze medal for architectural design. Bedingfield again won a bronze medal in a national competition's Medal and Prize List for his design for a house in 1894, the year he qualified as an architect, although he did not receive the prize as he already held higher awards for the same subjects. In his examinations, the work of Ralph W. Bedingfield was singled out for special remarks by the examiners. Among the examiners working with the College of Art at the time were William Morris, sculptor W. Hamo Thorneycroft , engineer Professor William C. Unwin and Walter Crane, so it is easy to see from where some of his Arts and Crafts influences came.[399]

While he was studying, Bedingfield was an architectural assistant with Leicester firm Goddard, Paget and Goddard. As well as working as an architect he also became involved in education. In 1903 he joined the Knights of Malta freemason lodge in Hinckley. He went on to introduce the first full-time courses in architecture at Leicester

399 Records of Leicester School of Art, 1888 to 1894, De Montfort University Special Collections, Leicester

School of Art, where he had studied himself, in 1919. As a committee member of the Leicestershire Archaeological Society he demonstrated an interest in the physical remains of the past. Ralph worked on the excavation of the ruins of Leicester Abbey, continuing work begun by his architect brother, Waller King Bedingfield. Ralph Bedingfield's obituary written by S.H. Skillington in the Leicestershire Archaeological Society Annual Report for 1940 remembered fondly that 'his innate unpretentiousness, his youthful spirit, his easy-going sociability and his constant sense of fun tended to obscure the vital importance of the work he did so well'.[400] These qualities, as well as his interest in history and archaeology, could be said to be inherent in his architectural designs for Western Park.

Of course not all or even most property developers and homeowners chose Bedingfield to design their homes, although he was closely involved in the development of Western Park Estate. Many of Leicester's leading early-20th century architects' work is represented among the properties of Western Park, including designs by Ernest H. Smith, and Fosbrooke and Bedingfield, Ralph's brother's partnership firm. The influence of the Arts and Crafts movement on all their work is apparent, although some clients chose to have a home in a more traditional style. Among Ralph Bedingfield's other work in the Leicester area are Lillie House on London Road and houses in Kirby Fields, where he made his own home in Ringwood, after moving from Narborough to Stoneygate Road with his wife Beatrice and children.

Letchworth Road and its first residents

The first plots to be developed on Letchworth Road were on its southern side, with large gardens sloping down with magnificent open views. The south side of Letchworth Road is situated on a high rocky ridge; the land falls away sharply behind the houses. This means that the architects and builders had to face the challenge of building on land that was not level. Using true Arts and Crafts principles, the architects and the landscape gardeners had to rise to this challenge by working with the terrain and incorporating it into their designs. Drawing on civil engineering skills, front and rear of the properties were on different levels, giving scope for large basements or storage spaces accessed at ground level from the garden. Many of the houses on this south side of the road had terraces and verandahs to give panoramic views across the park to the countryside as it was then. Gardens were laid out in terraces and reached by steps from the ground floor level.

The first house to be given planning permission by the Borough of Leicester in 1906 was the five-bedroom house known as Summer Hill designed by Ralph W. Bedingfield. This house was built for Ebenezer Hancock, an affluent draper with a business on the Haymarket, religious non-conformist, councillor and author of a

400 Leicestershire Archaeological Society, Eighty-sixth Annual Report, 1940, p.xx

Summer Hill, Letchworth Road, from sales brochure, c.1909.

booklet with the title *Keeping Young Past Eighty*. Ebenezer Hancock was born in Kent in around 1850, working his way up from a draper's assistant in Godalming where he began his career. Hancock may have already had connections with Bedingfield as he was chair of the Municipal Technical and Art Schools Committee between 1905 and 1908 and a co-opted member of the committee of this forerunner to De Montfort University until 1934. Ebenezer's daughter, Winnie, like Bedingfield, taught in the School of Arts. Hancock was also involved in the League of Nations Society from 1918, the year he had discussions with Frederick Barnes Lott of the Philosophical Society and Arthur C. Wates at Vaughan College. They were founder donors to the University of Leicester, who met in April 1918 to discuss the foundation of the new university college as a living war memorial.[401]One of Hancock's children, his son Albert John Woodgate Hancock, known as Joey, who was educated at Wyggeston School, became well known for his work in the fledgling motor car industry. After leaving school, Joey Hancock studied mechanical engineering at Birmingham Technical College and was a trainee pupil at J.W. Brooke and Company of Lowestoft in around 1901. Beginning his career with Humber, he joined the Wolsley Motor Company as a draughtsman then worked with Herbert Austin when the Austin company was formed in 1905. Joey drove for Vauxhall in the French Grand Prix of 1912 in Dieppe but had engine trouble after 15 out of the 20 laps of the race. Between 1919 and 1941 Joey was chief designer for Austin motor cars and became president of the Institute of Mechanical Engineers between 1935 and 1936.[402]

401 *Leicester Mercury*, 19 April 1918
402 Grace's Guide

John 'Joey' Hancock in his Vauxhall at the 1912 French Grand Prix at Dieppe. (Wikimedia Commons)

Hancock's home, Summer Hill, is now on Leicester's local heritage asset register because of its unusual and probably unique design. An understated, dark-brick, gabled frontage hides a creative solution to the problem of building on top of a slope. Ingeniously, it takes advantage of the sunlight and views to both south and west, by angling the breakfast and drawing rooms to the main body of the house, with the dining room at almost 45 degrees. The house had an integral cycle store at the front of the property.

Bedingfield designed another property for Hancock in 1909, intended to be built next door to Summer Hill, for use by the Abbey Gate Baptist Mission with Ebenezer Hancock as its superintendent. This proposed second property featured a carriage turn, and a library, kitchen and larder to the front of the property, with the main rooms enjoying a view of the garden and park. A slight complication here was that part of the house crossed the borough boundary into the county. It was agreed that all drains would be connected to Leicester's sewage and water system. However, there is no physical evidence of this property so there may be some doubt as to whether it was actually built.

Immediately next to Summer Hill is The White House, the ground plan of which matches the Ordnance Survey maps. However, in *Kelly's Directory of 1924* the Abbey Gate Mission with Hancock as superintendent is listed in between Summer Hill occupied by Hancock and The White House inhabited by William Harvey. Plans for

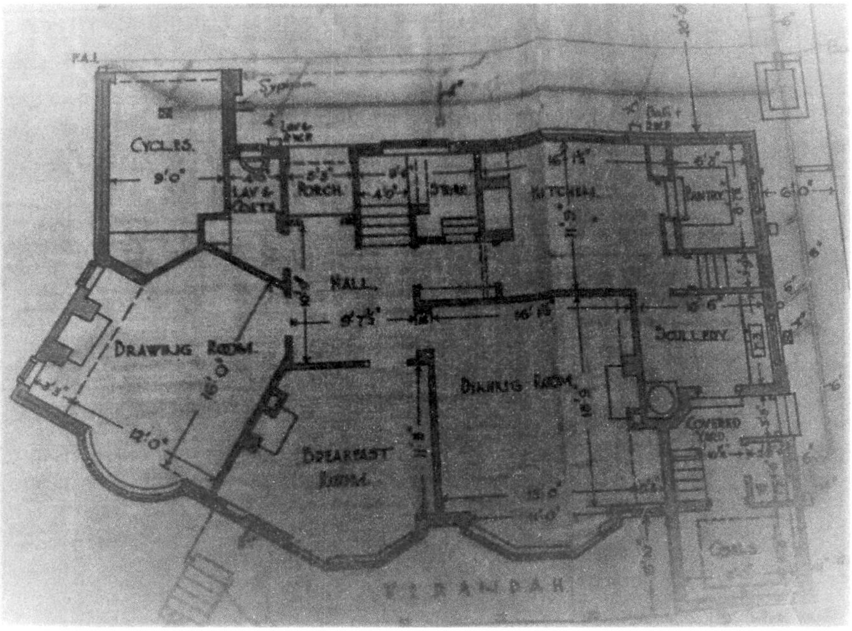

Summer Hill plan, by Ralph W Bedingfield, 1906. (Records Office of Leicester, Leicestershire and Rutland)

Plan for Abbey Gate Mission by Ralph W Bedingfield, 1909. (Records Office of Leicester, Leicestershire and Rutland)

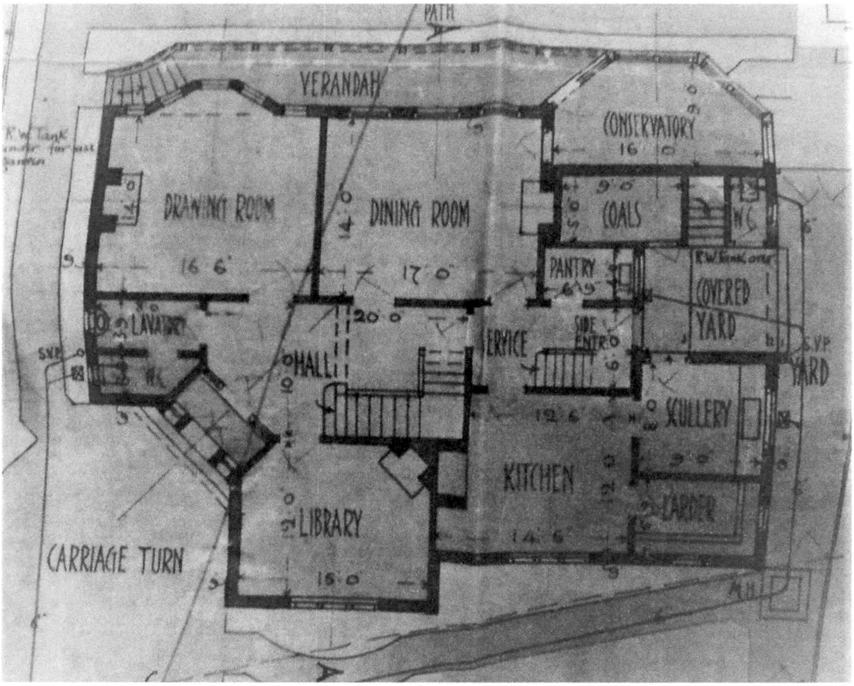

The White House, designed for Harvey by E.C. Harrison, were approved in September 1923. Perhaps Hancock ended up running the Mission from his own home.

Ralph Bedingfield was also the architect of the second development on Letchworth Road, a pair of five-bedroomed semi-detached houses, Overdale and Uplands, which received planning permission in February 1907. Just over a year later, the plans for the house that was to become Overdale, were amended to include a wash-house to the side and an additional bay window to the drawing room.

This pair of houses was again built for Liberal politician John Tudor Walters who sold them on their completion. The first inhabitants of Overdale were Wallace Price of Price Parsons and Company, Leather Factors, of 59 Halford Street and his family. During the 1920s, Sydney Pick moved into Overdale from Sunnycroft Road. He was the owner of Pick's knitwear factory on Wellington Street, credited with the creation of the patterned, sleeveless jumper for men. Pick was also a collector of Arts and Crafts style furniture by Ernest Gimson. Next door at Uplands was William Arthur Thompson, another businessman of W.A. Thompson Ltd, soon replaced as resident by William S. Cave, a yarn agent for Lee and Cave.

At the time *Kelly's Directory of 1909* was compiled, the only properties listed on Letchworth Road were Summer Hill, Overdale and Uplands, all names that reflect their position on the crest of the hill overlooking open countryside. Western Park Road contained 12 inhabited properties, Westfield Road four and Mellor Road six. These houses were beyond the built up area of Leicester, in extra-parochial land, still separated from the town by fields and allotments.

Houses overlooking Western Park, sales brochure, c.1908. (Records Office of Leicester, Leicestershire and Rutland)

Over the next few years more houses appeared on Letchworth Road. In 1907 plans were approved by the Borough of Leicester for two houses, each with four bedrooms, an attic and box room for builder W.G. Simons of Bolton Road. Further plans were given approval in March 1909 for four villas, a pair of semi-detached houses designed by Leicester architects Seale and Riley of 25 Horsefair Street for their client Orson John Wright, nephew of the prolific property Leicester developer Orson Wright. An auctioneer, estate and insurance agent, Orson John Wright had lived on Glenfield Road in 1901, moving to Gimson Road by 1911. At that time there were few buildings between Gimson Road and Western Park and one of Wright's neighbour's house was given the name 'Park View'.

Wright's four villas on Letchworth Road were opposite the existing three houses on the other side of the road. One of these pairs of semis was the Chestnuts and the Cedars. The first occupants of the Chestnuts were James Taylor from Lancashire, a commercial traveller selling oil cakes, a type of animal feed, and his family and servant. Next door at the Cedars, the first occupants were Ambrose Underwood, a railway shunter, with his wife, two sons and adopted son, plus four lodgers, a teacher with his wife and baby and a female nurse. This illustrates that not everyone living in this prestigious development were wealthy or middle class. The Cedars had two reception rooms, five bedrooms, and a bathroom. When it was advertised for sale in 1916, it was offered with or without a large, well-planted garden.

Houses constructed and occupied by 1912 were The Laurels, Overdale, Uplands, Summer Hill, Bradda and Red Gables on the present even-numbered side of Letchworth Road and on the other were Blythe Cottage, the Sycamores, the Chestnuts, the Cedars and the Western Park Estate Office near the site of St Anne's Church where Walter Cooper, an employee of John Tudor Walters's firm, Draper and Walters, lived and worked. Walter Cooper's own home, according to *Kelly's Directory of 1914*, was at 35 Meadhurst Road, an address that no longer exists, evidence that plots were sometimes combined and renumbered.

Cooper was suspended from his job after a scandal involving a teenage girl. Winifred Cooke claimed he was the father of her illegitimate child. Winifred was said to be from a respectable family. She had met Cooper, a married man in his forties, when she was in service at the Westcotes Hotel where he had stayed in 1912. Her mistress and employer had warned her against being involved with Cooper who had told Winifred he hadn't lived with his wife for many years. Winifred was dismissed from her job after she had been seen out with Cooper. She lost her next job at the Vegetaria Cafe when he caused a scandal by calling for her there. After that she went into service with Mrs MacDonald, who was away between Christmas and February 1913, leaving Winifred alone. Cooper repeatedly took her out, and 'misconduct' was said to have taken place at night in the Western Park Estate hut and during the day in the Coffee Room of the Empire

Hotel, after which Cooper was said to have taken her to the Oriental Cafe where he ate six poached eggs on toast. In court, Cooper denied anything inappropriate had happened between them, but Winifred was awarded payments to support her child.[403]

A complication when applying for planning permission was that the Western Park Estate lay within the jurisdiction of two local authorities, the Borough of Leicester and Blaby Rural District whose border passed through it. Sometimes the boundary passed through properties. Drainage and sewage pipes often had to be connected to those of the neighbouring council involving approval from both authorities. Matching the descriptions and plans to the correct properties has been complicated as at the time of construction and for several years afterwards, there were no house numbers, only names which sometimes changed as new residents moved in. For example, a pair of semi-detached houses on Letchworth Road were originally named Cromwell and Naseby. Cromwell, perhaps a controversial choice, was renamed Conegar but Naseby has retained its original name. In 1924, Mr C.B. Ward of Naseby applied for planning permission to add a garage to his property. There was another house with the name Cromwell on Letchworth Road, described in a 1930 sale advertisement as 'nearly opposite Sunnycroft Road'. By the time of the 1939 Register the houses were all numbered.

On 8 December 1911 the Mellor Trustees successfully applied to extend Letchworth Road beyond the county boundary. In 1912 Henry Bland's design for a house for J.S. Coltman was given the go-ahead, as was G.E. Clare's design for Red Gables for Scotsman James Gardner Grahame of Grahame Gardner outfitters, the suppliers of Gymphlex sports clothing for school and sports teams, remembered by generations of local people as the place they got their school uniforms. This was a three-bedroom house with a playroom, probably so called as it didn't meet the expected size for a fourth bedroom. A motor house was added to the plans for Grahame's house in an additional application the same year.

Bland was the architect chosen, also in 1912, by Mrs Benson when she had a pair of semi-detached houses with timbered gables built for her two sons, William and Thomas. Edgar Stevens and Company of Oadby obtained planning permission, again in 1912, for two pairs of semi-detached houses, one on Letchworth Road and similar ones on Westhill Roads. In the planning application these were described as 'proposed garden city houses'.

The years 1914 and 1915 were busy ones for developers on Letchworth Road. In January 1914 architect T. Henry Bowell of Market Place designed a four bedroom house for C.D. Everett near the corner with Westfield Road whose plans were amended a few months later. This was the first one of three contiguous houses designed by Bowell. Bowell is shown as the owner of these plots in the block plan indicating that as well as being an architect, he was a property developer building speculatively.

403 *Leicester Daily Post*, 7 April 1914

Semi-detached houses on Letchworth Road, designed by Ralph W Bedingfield. (Records Office of Leicester, Leicestershire and Rutland)

In July that year Ralph Bedingfield designed two pairs of semi-detached houses for Bradshaw Brothers who had already purchased the land. These four houses, opposite the entrance to Westhill Road were to have five bedrooms, a garden room and, a portent of the future, an integral motor store. They also had mock timber framing. They got the go-ahead from the Planning Committee in September 1915.

In September 1914 H. Bland, a surveyor, of 37 Danes Hill Road, submitted plans for approval on behalf of Archibald W. Smith, a boot polish and ink manufacturer, whose home was The Nook. Although in Blaby Rural District the plans were also submitted to Leicester Borough so the sewers could be connected. Like many other properties on this side of Letchworth Road, the kitchen was to the front of the property to take advantage of the views to the rear from the drawing room and dining room. These plans for what was to be a charming, pebble-dash stucco property with scalloped terracotta tiles hung between the upper and lower bay windows, had been modified to include three bedrooms and a playroom. Originally a four-bedroom house was proposed but presumably one of the bedrooms was too small and the plans amended. A similar situation seems to have arisen at the house on the north side of Letchworth Road designed for E.J. Williams by Harding and Williams of 13 New Street. The plans of July 1914 were resubmitted in 1915 with a small bedroom redefined as a dressing room 'in compliance with regulations'.

Another Letchworth Road property on Leicester's local heritage asset register was the home of seed grower Thomas Harrison and his family, Haycott House. This detached home was built using a distinctive pattern of red brick Flemish bond with darker, burnt brick headers, bay windows and an arched front doorway in decorative brickwork.

A sign of the affluence of the residents and their openness to innovation was their use of motor cars at a time when they were only available to a small minority. In 1914 plans for a motor house by Kites, Fosbrooke and (Waller) Bedingfield for R.C. Allen of Bradda, at the end of his garden, were accepted by Blaby Rural District with access from the end of Western Park Road where a bungalow is now situated.

Richard Charles Allen had started out as a traveller in the boot and shoe trade, living on Humberstone Road in 1881. After a change of career, he entered the brewing industry, owning his own factory on Oxford Street, perhaps assisted by his freemasonry as he was treasurer of St John's Lodge. The Allens lived at 29 Evington Road before moving to Bradda, maybe named as a reminder of happy holidays in the Isle of Man. Richard and his wife, Lucille, had three sons, Richard, Percy and Shirley. Percy lived at Chelston on the corner of Westhill Road. Shirley Allen became an accountant and in 1925 lived in a house called Lynford on Western Park Road, so perhaps he made use of his father's garage. Later Shirley moved to a much bigger house, The Beeches, on the corner of Letchworth Road and Meadway, designed by Norman Read for Mr Hales.

A splendidly complex, cantilevered construction designed by Ernest H. Smith for boot manufacturer William Merryfield Matthews was approved by Blaby Rural District Council in 1915. This brick-built property with a white-rendered front gable, named Lyndhurst, had four first-floor bedrooms with space in the attic for future rooms. Fronting the road were a motor house, scullery and coal store. In the basement was a large billiard room. At the rear were the main living rooms overlooking the huge garden and park beyond, with a verandah. The rear of the house towers majestically over the terraced garden. In 1918 permission was given for Bowles and Son to extend the property with the addition of a conservatory and new steps.

Matthews was another example of upward social mobility in the booming Leicester industrial scene. Born the son of a clicker in the boot and shoe trade in 1881, he spent his childhood in a shared property in Wheat Street in the poor Wharf Street area of Leicester. By 1911 Matthews, his wife and young family lived on Briton Street off Narborough Road and had a servant. The family moved on to Westcotes Drive for a short time before moving to Lyndhurst on Letchworth Road. William Matthews was also an early motor car owner and in 1920 he was fined ten shillings for having a car without lights.[404] This was perhaps for being parked without a hurricane lamp on the road side of the car, as was once required by law. In its entry in the 1939 Register, Lyndhurst was occupied by shoe manufacturer Sidney

404 *Leicester Daily Post*, 24 November 1920

Witton and his wife Helen. It also housed a female domestic servant, a builder's foreman, a carpenter, two plumbers and a couple of painters and decorators, perhaps indicating the house was undergoing renovation or alteration or was housing workmen employed on local building projects.

A nearby residence with the kitchen and coal store to the front designed by Norman Read for W. Cave which he called Holly Hayes was also approved in 1915 as was another Norman Read design for Louis H. Burridge, owner of a hosiery factory on Wellington Street and a director of Leicester City Football Club. In honour of his wife and daughter, both called Ida, the Burridge family home was named Ida Dene. This house had the kitchen, hall and a motor house to the front, and a billiard room in the attic space on the second floor.

G. Lawton Brown and Percy C. Jones's design for J. Johnson, The Croft had a front dining room. Taking advantage of views to the rear, like many others on the road, at the back it had a verandah and also a very large basement entered from the garden with which it was level. This house is made of brick with a mock-timbered gable to the front.

The Croft soon had new residents, barrister Captain Charles Edgar Loseby and his wife Dulcibella who moved in around 1922. Loseby had been gassed at Ypres and awarded the Military Cross during World War One. A freemason, Loseby was a member of the Lodge of the Golden Fleece. Between 1918 and 1922, Loseby was National Democrat and Labour Party member of parliament for Bradford East, although he later became a Conservative. Loseby was among the first lecturers at what was to become the University of Leicester. He taught Commercial Law on a part-time basis between 1922 and 1927. All his lectures took place in the evening to allow students who worked to attend.[405]

Loseby had an interest in the supernatural and was chairman of the Leicester Psychical Society in the 1930s. The trauma of World War One had led many of those who grieved to explore spiritualism. During Word War Two, Loseby was the defence lawyer for Helen Duncan, the last woman to be tried under the 1735 Witchcraft Act. In November 1941 Duncan, a fake medium, had held a séance in Portsmouth in which she claimed the spirit of a sailor told her that the battleship HMS *Barham* had been sunk. Although this was true, it was supposedly kept secret and so, because of security concerns, at a later séance in 1944 Duncan was arrested. Loseby lost the case and Duncan spent nine months in Holloway prison.[406] Loseby's book *Witches, Mediums, Vagrants and the Law* was published by the Spiritualist National Union in 1946. Loseby then moved to Hong Kong, before retiring to Guernsey in the 1950s.

405 University of Leicester Archives, Biographical details of seven members of staff, ULA/PER6/2

406 *Leicester Mercury*, 31 October 2017

In terms of the architectural history of Western Park, in 1924 Loseby commissioned A.J. Wood to design a garage for The Croft, however, Loseby may not have driven himself as in 1939 a live-in chauffeur and man-servant, Charles Waine, was a resident of the house.

Unusually, an architect who wasn't local, Robert Streather and Son of Four Oaks Warwickshire, designed a house for W. Turner, with a white-rendered front gable and cat-slide roof, incorporating a dormer window, in 1915. Another house designed by Streather's was Gorsecliff. When it was on the market in 1950, it was described as a 'superior detached modern residence built by Streather's, the principal rooms facing south, with extensive uninterrupted views over Western Park'. It had 'an oak hall, two delightful reception room views, kitchen, three double bedrooms, three further bedrooms and store rooms in the roof, bathroom, separate WC, a built in garage, central heating and a delightful garden'.[407]

On the opposite side of Letchworth Road, towards the junction with the future Glenfield Road extension, H. Cockram and Son of Halford Street designed Pensarn, a house for James E. Pendleton. This brick-built house appears older in style than other properties on the road, having the appearance of a symmetrical Victorian residence. Pendleton was in the construction industry himself; his father was a stonemason and the family lived on Southgates in Leicester. Young James was working as a carpenter in his teens and by 1901 was described in the Census as a builder and decorator. When James and his wife Ada moved to Letchworth Road the house on Southgates was rented out as his parents were staying in Bournemouth, either retired or on holiday. James, now retired, and Ada were all still living on Letchworth Road in 1939.

Next door to the Pendletons, the plot remained unbuilt on until 1922 when a bungalow, Nestena, was erected for Lizzie Fowkes and her husband Herbert William Fowkes, a boot and shoe manufacturer in business with his father. William Fowkes & Son had business premises on Loseby Lane. Fowkes was another resident who had been successful in industry, despite humble beginnings. His father William had started out as a hosiery trimmer who became a self-employed general dealer while Herbert himself began his career as an errand boy. When Herbert Fowkes and his wife Lizzie, a former cigar maker, moved into Nestena they had several children, Rowland, Phyllis, Doris, Herbert and Nesta. Perhaps they called their home Nestena in honour of their youngest child.

As a bungalow, Nestena is distinctive among the properties on Letchworth Road. It was designed by T. Henry Bowles with a medieval themed interior with stained glass windows featuring men in armour, inglenooks, wrought-iron light fittings and oak panels. There was a garage incorporated into the original design and an orchard and apple store in the garden. Nestena was for sale by 1928 but failed to find a

407 *Leicester Daily Post*, 25 February 1950

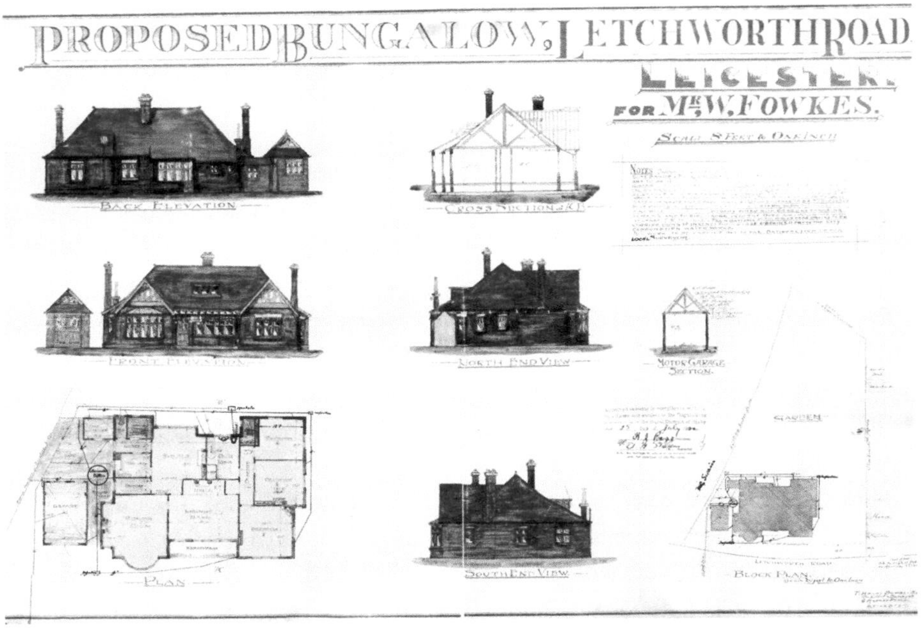

Plans for Nestena by T. Henry Bowles, c.1922 (Courtesy of Stephen Swabey)

buyer, even in an auction, until 1932 when Gerald T. and J.G. Edwards moved in. Gerald was an engineer with the water company and was still living at Nestena with his wife Rebecca in 1939.

Another property on the north side of Letchworth Road was Parkstone, a house covered with rough cast cement, built by W. Chambers of Western Road for Henry Cade. By 1939 insurance officer Thomas Poyser and his wife Elizabeth had replaced the Cades in the house.

Building could be and remains a potentially dangerous occupation. In July 1914, a bricklayer, E. Corby, fell from scaffolding surrounding a newly erected building on Letchworth Road on which he was working. Corby fell 16 feet and was badly hurt with broken ribs. To take him to the infirmary, the Fire Brigade ambulance van had to be requisitioned.[408]

Development continued in Western Park through and after World War One. In 1920 Frank Mayo received a government subsidy grant of £260 to erect a three-bedroomed bungalow supplied by Gascoigne Portable Buildings. The subsidy from the government was a response to solve the housing crisis by offering grants up to £260 as stimulus to 'anybody who builds a house in a satisfactory manner' by the end of 1921 under the Housing (Additional Powers) Act of 1919. The proposed bungalow sited on the corner of Letchworth Road and Sunnycroft Road was to be covered with Portland cement concrete and lined with asbestos. Thankfully because of health and

408 *Leicester Daily Post*, 17 July 1914

safety reasons, if the bungalow was ever constructed, it was not there for long as a pair of substantial semi-detached homes stands on the site.

Notable early residents of Letchworth Road, not already mentioned, were Samuel J. Pegg, of the local iron foundry, who lived at Hill Crest, originally owned by Mr J.S. Coltman who died in 1920 and the house sold. Hill Crest was described in the sales information as a 'charming detached house, in perfect condition, erected six years ago in the best manner, having electric light, plated hot and cold water taps, the walls to the scullery and pantry have white glazed dados, red tiled kitchen floors, and all fitments throughout are good. The principal rooms enjoy a most delightful view over the grounds towards Western Park and open country'.[409]

When the Harvey family left the White House, it became the home of Ronald Crawford Johnson, the grandson of the department store founder, Joseph Johnson. Ronald followed in the footsteps of his grandfather and father, George, as director of the business. In 1962 the department store on Market Street and Belvoir Street was taken over by Fenwicks.

Henry Hancock J.P., a draper like his apparently unrelated namesake Ebenezer, lived next door to the Peggs at Ruella. Henry was in business as a master draper with premises, The Beehive, in Cank Street and Silver Street. His father was a draper in Bristol from where Henry originated before learning the trade as an assistant in Oxford in the 1890s. Before moving to Ruella, Henry lived with his wife Emily, son Clifford and baby daughter Constance (Connie) on Kirby Road, a house that was also called Ruella, meaning 'path', perhaps a reference to his faith as Hancock was a Quaker, president of the Friends' Adult School and a Sunday school teacher at Westcotes Congregational Church.[410] Sorrow struck the family when Connie fell sick and died of Spanish Flu, aged eight, during the 1918–1919 pandemic. After losing their daughter, the Hancocks adopted another little girl, Margaret, known as Peggy.[411] As an adult Clifford worked as a soft furnishings salesman at Harris's Corner and Peggy had a job at the *Leicester Mercury*.[412]

Ruella's large dining room often welcomed distinguished guests to dinner, including the first Labour prime minister, Ramsey McDonald.[413] A less welcome guest appeared in 1928 when Henry Longford Bull, a Glenfield chiropodist, was discovered in the Hancocks' bathroom with his shoes in his pocket. Bull claimed to be unaware of where he was and said he had no memory of how he got there following a drinking session in the West End Inn on Duns Lane, later the Pump

409 *Leicester Daily Post*, 19 April 1920
410 Ned Newitt: *Who's Who of Radical Leicester*
411 Memories of Wendy Saville, shared by Su Bird
412 Memories of Wendy Saville, shared by Su Bird
413 Memories of Wendy Saville, shared by Su Bird

Rear of Ruella, before neighbouring property built. (Courtesy of Su Bird)

and Tap, despite police evidence that he appeared to be sober. To get into the house, Bull, said to be a chronic alcoholic, had climbed a post, mounted the verandah, and climbed through a bedroom window. Surprisingly he was found not guilty as he had no memory of the incident.[414]

Liberal-minded and progressive, Henry Hancock was a regular correspondent to the local press. During the war, in 1915, a letter of his expressing his sentiments for peace was published in the *Leicester Daily Post.*[415] In 1917 one of his letters argued for higher salaries to attract more skilled teachers and to inspire men and women from all ranks in society to enter the profession.[416] In another letter in 1920, he objected to the relaying of the golf course when the land would be better used for football and hockey as golf was for a small group of people only, unrepresentative of those sacrificed in the war.[417] He was also an advocate of building roads using reinforced concrete, a surface he said was extremely durable and economical.[418] Henry Hancock, a founder of the Workers' Educational Association in Leicester, and his neighbour Samuel Pegg, like a few other neighbours, were both founder donors to University College, Leicester.

In a letter to the *Leicester Daily Post* in support of this, Henry Hancock wrote that

414 *Illustrated Leicester Chronicle*, 20 October 1928
415 *Leicester Daily Post*, 2 August 1915
416 *Leicester Daily Post*, 27 July 1917
417 *Leicester Daily Post*, 19 October 1920
418 *Leicester Daily Post*, 5 August 190

To the Electors of Westcotes Ward.

LADIES AND GENTLEMEN,

Having been nominated to represent Westcotes Ward on the Leicester City Council, I beg to lay before you a brief statement of my qualifications and aims.

For the last 15 years I have represented West Humberstone Ward on the Board of Guardians. During the whole of this long period I have endeavoured to be a true Guardian of the Poor to all the sick, aged, and destitute people who have come to us for help. The children have been my especial care. During the year when I acted as Chairman of the Board, I was able, through the generosity of Leicester citizens, to fit up North Evington Infirmary with a complete Wireless Installation.

After many years' service on the Assessment Committee I have been appointed the first Chairman of the new City Committee appointed under the Rating and Valuation Act, 1925.

I am deeply interested in the Adult School Movement, the Workers' Educational Association, our University College, and Kyrle Society, and other organisations whose purpose is the enrichment of life. I am no narrow party man, and am glad to count amongst my friends good men and women of all parties.

Although I fully recognise the contribution which all sincere people may make to the common good, yet I believe that the Labour Party is right in insisting that the claims of Life and Personality should come before the rights of Property, Privilege, Capital and Industry. All these things are valuable only in proportion that they help to make happy and noble men and women.

Therefore, if elected to the Council, I shall whole-heartedly endeavour to increase the possibilities for obtaining Good Homes, Pure Food, Physical Health, and Equality of Educational Opportunity for all.

Yours very sincerely,

"RUELLA," LETCHWORTH ROAD.

HENRY HANCOCK.

With the Compliments of

HENRY HANCOCK,

The Labour Candidate.

Central Committee Room :

20 NARBOROUGH ROAD

Election leaflet for Henry Hancock, 1927.

the founding of university college was a fitting memorial to those lost in the war and could lead to it eventually becoming a full university, 'Money spent on education is the very finest investment we can make, and one which, in the ultimate, will bring the very best returns. It should be free and open to all mentally capable young citizens, whether from the state elementary or private schools and would commend itself to thousands of our manual workers, who are just beginning to realise that equality of educational opportunity must precede any thought of social equality.'[419]

Politically active, Henry Hancock was elected as a Guardian of the Poor in 1913, becoming chair of the Board of Guardians in 1924. During his time as a Guardian he arranged Summer Holiday Camps for Leicester's Poor Law dependent children, acted as Father Christmas at the Children's Home Christmas parties and introduced wireless for the sick in the North Evington Infirmary, now the General Hospital.[420] He stood as a Labour candidate for Westcotes Ward in the council elections of 1924 where he was beaten by William Francis (Frank) Gadsby, of the well-known picture framing business. The tables were turned in 1927 when Hancock was elected as councillor for Westcotes. After breaking the Labour whip by nominating the Conservative J.L. Harrison as chairman of the new Public Assistance Committee instead of Labour's Amos Sherriff, he did not stand for re-election in the 1930 council elections.[421] By 1931 Henry Hancock had retired but spent time travelling to the US in 1931 when he returned from New York on board the Samaria. He then visited Australia, returning from Brisbane on the Moldavia in 1933.

The two plots next to the Hancock's, on the north west side between Ruella and one owned by Mrs G. Clements were bought from Tudor Walters by Ann Eleonor Lucas, the wife of baker George Lucas of Northgate Street in 1914. Tudor Walters paid the money received to Helme, towards paying off his loan. The Lucases never did build a home there and the plot was sold again to Hannah Elizabeth Walsh, wife of Merit Alfred Walsh, an optician of Gallowtree Gate, for £340 in 1919. The Walsh's house, Fairview, was designed by Henry Bland, with a front kitchen and a rear terrace. This house had three bedrooms and a sewing room in the smallest upstairs room. The remaining plot between the Walshes and the Hancocks was bought by Henry Hancock who had an extension to Ruella built there, providing a small laundry room and tradesman's door. The rest of the plot was sold in 1923 for £386 7s 6d to Rose Blockley whose husband Frederick was a pharmacist, who owned the Fosse Pharmacy on Woodgate.[422] The Blockleys built their house, Kosineuk, but didn't enjoy it as a couple for long. Rose died in 1925 and the following year Frederick married again to Edith Rogers.

Among other notable early residents were Councillor Sydney Perry, a director of pattern makers G. Perry and Sons of Hall Lane, who moved into Denton on the corner of Meadway. The owners of Squires Bakery lived close to each other, Gordon Albert Upton Squires at Whyborough on Letchworth Road and Andrew Fred Squires on the Meadway. Doris V. Howard, Leicestershire ladies' table tennis champion also lived on Letchworth Road.

---

419 *Leicester Daily Post*, 21 November 1917
420 *Leicester Mail*, 23 November 1929
421 Ned Newitt: *Who's Who of Radical Leicester*
422 Abstract of title 1923, loaned by Su Bird

Letchworth Road, February 1940. (Courtesy of Su Bird)

House building continued at the other end of Letchworth Road, through the 1920s, leading towards its junction with Wynfield Road. Among some fine individual houses, three similar white, double-gable fronted, detached houses appeared on this stretch of road in around 1929. One of three similar white-rendered houses on that end of the road was named Tapanui, after a place in New Zealand. In 1939, music teacher Susana Turner lived in this house with her sister Mary who was in the gown and millinery business.

Westfield Road

Westfield Road contains houses of several types. The oldest part of the road, nearest to Hinckley Road was set out by May 1908, with plans by Ralph W. Bedingfield for six four-bedroom semi-detached houses on the odd-numbered side of the street. To start off with there were only houses on the odd number side and none above Letchworth Road. Over the road, Bedingfield designed and built four more houses, which were approved in September 1908, one of which was given the name Biskra. Further houses were built by Bedingfield and the Bradshaws on this lower section within a short space of time.

As both architect and applicant for planning permission, Bedingfield may have been acting as an agent here, perhaps for Bradshaw Brothers. These semi-detached houses had a kitchen with a range and in the separate scullery there was a copper, mangle space and sink. Bradshaws erected another eight semi-detached houses in 1911. The last house on this lower section of the odd-numbered side of Westfield

Road, near the corner of Letchworth Road, does not match the other side of the semi-detached property. Bradshaws applied for permission to modify the plans to make this a larger, two-bayed house. This house was to be occupied by Charles F. Bradshaw, the brothers' father. In March 1914, further permission was sought to build what was referred to as a motor shed to the rear of his property, entered from Letchworth Road.

A couple of doors down, a four-bedroomed house, given the name The Hut, previously occupied by Mrs Robinson, was described in 1929 as 'attractive, planned on labour saving principles, close to electric car route park and golf links'.[423] It had a modern fire grate with a green-tiled hearth and mahogany surround in the drawing room and another fireplace and electric heating plug in the dining room. In the kitchen was a Melrose single oven range with store cupboards and drawers at the sides. The scullery contained a glazed earthenware sink, with hot and cold taps plus a soft water pump, a copper and a recess for a gas stove. The bathroom had a heated towel rail. In the garden was a wireless mast. The description of this home illustrates the transition towards a modern lifestyle in the first decades of the 20th century.

In 1913, the Mellor Trustees submitted plans to extend Westfield Road and Westhill Road beyond the Leicester borough boundary into Blaby District. Beyond Letchworth Road, Westfield Road was developed with higher-specification, individually designed properties rather than semi-detached houses. The earliest identified on this stretch of the road was a school building designed by Ralph Bedingfield in 1912, now much altered and in use as a place of worship. The initial plan was not approved by Leicester's planning department due to issues about paving outside the school and the amount of space allocated to each scholar, even though the footway was actually in Blaby Rural District, outside the borough council's jurisdiction until 1935 when Leicester's boundaries were extended.

Plans were eventually approved in November 1912. Bedingfield's plans for the property show a smaller building than the present one. On the drawings it was indicated that there was space either end for future classrooms. The Froebel School, run by the Misses Andrews, was listed in contemporary directories as a Prep School. Friedrich Froebel was a German educationalist whose holistic ideas on learning through play and educational toys created the idea of the Kindergarten for young children. The school building was sold by auction in July 1956, when it had a large hall, a classroom, furnace basement and a playground, making it suitable for a new use.[424]

On the same part of Westfield Road, a four-bedroom detached house for Frederick H. Strawson, who was in the wholesale provisions business, was designed by Ralph Bedingfield and a similar-sized property for Mr Cubitt was designed by Ernest H.

423 The Hut, sales particulars, 1929, ROLLR DE4674/371
424 Sale particulars, Warner, Sheppard and Wade, 25 July 1956, ROLLR DE4674/1134

Design for his home on Westfield Road by Arthur J. Wood, 1914. (Records Office of Leicester, Leicestershire and Rutland)

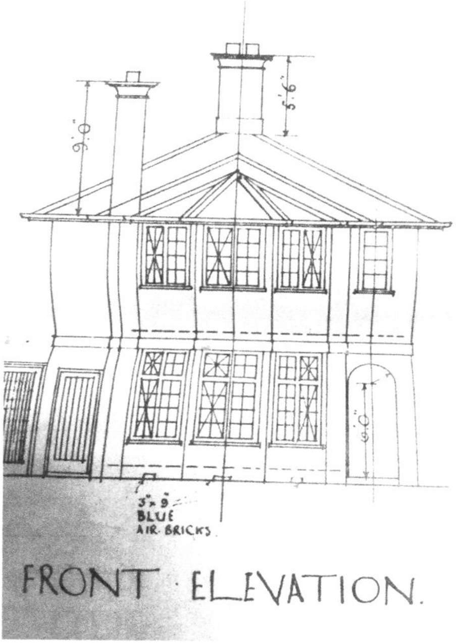

Smith in 1913. This brick-built property has a front gable with bay windows, a white stucco front studded with spaced, red brick quoin at the front corners. In 1914 a wonderfully individual house with an imposing bow front with the front door and that of a cycle store set back from the building line was designed by Arthur J. Wood as his own home on the Blaby side of the boundary. Other developers of detached properties were R. Salter and Sons (builders) for Charles W. Leake (1916), Broughton and Dudgeon (builders) for Mr Geary (1916), H. Gretton for W. Harrison which was brick built with a cross-hatch pattern in blue bricks above a wooden-beamed porch in a front gable (1916), Clement Stretton for H. Linney, and Fosbrooke and Bedingfield (the firm of Ralph's elder architect brother Waller) for H. Wells in 1924. This house had a large kitchen in a front room with a scullery to the rear. Westfield Road continues on the other side of Glenfield Road, where it connected with Hilders Road in the 1930s and since World War Two has led to Lindfield Road.

The earliest plans for the Western Park Estate show an additional unnamed road running from Westfield Road between Letchworth Road and Glenfield Road to what was to become Eastfield Road, originally planned to join Glenfield Road. This road was never built, the upper end of Eastfield Road became a cul-de-sac and part of the space allocated was occupied by the Dane Hills Tennis Club until 1955 when the facilities were taken over by Westfields Tennis Club. Founded as Westcotes Church Tennis Club in 1924, the club leased two grass courts from the Westcotes Estate on what became part of Western Park. In 1932 the club changed its name to Westfields Tennis Club when it was joined by 20 members from the Church of the Martyrs which saved it from financial difficulties. The club occupied several sites before finally settling down at the top of Eastfield Road.

Westhill Road

Work began on developing Westhill Road when plans for drainage were submitted to both Blaby Rural District Council and to Leicester Borough, approved on 22

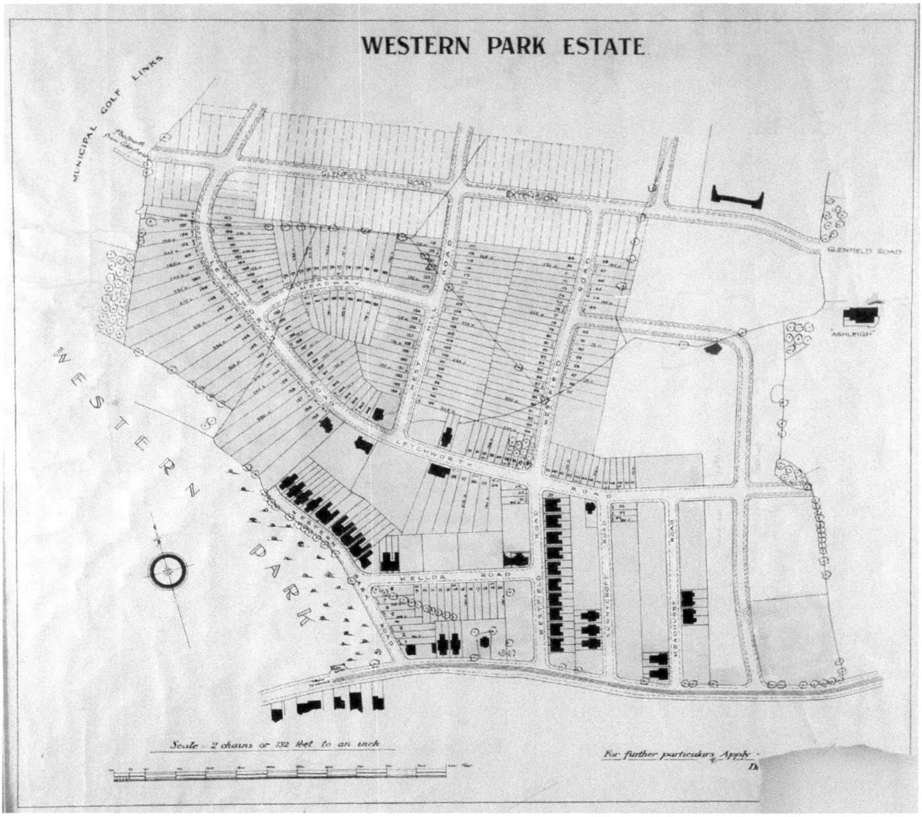

Plan of Western Park Estate.

December 1911. The first designs were again by Ralph W. Bedingfield, for a four-bedroom house, this time for print manager Charles S. Pye, who gave his home the name Bickleigh House. Building did not necessarily take place immediately. For instance plans for Mrs Marian's drains were approved in 1912 but the final plans for her house Barncroft, another Ralph Bedingfield design, were not submitted for consideration until 5 March 1920, possibly due to wartime labour shortages. Ralph Bedingfield himself was occupied with wartime service, being made a Captain in the Leicestershire Regiment Territorial Force Reserve, reinstated to a commission he had resigned in 1913. Mrs Abbott's daughters, were both business women. Evelyn was director of a hosiery manufacturing business and Edith a cardboard box maker and private secretary. Cartref, which means 'home' in Welsh, was also built around the same time, designed by Norman Read for T. R. Pryce and Company in 1921. Cartref may have been renamed as Sunnyholme when new owner, hosiery manufacturer, Alfred Leeson moved in.

By 1914 there were nine occupied houses on Westhill Road, numbers 2 to 16, with a gap at number 8 on the evens side. Two properties on the other side of the

I apologise for these small mistakes. I hope they don't spoil your enjoyment of the book.

Page 200 - "Mrs Marian's drains" should read "Marian Abbott's drains"

Page 236, photo description - "Swannington Road" should be "Danehurst Avenue".

Plans for Barncroft by Ralph W. Bedingfield, 1912. (Records Office of Leicester, Leicestershire and Rutland)

road were Highcliffe, occupied by engraver William Thomas Freeman and The Oaks, another Bedingfield design, the new home of Thomas Herbert Wathes of the successful Leicester electrical firm T.H. Wathes and Co. Ltd. Wathes had moved to Westhill Road from Stretton Road. Another of the early houses to be approved for building on Westhill Road was one for Samuel John Wathen Wigg, of 27 Kirby Road in July 1914. An architect himself, Wathen Wigg's home, unusually for the time and class of property, had a kitchen only with no scullery. It also had a front cycle store. 'Hawkestone' was the home of John Hayes of Harrison Hayes, hosiery manufacturer.

Westhill Road, in Blaby Rural District at the time of development, contains two properties on Leicester's local heritage asset register. Number 1, on the corner with Letchworth Road, was designed by Francis Morley of 10 St Stephens Road Leicester for Percy Allen. Percy was the son of Richard Allen of Bradda and the brother of Shirley Allen of The Beeches, both on Letchworth Road, so the family remained living close to each other. This five-bedroom house, Chelston, was designed over three floors in 1920. Chelston was also the name of Percy's previous home at 6 Fosse Road South. Percy had taken over as managing director of R.C. Allen Limited, his father's bottling business on Oxford Street. A glass-walled, flat-roofed extension was added to this detached house by its 21st-century occupants, the Bebbington family, and was the winner of Procon Leicestershire's Small Residential Scheme of the Year Award 2017.[425] Designed by Carl Bebbington, creative director of Newenglish Design, the extension went on to win the RIBA East Midlands Award 2017 which was presented to the Bebbingtons as the architectural designers, and architects SGP who provided technical support.[426]

The other Westhill Road house on the local heritage asset register is Green Gables whose architect was A.S. Phipps of 39 London Road, commissioned by

425 ProCon Leicestershire website
426 newenglish.co.uk website www.newenglish.co.uk

Westhill Road, 2020. (Courtesy of Carl and Wendy Bebbington)

Leslie William Matthews. This superb example of an Art Deco house has white walls made even more striking by a green, glazed-tiled roof. It was built using brick, stucco and tiles, with a garage and four bedrooms. It incorporates the letter 'M' in the front door, the initial of its original owner, Leslie Matthews, who was the son of William Merryfield Matthews of Letchworth Road. These original external features have survived into the 21st century and the house is one of the two or three finest Art Deco houses in Leicester. Leslie Matthews, director of a hosiery business, married Dorothy Cubitt in 1934, who had lived nearby with her parents on Westfield Road.

Westhill Road includes a pair of semi-detached villas by builder Edgar Stevens and Son in 1911: Chesterfield occupied by telegraphist John Wigley, and boot and shoe designer Edward Dixon's home, The Mount. Other properties are a three-bedroom house by architect R. Salter for William R. Lathkill Hooper in 1915 and another for leather agent Alfred E. Cowling. Sekondi was designed by Norman Read for solicitor Edwin Dixon in 1912. Mr Castle's house was the work of S. Henry Langley in 1916. Slightly later than the others, showing the emerging 1930s double-bay windowed style, was one by S.M. Stanage of 69 Danvers Road for S.C. Wright in 1931.

Meadway

Development began on Meadway slightly later than the other roads while it was in

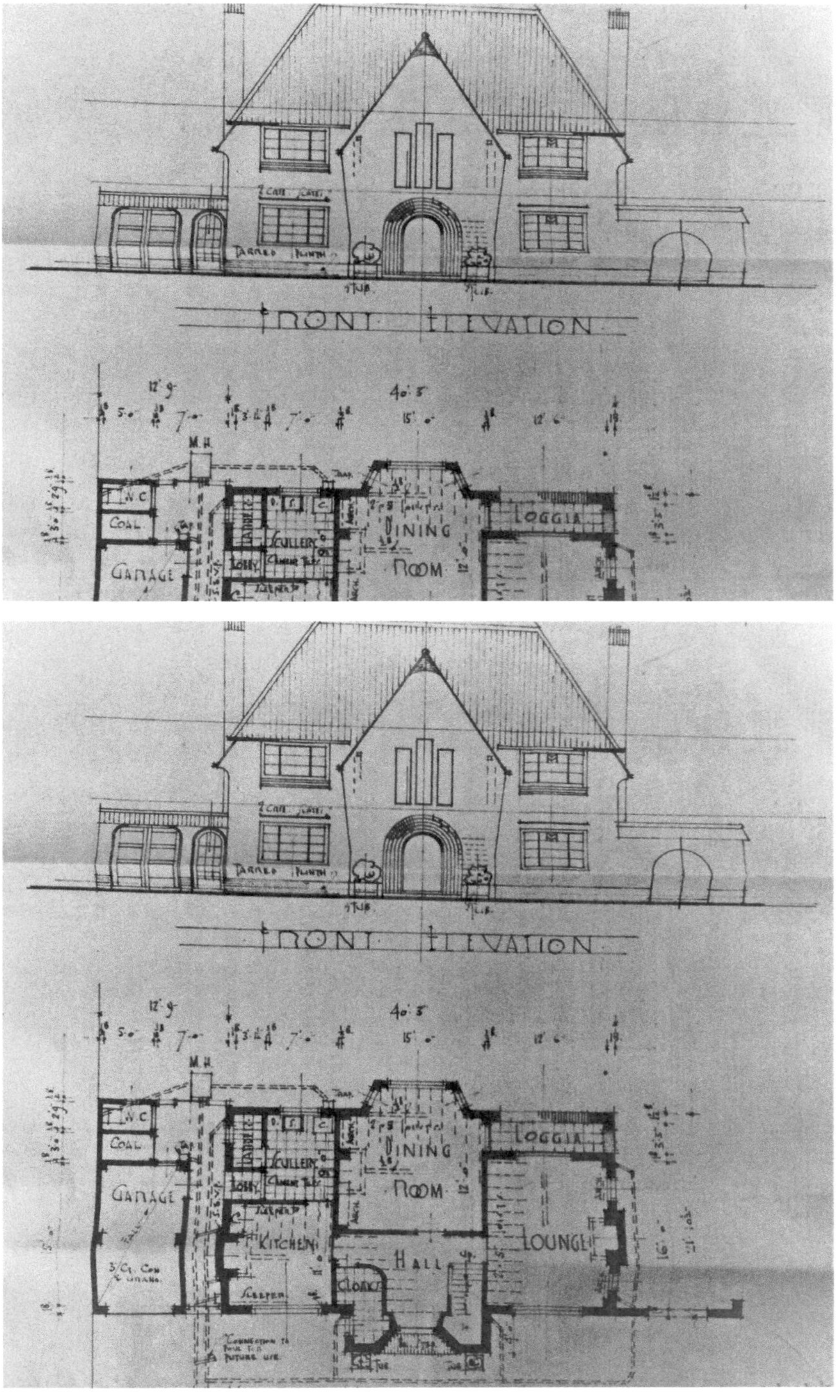

Plans for Green Gables, Westhill Road by J. S. Phipps. (Records Office of Leicester, Leicestershire and Rutland)

Blaby District. Drainage plans for Meadway were submitted between 1913 and 1919. The first house to be occupied was Sancta Via which is shown by *Wright's Directory of 1914* as the home of Alfred Kirk, warehouseman. Again this road contains mostly detached, bespoke four-bedroom homes, for example the house designed and built by William Humphris of 2 Luther Street for Agnes Waters Leavins in 1914. The four-bedroomed house with separate kitchen and scullery, designed by Ernest H. Smith of 7 Welford Place for Cecily Pryce in 1914, was said to have honeycomb sleeper walls, to prevent damp floor boards.

Another property was by R. Salter and Son, builders of Gwendolen Road for Alice L. Dunmur, the wife of accountant Theodore Dunmur of West Street. This 1915 property was a half-rendered house, one of the few in the area to have just a kitchen and no scullery, reflecting the change in domestic arrangements. Another was by Frank H. Jones, architect of 5 Greyfriars for Messrs S. Broughton and Sons in 1915. A house with the unusual name of Tilques sharing its name with a place near St Omer in northern France, perhaps named after some wartime memory or experience, was by H. Bland for J.W. Faulk, approved in 1919. Another popular choice of architect for homes on Meadway was Norman Read. He designed three houses there in 1923: Westholme for C. Edwards, Bretten Court for W. Smith and another for T.B. Woodward. On the other side of the road, Brecon or Bracken Lodge was a white pebble-dash house with a distinctive rustic appearance and a central gable.

A particularly distinguished house, on the corner of Meadway and Westhill Road was designed for George Gibson by William Keay of Pick, Everard and Keay in 1923 and built by Herberts. Given the unusual name of Croigland, perhaps a pun of his Lincolnshire birthplace of Crowland, and built of dark brick, the house is a T-shape.

Bracken Lodge, Meadway, 2021.

Croigland, Meadway, design by William Keay of Pick, Everard and Keay, 1923. (Records Office of Leicester, Leicestershire and Rutland)

Its kitchen contained a modern Triplex combination grate with a stove and oven which could heat water as well as provide warmth. Croigland had a separate scullery. The bay window of the kitchen faced Westhill Road and that of the dining room, next to the kitchen, faced Meadway. The drawing room was at the opposite end of the house, overlooking the garden. The house had both electricity and gas. The garage, with water installed, was at the bottom of the garden, accessed from Meadway.

Extending the estate

The suburban development of Western Park spread inwards towards Leicester, with more streets of houses appearing between Westfield Road and Gimson Road. Sunnycroft Road was under construction by 1911, and Meadhurst Road by 1913, the closest the development came to the town. The beginnings of Eastfield Road were laid out at the same time as Hinckley Road School, with houses built by the mid-1920s.

Building sites were often a source of adventure for young people. During the construction of a house on Sunnycroft Road in 1912, five boys aged 14 and 15, from New Parks Street and Leomington Street in the West End, broke into a builder's hut and took a pick and a shovel belonging to a plasterer's labourer, James Wilson, who was working on the house. The lads used the tools to dig themselves a cave in one of the nearby sand holes, where they were caught by a policeman, taken to court and fined.[427]

Plans for Glenfield Road, together with extensions to Westfield Road, Letchworth Road and Westhill Road, were submitted by Sir John Tudor Walters as landowner,

427 *Leicester Daily Post*, 25 November 1912

Houses on Meadhurst Road probably by Ralph W. Bedingfield, Western Park Estate sales brochure c.1909. (Records Office of Leicester, Leicestershire and Rutland)

on behalf of the Housing and Town Planning Trust Limited of London in February 1929. This application included specification for roads and drainage. Housing began to be built on this new stretch of Glenfield Road from 1930 by developers such as S.C. Wright, Clement Stretton and A.J. Wood, transforming that section to

Design for St Mary's Glenfield Road, by Ralph W. Bedingfield, 1930. (Records Office of Leicester, Leicestershire and Rutland)

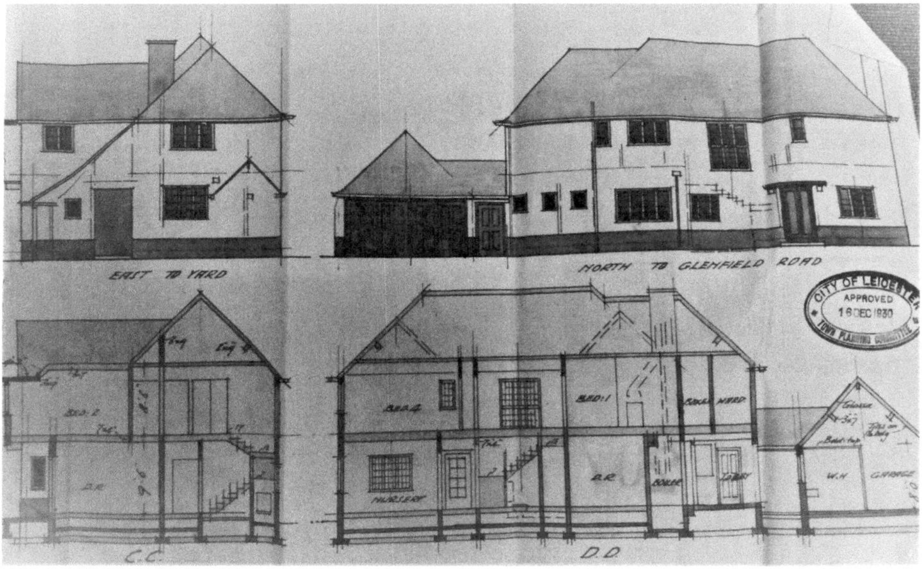

a road from a footpath. Bradshaw Brothers built pairs of semi-detached houses there between 1931 and 1932, as did Clement Stretton for Mrs E. Winterton, Walter Brand and Drew Edwards for Messrs J. Bentley.

More distinguished detached properties appeared on Glenfield Road too, most notably the two striking white houses designed by Ralph Bedingfield. The last house before the park was St Mary's designed by him in 1930 for W. Sidney Russell, a company director. This large pebble-dash rendered house was designed with five-bedrooms. Next to it, on the corner of Letchworth Road Bedingfield built another white pebble-dashed house in September 1933, marking an association with the design of the Western Park Estate, lasting almost 30 years.

The business relationship between the Mellors and Sir John Tudor Walters continued through the 1920s but a new builder had become involved in the development. Tudor Walters purchased another parcel of land from the Mellors in October 1923. In January 1924, a plot from this land, on the corner of Letchworth Road and the upper cul-de-sac end of Eastfield Road, was conveyed to Smith Housing Company Limited, a business formed in January 1921 to build houses, and deal in stone, sand, lime, bricks, timber, hardware and other building materials. It was a local company, a partnership of William Tompkins of Fosse Road South, and William Archibald Tompkins of Westleigh Road, with its registered office on Harrow Road, all in the West End of Leicester. Perhaps for the Tompkinses, the company was a financial investment as they were boot and shoe manufacturers, owners of W. Tompkins and Son Ltd. The third partner, from whom the company took its name, builder Samuel Walter Smith, lived initially on the other side of the city in Sawley Street.[428]

The Smith Housing Company bought a parcel of land from the Gimson trustees on which were laid out Wynfield, Clarefield and the west side of Gimson Road. Labelled the Dane Hills Estate, this land was divided into plots for house building.[429] This advertisement appeared in the local newspapers in March 1926, 'Semi-detached modern villas for sale, room for garage, large gardens, best position in the city, Hinckley and Gimson Roads and adjoining estate, ¾ can be obtained on a mortgage. Estimates given for building houses on estate. Plots for sale.' The address for enquiries was 421 Hinckley Road, on the corner of Westfield Road.[430]

'You must see Leicester's ALL ELECTRIC HOUSE on Clarefield Road,' proclaimed a large advertisement in the *Illustrated Leicester Chronicle* in January 1927. The house was to be officially opened by Mrs Swain, wife of a councillor, at 3pm on 17 January and was open daily, 2pm to 9pm between 17 and 29 January.[431]

---

428 *Leicester Daily Post*, 21 January 1921
429 Dane Hills Estate plan, ROLLR 22D68/136
430 *Leicester Mercury*, 24 March 1926
431 *Leicester Chronicle*, 15 January 1927

The Smith Housing Company operated as both speculative developers building houses to sell, and as builders commissioned to build individually designed properties. One of the plots bought from Tudor Walters in January 1924 was sold to George Russell in May 1925.[432] George Russell was the son of Samuel Russell of iron founders S. Russell and Sons. He had an attractive detached house with weatherboard cladding built on the plot, which he named Sandilands, perhaps because of the sandstone quarries nearby or in memory of seaside visits to the Lincolnshire coast, where there is an area of the same name near Sutton on Sea. George Russell moved to Eastfield Road, from Winchester Avenue, with his wife Margaret and her mother Helen Oakley but his mother in law died in 1931 at the age of 72. The couple also had live-in domestic help, the bells to call the servant still remain in the house. Louise Musson was in domestic service with the Russells in 1939. Other members of the Russell iron foundry family had also moved to Western Park. Parents Samuel and Fannie had moved from Winthorpe on Westcotes Drive to Newstead on Meadhurst Road and brother Percy was also on Meadhurst Road, five doors down from his mother and father. Another brother, Samuel Hibbert Russell lived on the Hinckley Road end of Westfield Road. As already mentioned, another brother, William Sidney lived at St Mary's on Glenfield Road. The iron foundry had moved to Bonchurch Street by the mid-1930s, so it was easy walking distance from their homes.

On the corner of Eastfield Road and Hinckley Road was the Meteor Garage run by Jowett Cars, where second-hand motors, such as Austin 7s, were sold. There was also a driving school there by 1939, Crumpton's School of Motoring, where tuition was offered in dual controlled Morris cars.[433] The site is still used as a garage for motor repairs and a petrol filling station.

The exact position of the border between the Mellor-owned land and that of the Gimsons appears to have been between Eastfield and Wynfield Roads. William Gimson and Sons, who owned the land around Ashleigh where Albert Starkey Gimson lived, were advertising land for sale in 1920. This land between Eastfield Road and Gimson Road was developed as the Dane Hills Estate with land fronting Hinckley Road, Gimson Road, Clarefield Road (perhaps named after Smith's wife, Clara) and Wynfield Road offered for sale in lots for individual development by 1930.[434] This area was purchased as a whole by the Smith Housing Company.

The Smith Housing Company was one of the developers involved in building this part of the Western Park Estate. Between March and April 1931, the company was advertising for sale in the *Leicester Evening Mail,* modern semi-detached villas, near completion, in the select residential development of Western Park Estate. Prices and

432 Register of title, loaned by Chris Freeman
433 *Leicester Mercury*, 29 August 1939
434 ROLLR, 22D68/136

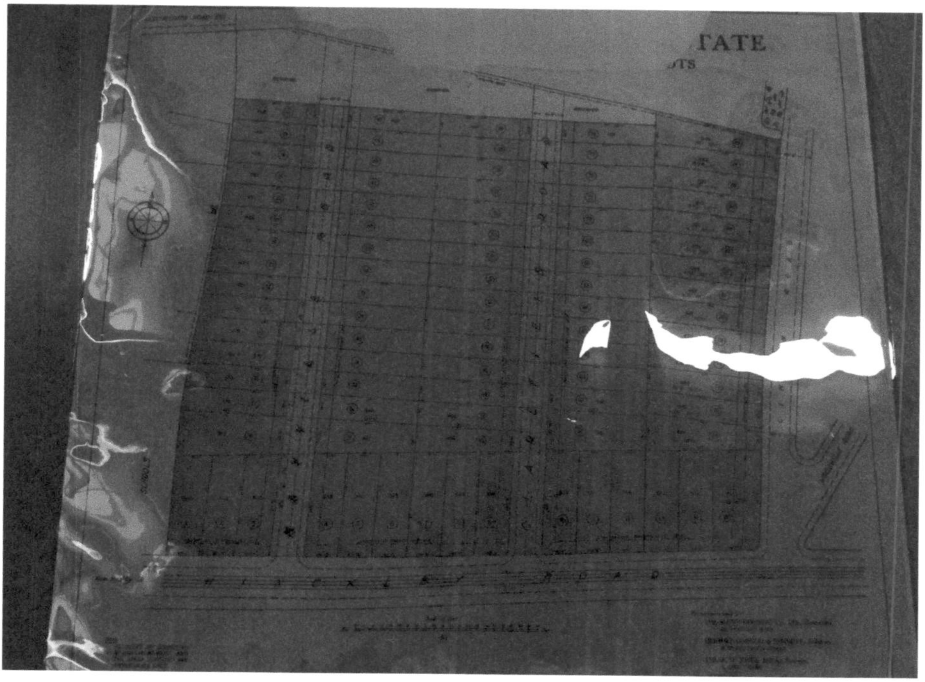

Plan of plots on Wynfield, Clarefield and Gimson Road for Smith Housing Company, 1920s, original damaged. (Records Office of Leicester, Leicestershire and Rutland)

particulars were available from 28 Gimson Road.[435] Samuel and Clara Smith had left Sawley Street and made this house their home. The couple had travelled to Canada where they married and where their first son, George, was born, followed soon by Eric. They lived on Gimson Road for the rest of their lives, until Clara died in 1950 and Samuel in 1962. During World War Two, Samuel served as in the ARP specialising in Demolition.[436] Like many other men at the time, Samuel Smith was a freemason in the Temple Lodge.

It didn't take long for these homes in Western Park to sell. By October 1931, there was only one left: a six-roomed modern villa, in a pleasant position, with room for a garage, priced at £800.[437] Smith Housing Company appear to have been operating as developers and builders as well as dealers in land.

The former garden and stable yard of William Gimson's Ashleigh House, still housing horses, occupied the space that now contains Denis Close and the more modern part of Nevanthon Road until around 1972. Perhaps the original plan had been for Letchworth Road to be continued through to Woodville Road or the top of Clarefield Road, as there are no house numbers lower than 50. That end of Letchworth

435 *Leicester Evening Mail*, 16 March–8 April 1931
436 1939 Register
437 *Leicester Mercury*, 2 October 1931

Road was actually a cul-de-sac, ending with a gate near the top of Wynfield Road. It remained unadopted until this area was built on in around 1970. Even though the road was adopted by Leicester City Council when the cul-de-sac was opened up to join with Nevanthon Road, the pavement remained the responsibility of householders, some of whom took out insurance policies to cover themselves in case someone had an accident outside their house. The Letchworth Road pavement was finally adopted by the Council in September 2007, as was that of the cul-de-sac Danehurst Avenue, off Glenfield Road, completed by Jelley's in 1939.

Despite the suburban development of the early 20th century, Western Park retained its rural ambience for several years. St Catherine's Convent's 'Home For Incurables', built in the early 20th century, on the opposite side of Glenfield Road, later Highpoint Conference Centre and now a care home, had additions designed by Waller Bedingfield and Grundy, and Fosbrooke and Grundy. These were new farm buildings and also included a cowshed and pig sty by architect S.H. Langley illustrating that much of the work of an architect is far from being grand designs. Beyond it, across the Glenfield footpath from the new Western Park Estate, until 1936, was Bird's Nest Farm.

Nearer to the town, opposite Ashleigh, was an imposing, red-brick, Queen Anne Revival-style semi-detached property built for William Gimson in 1884. This building contained two houses: Melbourne House, on the corner of Sandhurst Road, had 12 bedrooms over four floors, used as a boarding house, and Craigside with 11 bedrooms, occupied by the Misses Baker, grand daughters of William and nieces of Albert Starkey Gimson. During World War Two these houses were requisitioned by the War Office.[438] The building survives today as flats, thanks to a campaign to prevent its demolition. The Victorian building is now part of a larger development and is linked to a modern block of flats with laundry facilities and car parking, known as Michael Lewis House. After Albert Starkey Gimson of Ashleigh died, the remaining 13 acres of what was described as the Dane Hills Estate, associated with the Gimson family for over 80 years, was sold by auction in 1945. Ashleigh itself contained nine bedrooms, a vinery and conservatories. Nearby were two cottages, farm buildings, a pigsty, cowshed, garage, greenhouse and stables. There were three hard tennis courts off Sandhurst Road, and a market garden in the former gardens of Ashleigh. A plot at the top of Clarefield Road and Wynfield Road with a pond in the middle was offered for sale in a separate lot. Development began here on Nevanthon Road and there were plans for a circular road around the plot but there was no further building until Denis Close was built nearly 30 years later.

At the top of Glenfield Road, opposite the park, there remained, for the time being, the Municipal Golf Course with its pavilion erected in 1921. On the southern

438 Residential development known as Ashleigh, sales brochure, 1945, ROLLR DE4674/830

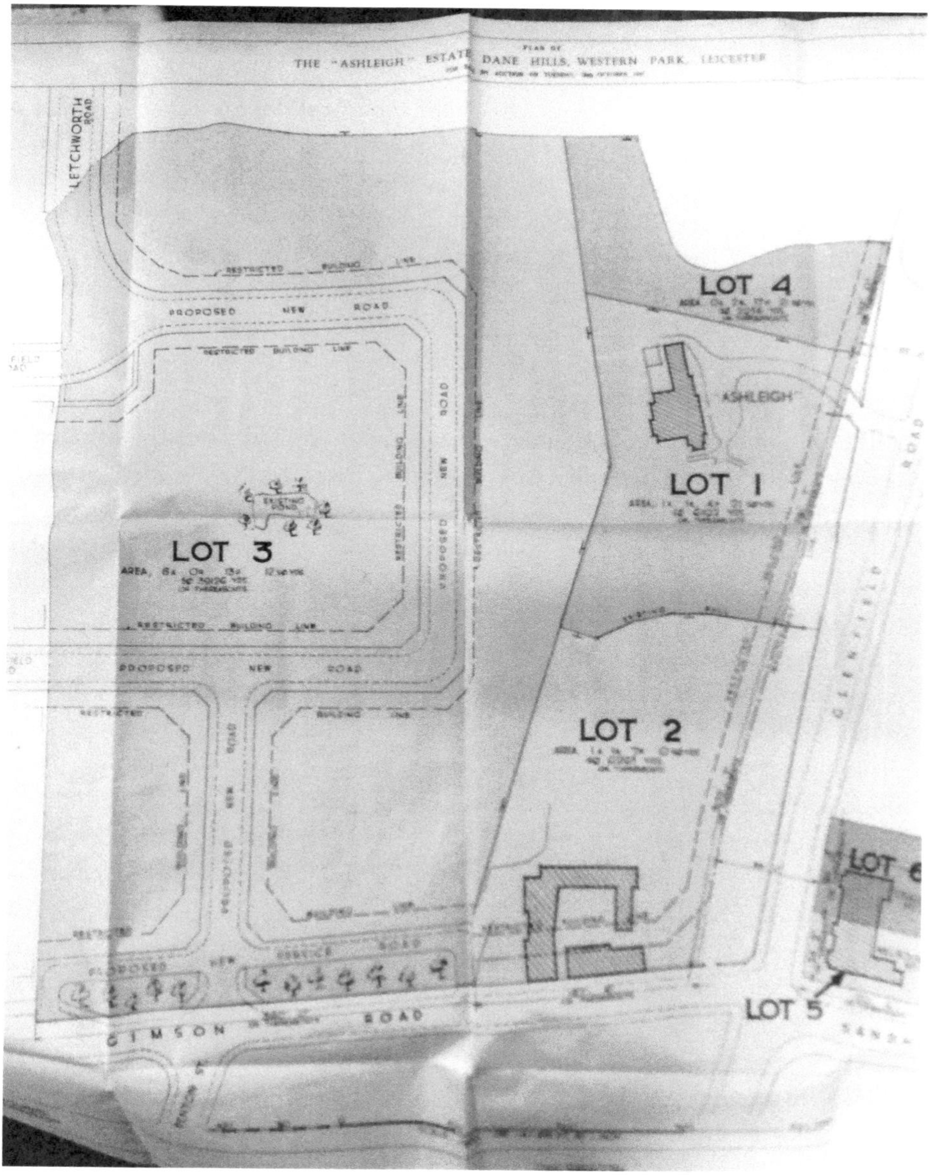

Gimson land and Ashleigh, for sale in six lots, 1945.

side of the estate, the land opposite on the other side of Hinckley Road survived as countryside with fields and allotment gardens until the mid-1930s. Despite this seeming remoteness, there was a frequent and regular tram service from the centre of Leicester.

An observation of the kind of people who had houses built in the Western Park Estate development shows that most of them were successful in business, industry and trade. In the previous century, men (they almost always were men) who were successful in the world of commerce had sought country houses to enhance their status and give the appearance of living the lives of country gentlemen farmers in the way that the landed elite of previous generations had done through inheritance. Now these newly wealthy or at least moderately financially successful people were choosing to live in bespoke properties, emphasising their individuality and embracing a progressive, modern way of life. They also bought into the suburban lifestyle and garden city ethos, moving to an area close to the urban centre of Leicester where their businesses were situated and easily accessible by tram, on foot or even motor car but modelled in a way that imitated a rural idyll, including large private gardens for leisure.

The new residents also established strong community links, as demonstrated by their involvement with St Anne's Church which offered a focus for social activities. Many supported charitable and educational institutions that benefited the citizens of Leicester as a whole. An interesting feature apparent in several of the property deeds for houses in Western Park was the high number of purchases made by married women. Perhaps this is because this newly prosperous middle class, dependent as they were on trade and industry, were insecure in their success and felt the need to separate their investment in a home from their business affairs by keeping their domestic arrangements in the names of their wives in case of future financial problems.

As industry in Leicester prospered in the late 19th and early 20th centuries, thanks to the application of powered machinery in the hosiery, boot and shoe and light engineering or in the service sector that catered to the increasingly better-off section of the community, there were many more included in this new middle class. Even if they had aspired to become country gentlemen, there were just not enough appropriate properties to go round. The country estates, including that on which Western Park was built, were being sold off and packaged into parcels of land for housing development to meet the needs of the growing population.

St Anne's Church

It wasn't long before the emerging Western Park community was big enough to need its own place of worship. In January 1914 the Church Extension Board submitted plans by J. Stockdale Harrison, proposing to re-erect the dismantled corrugated church of St Thomas's on East Park Road on Letchworth Road by the corner with Westfield Road. This prosaic building, affectionately known later as 'Tin Annie', was in use for Anglican worship before the permanent, brick-built church of St Anne's was erected by its side.

The tin church opened its doors to worshippers in 1914, as St Anne's District within the parish of St Mary de Castro, under the pastoral and spiritual care of priest-

Inside Tin Annie when in use for worship. (Courtesy of St Anne's Church)

in-charge Canon Tolhurst. Although it was only a tin building, many weddings took place there, such as that of Winifred Harvey, whose family home was the White House on Letchworth Road. She became Mrs Gerald Nethercot on New Year's Day 1931. Winifred was said to have presented 'a charming figure in a pearl grey satin gown and attractive little grey velvet cap, with shoes to match'.[439] Another couple who were wed in the tin church was Evelyn Dumelow and George Siser in April 1932.[440]

Building a permanent church for the Western Park community remained an ambition for the first 20 years of the St Anne's congregation, which set to work to raise the funds needed to pay for one. Various initiatives for the benefit of the St Anne's Permanent Church Building Fund entertained, strengthened social bonds and networks, and, importantly, contributed towards the costs of a new church. One of these events was a concert organised by Edith Marlow, featuring the rich soprano voice of Phyllis M. Wright, a popular performer with the women of the Swain Street Institution, otherwise known as the workhouse.[441] Phyllis herself was another bride who married in the tin church when she wed Eric Ordidge in April 1933.[442] Another way of bringing in cash for the fund was an appeal by jeweller George Tarratt of 19 Market Street in Leicester. Tarratt advertised in the local press that readers could help

439 *Leicester Chronicle*, 3 January 1931
440 *Leicester Chronicle*, 16 April 1932
441 *Leicester Chronicle*, 10 January 1931
442 *Leicester Chronicle*, 16 April 1933

build the new church by sending him their 'odd gold and old trinkets' as gifts.[443] In February 1931 the St Anne's Dramatic Society put on a production of the play *The Bishop's Candlesticks,* with money from ticket sales donated to the church building fund.

A novel way of raising funds for the church was a 'jolly golf competition'. Two cups, men's and ladies', were donated as prizes by Dulcibell Loseby and William Salt. Games of golf could be played on any course as long as all scores were verified.[444] Revd Harland was a competitor in the contest. Maurice H. Harland had replaced Canon Tolhurst as vicar in 1927. Revd Harland remained at St Anne's until 1933 when he moved to Leeds.[445] The final of the St Anne's Church Open Golf Tournament was played the following October on Western Park Golf Course on Glenfield Road. Miss Yeo of Western Park was the victor against Miss Burton of Longcliffe Golf Club in the ladies' final. In the men's competition it was an all Western Park final when Mr Timson defeated mechanical engineer R. Hallam of Grace Dieu on Letchworth Road. Charles E. Loseby of Letchworth Road, the husband of one of the prize donors, presented the winners with their trophies.[446]

A Christmas Fair held at the Edward Wood Hall on London Road, now the University of Leicester's Fraser Noble Hall, gave a boost to the funds in November 1931. The Fair was held over three days with the Duchess of Rutland performing the opening ceremony on the first day, and Lord Castle Stewart MP doing the honours on the third and final day. This was no ordinary church fete but featured classical and variety concerts, miniature golf and games. A highlight was an auction. The most sought-after lots were a picture and other gifts donated by Queen Mary. As an additional attraction, people were invited to view the Queen's donations before the sale.[447]

The whole community got involved in the fund raising in some way but special mention was made in the local press of keen church worker Mr F.W. May of Westfield Road, who had supported St Anne's since it opened in 1914. In his role as people's warden of the church, he was a pioneer of social events for the community, such as dances, bridge and whist drives.[448] In November 1931, Mr May organised a dance at the Palais in town. Another indefatigable worker for the church was Joseph Ward, the vicar's warden, who was a rate office official in his day job. He and his wife held fund raising whist drives in their home, Trentham, on Letchworth Road.[449] Mrs Ward was involved with the Women's Working Party, a group which also raised large sums for the church.[450]

443 *Leicester Chronicle*, 17 January 1931
444 *Leicester Chronicle*, 6 May 1931
445 *Leicester Chronicle*, 5 August 1933
446 *Leicester Mercury*, 20 October 1931
447 *Leicester Mercury*, 24 November 1931
448 *Leicester Chronicle*, 21 October 1933
449 *Leicester Chronicle*, 30 January 1932
450 *Leicester Chronicle*, 19 August 1933

St Anne's Church, with Tin Annie in the left background. (Image Leicestershire)

By late 1932, an architect for the new church building had been selected, Arthur F. Bryan ARIBA was a man with plenty of experience of working on local ecclesiastical buildings. Some of his previous projects were the reconstruction of St George's church tower, rebuilt following a great fire in that part of Leicester in 1911, the restoration of St John the Divine, and repairs to St Mary de Castro.[451] During the church's construction, Bryan lived close by at 47 Westfield Road. A house opposite St Anne's on the corner of Letchworth Road, was also the work of Arthur F. Bryan. In December 1932, the Bishop and other clergy took part in a ceremony to break the ground on the corner next to the tin church, ready to begin building.[452] Just a few months later, on 1 April, the foundation stone was laid in a consecration ceremony performed by Revd W. Foxley Norris, the Dean of Westminster.[453] By the following summer, the church was practically completed.[454] The first portion of the church was consecrated on 9 July 1934, by the Right Reverend Cyril Bowman Bardsley, Bishop of Leicester. By this time Revd Harland had left for Leeds and been replaced by a new vicar, Revd L.E. Dashwood, previously curate of St Peter's.[455]

451 *Leicester Chronicle*, 10 December 1932
452 *Leicester Chronicle*, 17 December 19323
453 *Leicester Chronicle*, 8 April 1933
454 *Leicester Chronicle*, 2 June 1934
455 *Leicester Chronicle*, 23 September 1933

After a two year engagement, among the first couples to marry in the new church building in April 1936 was Dennis Ewart Sharp of Millborough on Meadhurst Road and Ida Burridge, daughter of Ida and Louis H. Burridge (1882–1945), hosiery manufacturer and chairman of Leicester City Football Club, of Ida Dene on Letchworth Road.[456] The groom, Dennis Sharp, was a director of D.E. Sharp and Company, hosiery manufacturers. Also a musician, Dennis was the organist at St Anne's.[457] Ida's brother Jack (John) Burridge was honorary secretary and a player member of St Anne's Football Club.[458] Following his father's footsteps, John Burridge (born 1917) became managing director to L.H. Burridge and Company Limited, hosiery manufacturers of Wellington Street, and a director of Leicester City FC.

The permanent church of St Anne's was built of buff-coloured, brindle brick with some stone dressings and a slate roof. Its style is described by Historic England as Free Late Gothic. The interior is spacious and imposing although the nave remains unfinished on the west side although this is hardly noticeable. Inside, the main features are of stone with plastered walls with boarded keel roofs to the nave and the chancel which has richly carved fittings. The Lady Chapel, added in 1956, has a stained glass east window by L.C. Evetts.[459] The organ was built by Liverpool firm Rushworth and Dreaper. A new stained glass window commemorating servicemen of World War Two, designed by Claire Williamson, was installed in 2011. According to Historic England, this well-designed church has fine brickwork with unusual layering and rich interior fittings. The unfinished west end does not detract from the spacious and imposing interior. It is listed by Historic England at Grade II.

With a new church for religious worship and events, the tin hut was free for more secular activities and celebrations, such as the coming-of-age-party for Lorna Shaw of Fran Lyd on Letchworth Road.[460] Fundraising continued even after the new church was completed in 1934, with events that provided entertainment and helped strengthen community ties. Leicester Fencing Club took part in a match against Derby Garrison Sherwood Foresters in the Parish Room, the relegated but still important status of Tin Annie. This event introduced the sport to many locals with a demonstration of how 'beautiful to the eye and beneficial to the health and figure exercises with foil, sabre and epée can be'.[461] The first time the parish hall was used to stage a production by the Dramatic Society was when the group performed three one-act plays in December 1936: *The Boy Comes Home* by A.A. Milne, *The Christening* by Gertrude Jennings and *The Green Monkey* by Victor Bridges.

456 *Leicester Chronicle*, 25 April 1936,
457 *Leicester Chronicle*, 28 April 1934
458 *Leicester Chronicle*, 28 March 1936
459 Church of St Anne, https://historicengland.org.uk/listing/the-list/list-entry/1389695, accessed 14 August 2020
460 *Leicester Chronicle*, 24 October 1936
461 *Leicester Chronicle*, 20 October 1934

In the late 1950s the front section of the Hall was replaced by a new two-storey extension, designed by Roy Bordoli, church architect. The rear end of the Hall had deteriorated and in 1986 was replaced by a brick extension designed by local resident and architect Philip Dodd of Welch, Dodd and Wright.

Tin Annie remained as the central section of the building and was still in use by the community when during St Anne's centenary in 1914, church members and vicar Revd Stephen Burnham decided to celebrate with a year of fundraising to build a completely new Hall. There was already £15,000 in the fund, thanks to a generous bequest from the estate of Margaret Russell, made 30 years before. Mrs Russell, of Sandilands on Eastfield Road, who died in December 1987, was the widow of George Russell of the iron foundry. Her legacy and profits from the use of the Hall meant that the fund opened with about £45,000.

As in the fundraising efforts in the previous century, the community shared its enthusiastic support for the Spring and Autumn Fairs, quiz evenings, cake sales, pop-up restaurant and a Street Party. Combined with other events, coupled with £89,000 in donations, £105,000 was raised during the year. Cinema evenings, Buy a Brick, Western Park Open Gardens, a talent show and a beer festival added to the fundraising momentum during 2015. Further contributions came from local businesses and organisations, such as the Co-op, Biffa, the Corah Foundation, Leicestershire and Rutland Freemasons and the ward councillors' community budget, which brought the total up to £280,000. The remaining amount needed for the new £400,000 Hall came in the form of a grant from the Diocese's Capital Fund in 2016. Plans were drawn up by architects LE1 and local firm Henderson's was engaged to carry out the construction. Work was completed by Christmas 2016.[462] The retained front section was improved and the official reopening, performed by Archdeacon Tim Stratford, attended by ward councillors and around 200 members of the church community took place on 6 May 2017.

An asset to the locality, in February 2018 the Hall opened its doors to displaced or distressed members of the community affected by the traumatic explosion that destroyed some of the shops on the shopping parade on Hinckley Road that tragically killed five people. The noise and shock waves of this were felt across the community and beyond. Those who had lost their home or were not allowed access because it was unsafe, or due to the ongoing investigation, were supported by gifts of toiletries and clothes or someone to talk to at the Emergency Centre that was set up in cooperation with the Council's resilience team. During the Covid-19 pandemic of 2020 and 2021, despite being closed due to the prohibition of community activities, the Hall provided a drop-off point for people to donate food to share with the local food bank at Braunstone Frith.

462 Information supplied by Philip Dodd and Cathy Harrell of St. Anne's

The Hall remains the focal point of the Western Park community and continues to provide a venue for many local events, such as the Western Park Beer Festival, Pop-Up Tea Rooms, parties and meetings as well as providing space for a day nursery and meetings of groups associated with the church.

1930s Housing Development and the growth of owner occupancy

It wasn't until the middle of the 1930s that building began on the other side of Hinckley Road. Between the two world wars, government subsidies had encouraged council house construction and this building boom later extended to private dwellings. A high level of depositors' funds invested in building societies meant that the societies needed to persuade more people to buy their own homes. Money borrowed earlier in the century for building projects was mostly repaid and building societies sought new investments for their funds by recycling them as capital. The length of time to pay off a mortgage was extended at the same time; for example in 1933 the average length of a mortgage was 12 years, up from just ten years in previous decades. By 1938 the average time it took to repay a mortgage grew to 16 years.[463] House buyers needed smaller deposits too. In 1931 the Leicester Temperance Building Society was offering mortgages of up to 75 per cent of a property's value.[464] By 1935 mortgages of up to 90 per cent were offered.[465] This and lower interest rates, provided easier access to mortgages for people in steady employment, who were now encouraged to become owner-occupiers rather than renters. This improved the market, increased demand and raised prices for building land.

Leicester Temperance offered to 'make everyman his own landlord' and in 1937 the society's assets reached £937,972 with 97 per cent of mortgages being loans of less than £1,000.[466] For the Leicester Permanent Building Society, 1936 was a record year in which increases in wages had maintained demand for house purchases and savings. That year £2,832,000 had been loaned for house buying, a rise from £2,584.000 in 1935 and £1,839,283 in 1934.[467] Its newspaper advertisements encouraged ordinary people to buy a house for the first time with,

> 'Gone are the difficulties of house purchase when you buy the home of your choice through the Leicester Permanent Building Society. A mortgage with this popular and trusted Society is simplicity itself, and the weekly repayments are often LESS than you pay in rent. Let us do for you what we have done for thousands of others. Make the house your own now.'[468]

---

463 *The Economist*, 1 July 1939, p.17
464 *Leicester Evening Mail*, 17 March 1931
465 *Leicester Evening Mail*, 27 March 1935
466 *Leicester Evening Mail*, 27 October 1938
467 *Leicester Evening Mail*, 5 January 1937
468 *Leicester Evening Mail*, 9 April 1936

Building firms became developers, concerned with an entire housing scheme, including the layout of roads and plots, rather than just building houses. These developments were usually speculative, medium density with houses built to a standardised, almost universal plan for semi-detached properties rather than individual, bespoke designs by architects.[469]

Housing development on the south side of Hinckley Road had begun with some ribbon development along the road opposite Western Park around the turn of the 20th century, with late Victorian-style houses. Wyggeston's Hospital owned land between the road and the railway line, what was part of its endowments in the manor of Bromkinsthorpe, probably that given by Hastings, Lord Huntington in 1576. In an auction catalogue of 1925, the land was described as 'part of the ancient possessions of the Charity'.[470] The governors of Wyggeston's Hospital, an alms house charity established in 1513, endowed with considerable lands through the legacy of its founder, William Wyggeston, and subsequently added to, began to investigate the possibility of selling some of this land off Hinckley Road for housing in the 1920s. This conflicted with Leicester Corporation's Town Plan which designated that same land for permanent allotments, continuing its long-standing use. Wyggeston's agent investigated whether the charity should receive compensation for this.

Concerns of the City Surveyor about a potential heavy claim for compensation that could have arisen because of the impact of the Town Planning Scheme on Wyggeston's Hospital led to a compromise. The Town Clerk suggested that Wyggeston's governors should make an application to develop part of this land under Town Planning (General Interim Development) Order 1922.[471] Plots of land with frontages facing Hinckley Road were planned with the approval of the Corporation, including a strip of land for road widening, with reserved prices of ten shillings a square yard. The Corporation turned down the offer to buy land fronting Hinckley Road for future widening of the road and so this was included within the plots. The Allotment Society took over the land behind the plots offered for development and was offered a new tenancy agreement in 1925 at a rent of £63 a year for the six acres three roods and 38 perches of land.[472]

Seeing no financial advantage from developing the site itself, Wyggeston's arranged for the building plots to be sold at auction by Tarratt's. There were 16 lots available of three different sizes, 11 of them 45 feet in width, two at 60 feet and another two at 61 feet wide, with variations in area. Tarratt's sale catalogue told potential bidders,

---

469 R. Best: *The Future Urban Acreage*, Town and Country Planning, 32, (1964), p.220

470 Auction catalogue produced by Tarratt's, 8 July 1925

471 Wyggeston's Hospital Estates Committee Minutes, 7 January 1925

472 Wyggeston's Hospital Governors' Meeting at Clerk's Office, Market Street, Leicester, 28 January 1925

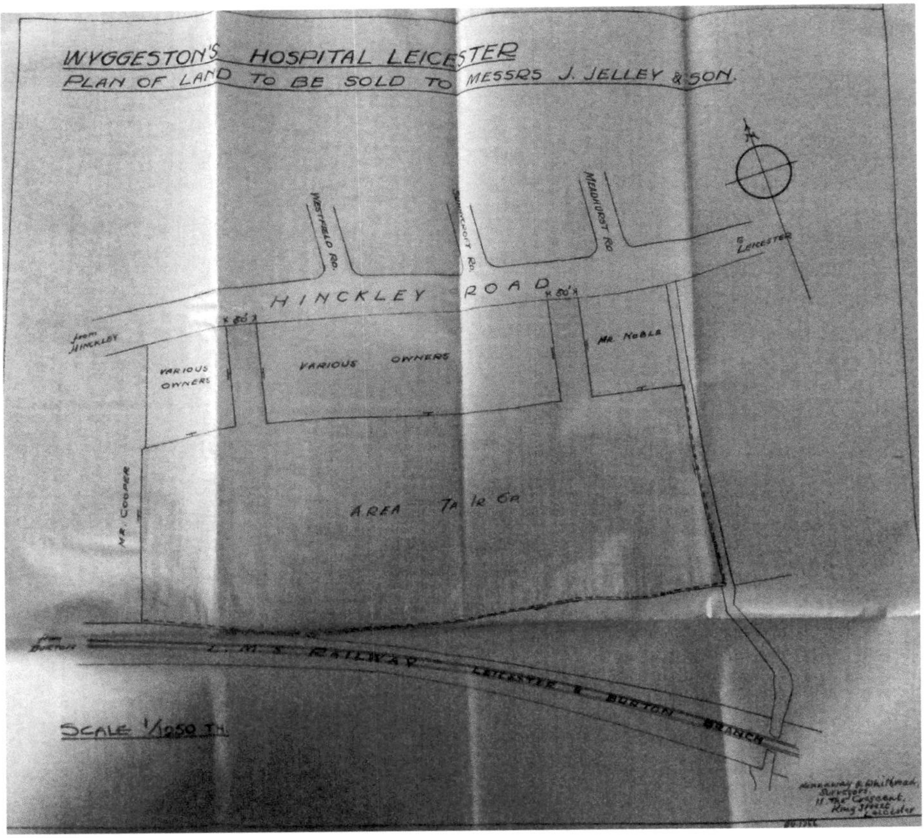

A plan of Wyggeston's Hospital land for sale on Hinckley Road, 1925. (Wyggeston's muniments room)

> 'The whole of the Lots are situate on a Main Road, and are of a convenient size, and suitable for the erection of a good class of Residential Property. Gas, Electric Light, Water and Draining Services pass the respective Lots. No building (except bay windows or porch or projective not exceeding 3 feet) to be set nearer to Hinckley Road than 20 feet from the line marked for future widening of Hinckley Road except a fence up to 5 feet high. Only private dwelling houses.'[473]

Surprisingly, in spite of the popularity of the emerging community across the other side of Hinckley Road, none of the plots were sold at the auction, perhaps due to financial recession or maybe the reserve price of ten shillings a square yard was too high. However, a potential purchaser came forward afterwards offering to buy all of the plots for 5s 6d a square yard, well below the price sought. The governors resolved that they would accept 8s 6d.[474]

---

473 Auction catalogue produced by Tarratt's, 8 July 1925
474 Meeting of the sub-committee of Wyggeston's Hospital Estates Committee, 7 July

Prospective purchaser Joe Noble, who was the former landlord of the Globe pub, had run the refreshment business at the Cattle Market and stood unsuccessfully as a Conservative candidate in the 1896 local elections, lived opposite at Villa Hinckley Road. He made several offers below the asking price to buy the whole 15,000 square yards over the following months. Keeping the land unsold and empty was costing Wyggeston's money; they had been obliged to pay £105 17s 7d for a chestnut pale fence between the land for sale and the cultivated allotments and then had to reduce the Allotment Society's rent for the year by £11 5s 3d because erecting the fence had damaged some of the gardens running beside it.[475] Two new entrances to the allotments had to be created along with new gates. Although Noble was told repeatedly that his offer of 6s 6d would not be accepted, dropping their own price to seven shillings per square yard, eventually the governors gave in. The offer of 6s 6d was finally accepted in June 1926 and a final price of 6s 9d per square yard was secured from Noble. The sale of the land was completed by October that year.[476]

Unless he had bought the land as a medium-term investment waiting for its value to rise, Noble doesn't seem to have found it any easier to sell the plots than Wyggeston's had done. By July 1931, five years after his purchase, Noble was still advertising nine plots of land near to Western Park gates on Hinckley Road to builders at a 'very low price' or even to exchange for houses.[477] By the end of 1931, though, there was only one plot remaining.[478] The houses on this stretch of Hinckley Road, between the path leading to Dane Hills Farm and Braunstone across Ainsdale Road and the Western Park View care home, are of a variety of designs, evidence of the sale of some individual plots to different purchasers. Some are semi-detached and appear to be the work of a single speculative developer, perhaps J. Jelley and Son, while some appear to be bespoke. One detached house bears the date 1933.

When William Gimson died in 1930, his sons and executors, Albert Starkey Gimson and Henry Hay Gimson, sold parcels of land for building on the south side of Hinckley Road in 1933 and 1934. This was purchased by members of the Jelley family of builders, James and his children James Herbert and Florence. The developer J. Jelley and Son was a building firm based on Shenton Street in Leicester. The first advertisement for houses in what was initially marketed as the Wyngate Drive Estate appeared in the local press in November 1933.[479] Building began on what had been Gimson's land, on Ainsdale Road, Oakthorpe Avenue, Dorchester Road and Kingswood Avenue, up as far as the footpath to Dane Hills Farm, which survives as

---

1925 (nb this date may be recorded incorrectly as it is the day before the auction).

475 Wyggeston's Hospital Estates Committee Minutes, 24 March 1926

476 Wyggeston's Hospital Governors' Meeting minutes, 22 June 1926; Wyggeston's Estates Committee Minutes, 6 October 1926

477 *Leicester Evening Mail*, 10 July 1931

478 *Leicester Evening Mail*, 3 December 1931

479 *Leicester Evening Mail*, 17 November 1933

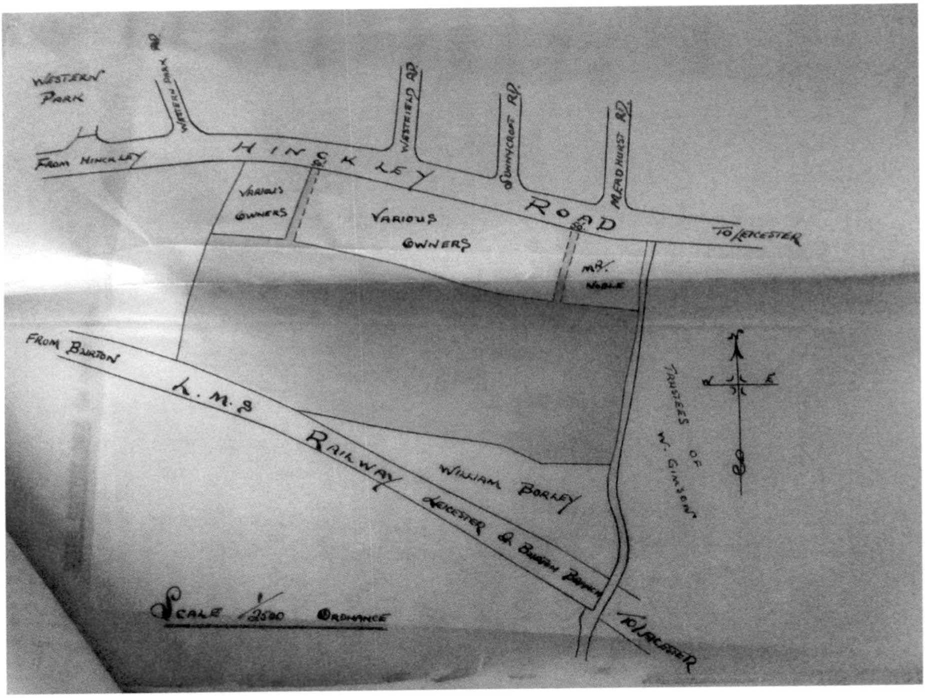

A plan of the road layout on part of former Gimson land by Jelley and Sons, c.1936.

the Black Pad or jitty from Hinckley Road, across the railway line, to Braunstone Estate. The farm had been on the other side of the railway track, where Wodehouse Road is now. The new houses were advertised by Jelley's as being closer to the town than the tram terminus and adjacent to schools. Florence Jelley made her own home on Hinckley Road at the corner with Kingswood Avenue, where she was joined by her husband George Stubbings, whom she married in 1943.

Wyggeston's Hospital began negotiations to sell seven acres of land off Hinckley Road to Jelley's who planned to extend their estate beyond Wyngate Drive, Dorchester Road, Kingswood Avenue and Ainsdale Road, on land already purchased from Gimson's and laid out. They planned to build more houses for private purchase on an extension to Ainsdale Road, beyond the Dorchester Road junction and the footpath. Ainsdale Road was to end in a cul-de-sac with the part of the road connecting it with Hinckley Road to be named Brampton Road, according to the Ordnance Survey map of 1938, published in 1944.[480] However, the short stretch of road linking up with Hinckley Road became a continuation of Ainsdale Road. The name Brampton must have had some significance to the builders as building began on Brampton Avenue off Glenfield Road after the War.

480 Ordnance Survey 6in map, Leicestershire XXXI.SW, revised 1938, published 1944

Wyggeston's Hospital Estates Committee heard on 7 June 1933, that the Charity Commissioners approved the sale of the land that was being used as allotments. Leicester Corporation also had to approve a change of use for the land as it was still designated as permanent allotments. The allotment holders weren't happy about this, as it meant they would lose their plots less than a decade after the earlier disruption. They had spent more money on developing their gardens than they might otherwise have done, as they had felt secure in the understanding that the plots were scheduled as permanent allotments. The treasurer of the Allotment Society, Mr A. Blunn, wrote to Wyggeston's governors, through their agent, pleading the case for the allottees to receive some compensation for their losses. Alfred Blunn, a retired commercial traveller, lived with his wife, Helen, at Westfield Road, just the other side of Hinckley Road from the allotments.[481] Blunn emphasised that the loss of their plots could 'inflict great hardship' on the allotment holders, 'many of which had held their allotment for a considerable number of years, and in some cases they had invested money they can ill afford to lose'.[482]

The issue of compensation for allotment holders had still not been resolved by the beginning of 1934, even though they had been asked to quit by the following February, after the sale of the land was agreed in September the previous year. The Wyggeston governors' Estates Committee had still made no decision on paying compensation. Blunn wrote again to the governors, reminding them that the Allotment Society had received notice to quit the land by 1 March and renewed the appeal for compensation, recognising that there was no legal claim but trusting the governors would give it 'sympathetic consideration' as the tenants, many of whom were 'elderly men drawing small wages or entirely dependent upon their old age pensions', suffering considerable loss and inconvenience'. The annual rent paid by the Allotment Society was £63 18s 6d.[483]

Anticipating having to abandon their allotments, many allottees had already given up their plots which were left vacant, causing additional problems for the Allotment Society which remained responsible for the full rent, now paid to the new owner, the developer Jelley and Son.[484] However, the advice given to Wyggeston's governors by their agent was that within the agreement under which the allotments were held, he did not think that any compensation was payable, provided that formal and legal notice was given to terminate the tenancy. Nevertheless, Wyggeston's' governors agreed to pay the Allotment Society a grant of just £10.[485]

Jelley's came into conflict with Leicester Corporation which ended up in a Ministry of Health Inquiry at the Town Hall in 1938. The Corporation refused to grant Jelley's

481 1939 Register for England and Wales
482 Wyggeston's Hospital Estates Committee Meeting, 7 June 1933
483 Wyggeston's Hospital Estates Committee Meeting, 3 October 1934
484 Wyggeston's Hospital Estates Committee Meeting Minutes, 10 January 1934
485 Wyggeston's Hospital Estates Committee Meeting Minutes, 19 June 1934

its approval to build an ash-surfaced access road to garages behind some of the houses on Ainsdale Road. Although the road did not conform to Corporation requirements for a concrete surface of six inches and a minimum width of ten feet, Jelley's representative argued these requirements were excessive for a closed road which had to bear no traffic except the occasional passage of a car to a garage. A garage belonging to Mr Bailey had already been constructed in 1935, although the Corporation said there was no evidence of an application for planning permission and no access road had appeared on Jelley's plans. Several residents made statements in favour of the road but one, Henry Willett of Hinckley Road, objected. Mr Willett was worried that a proper road would 'encourage hawkers, rag and bone men and the scum of the earth to skulk round the back ways of the houses'.[486] Jelley's must have won their case, as the access road remains, as does a similar one behind Wyngate Drive, although now gated for security.

The allotment land was sold to Jelley and Son for £800 an acre plus the expenses connected with the sale, a total of £5,700, subject to the restrictions imposed on the land by Leicester Corporation being withdrawn, which they were. The contract was signed and the deposit paid by October 1934.[487] Selling the land for housing development brought in a much more substantial sum than could be expected from the sale of agricultural land that had declined in value, funds that were invested elsewhere by Wyggeston's Hospital to support the work of the charity.[488]

By 1936 houses were ready and for sale on the former Gimson owned land, as far up as Kingswood Avenue, where in November that year a mock-Tudor, gable fronted semi-detached house with a garage on that road, sold for £775 on a mortgage from the Leicester Permanent Building Society at 4.5 per cent interest with repayments of £4 4s 9d a month. The first owner, Thomas Rawlinson, was a civil servant, indicative of the expansion of the white collar workforce in secure employment, able to buy their own homes from this time.[489] This mortgage was finally paid off in 1959. Soon building was under way on the section of land that had been bought from Wyggeston's Hospital. The houses sold quickly and by the spring of 1939, just six detached houses of various types and aspects, some with garages, were still for sale at prices from £725. Three semi-detached homes remained available at £635.[490] By June 1939, only six houses out of 500 remained unsold on the 'high class residential estate'. This was announced in the local press, as 'positively the last chance to buy'.[491]

486 *Leicester Evening Mail*, 17 March 1938
487 Wyggeston's Hospital , Estates Committee Meeting, 3 October 1934
488 James Thawley: A Certain Hospital Forever, p.79
489 Deeds loaned by Beverley Lambie
490 *Leicester Mercury*, 10 April 1939
491 *Leicester Mercury*, 12 June 1939

View of Wyngate Drive under construction from Braunstone Avenue, c.1935.

In 1935, the two sections of the development on the former Gimson's and Wyggeston's land were advertised as Wyngate Drive Estate, only 15 minutes' walk to Leicester Market Place, before being rebranded as the Western Park Estate. Prices ranged from £575 to £650. For prospective buyers to look round and make enquiries about buying a new home in the development, Jelley's opened a show home at 2 Wyngate Drive which was furnished by Goodly's, a Worcestershire firm with premises on Market Street and Pocklington's Walk. Another development by Jelley's was described as 'off Eastfield Road' where building was restricted to properties that sold for between £750 and £850. The district was promoted as 'the healthiest position to live', where 'homes stand as high as the Dane Hills, in the best residential district, which is restricted to protect your investment'.[492]

Others involved with the development of the area were solicitor Cecil Harris of the Westcotes Estate, along with the architects and surveyors Pick, Everard, Keay and Gimson. Four shops were erected on Wyngate Drive, serving what was then also known as the Westcotes or Sykefield Estate.[493] Some of the land on which a part of Wyngate Drive on the even-numbered side east of the brook, the shops, and the Westcotes end of Braunstone Avenue were built was owned by Westcotes Estate Limited, the company formed by Joseph Harris of Westcotes and left to his three sons,

492 *Leicester Evening Mail*, 11 July 1935

493 ROLLR DE9149/11 Papers relating to the development of the Westcotes Estate land housing development.

Houses by Bax and Company, built c.1931, Letchworth Road extension, taken 2021.

Montague, Henry and Cecil. Houses on one end of Braunstone Avenue, built in the decade up to 1935, were individual bespoke properties.

Towards the junction with Wyngate Drive semi-detached houses were built speculatively by builder George Charles Pook for the Westcotes Estate in an area described on deeds of 1937 as part of the Sykefield Estate. A block of three houses was built nearest the junction with Wyngate Drive and sold in July 1937 as a group for £2,200 by Pook to William Lawrence, a pork butcher of Westcotes Drive. William Lawrence moved into a detached house on Wyngate Drive, opposite the shops, the garden of which was adjacent to the rear of the three houses. At least one of these were then rented out, before being sold to owner occupiers in around 1951, when Lawrence died.[494]The plot on the corner of Wyngate Drive and Braunstone Avenue was bought from the Westcotes Estate by the trustees of the York Street Hall, a non-conformist church based in the city centre, who built a small church, Braunstone Avenue Hall, there in 1934. This provided a place for worship and meetings for a group that had been meeting in the house of Mr Bond, a York Street church member, on Rancliffe Crescent in the new Braunstone Estate. Mr Bond had run a Sunday School in his own home before the new church was built. It is still one of three churches owned by the York Street Hall trust.

Jelley's was also developing the area north of Glenfield Road as the Dane Hills Estate, near what it referred to as the Glenfield Road extension, indicating its transformation from footpath to metalled road. Letchworth Road was extended on the other side of Glenfield Road; three houses built by Bax and Company received planning permission in 1931, one with a garage in June and two more in October. The builder himself or a family member lived in one of them. Frank C. Bax, whose

494 Deeds relating to houses on Braunstone Avenue, 1937.

occupation was given as a hosiery dyer foreman, lived there with his wife Winnie in 1939. By this date, houses were built and occupied as far down as number 174. This was the beginning of the road leading down the 'Letchworth Road Dip' and, later, on into New Parks. An advertisement for the development, placed by Jelley's in January 1939, drew the attention of *Leicester Mercury* readers with the heading 'The West End is the Best End'. It declared, 'You may not know it is still possible to reside nearer the centre than the car [tram] terminus, and only 20 minutes' walk to the Market Place. Think what this means during the foggy and frosty winter. We have a limited number of modern houses in this area, situated near Wyngate Drive and Dane Hills Estates. Various types, detached and semi, with or without garage room.'[495]

The Dane Hills Estate was promoted to prospective buyers as the 'highest part of the city', close to the bus terminus.[496] It had excellent views across Leicester. Most of Hilders Road, with houses of a more varied design, was inhabited by 1939. Modernity and convenience were key themes in all advertisements for new houses, and electricity had become standard. One on Hilders Road was marketed as an excellent detached residence, with three bedrooms, a garage, power plugs and no road charges.[497] Road charges were a fee paid to the local authority, based on the width of a property's frontage, a financial contribution for making up the road outside. In some areas, the roads remained unadopted for years, before being adopted by the Council which took on responsibility for their maintenance. While a road remained unadopted, individual householders were responsible for the upkeep of the stretch outside.

Purchasers of new houses, which were mostly of a similar type, what became the standard type across Britain in the 1930s and 1950s, were offered a choice within the range of housing types available. Each semi-detached or detached house, with a double bay-windowed front and porch is subtly different, in what could be described as 'mass-produced individuality'. Some have arched entrance porches, others have a straight lintel. Some have mock beams in a gabled roof, the so-called 'tudorbethan' style popular in the early 20th century. Many others have a straight roofline. Some houses have a wider frontage as they incorporate a garage built at the side, some of which have a fourth bedroom above, while other garages are single-storeyed. Many have art deco design features, particularly in the stained glass of their front doors or windows, and interior doors.

On Ainsdale Road there are a few built in a 'moderne' style, although with the architectural compromise of pitched rather than flat roofs. All were built with electricity, bathrooms and two toilets, one upstairs, either separate or in the bathroom and another outside next to the coal house. Homeowners were free to decorate their homes as they chose and they created attractive front gardens to impress passers-by and express pride in their property.

---

495 *Leicester Mercury*, 10 January 1939
496 *Leicester Mercury*, 31 August 1939
497 *Leicester Mercury*, 2 March 1939

Ainsdale Road, taken in 2021.

A few houses were still looking for purchasers or tenants on the eve of World War Two and during the phoney war in the latter part of 1939. One such was a modern detached house with all conveniences for £800. The impending war obviously had an influence on the housing market and vendors were eager to emphasise any safety features of their property. One advertisement placed by Jelley's, offered a semi-detached, modern house on Oakthorpe Avenue with a reinforced concrete floor that could 'be used for an ARP basement', newly built for £635.[498] Another advert placed by local house builder S.C. Wright of Westfield Road, drew attention with the heading 'A Regrettable Necessity is a reinforced concrete air raid shelter'. This was incorporated into a modern house for sale, situated on Hilders Road, which also had (almost as secondary features) three bedrooms, two reception rooms, a kitchen with fireplace and a garage; decoration would be to the purchaser's own choice.[499] During the War, borrowers who enlisted for military service were charged interest only on their mortgages.

For some residents of Western Park, the realisation of how life-changing the War would prove to be was not immediately apparent. One advertisement placed in the local paper in November 1939, was seeking 'a reliable young woman, three mornings weekly', perhaps showing an unawareness during the 'phoney war' of the need for all women to be engaged in some form of war work, making domestic service positions difficult to fill.[500] As part of the preparations for attack by the Luftwaffe, designated ARP wardens' posts were established, often in domestic premises around the community. Around Western Park, which was in G Division, there were posts at 247 Hinckley Road, 21 Meadhurst Road, 16 Westhill Road, 34 Hilders Road, 115

498 *Leicester Mercury*, 10 and 15 May 1939
499 *Leicester Mercury*, 28 August 1939
500 *Leicester Mercury*, 20 November 1939

Dorchester Road, in the basement of 126 Westcotes Drive, in a garage at the corner of Western Park Road and Hinckley Road, in Hinckley Road School (Dovelands) and in the kitchen of Westcotes Congregational Church.[501] These were in addition to the ARP Depot inside the Western Park gates.

By the time World War Two broke out in 1939, the neighbourhood that took its name from the now 40-year-old Western Park was more or less complete and a new suburban community created occupying the space between the Midland Railway line and the park, down to Gimson Road formerly Ashleigh Road (renamed in memory of the family who had lived in the large house, now Christ the King Junior School) and Braunstone Avenue and the top end of Westcotes Drive. This reflected a new way of living for a substantial proportion of the population, not just in Leicester but across Britain. Public transport allowed people to live further away from their places of work.

The last quarter of the 19th century had seen a rise in real incomes and reduced working hours in many occupations. There was also an increase in the number of people employed in education, administration, clerical and skilled manual trades, which offered the security of regular hours and good pay. Improved education provided opportunities for working-class people to access better paid and more secure employment. The expansion of British industry and commerce, assisted by colonialism, created a need for an expanded professional class and also a wider pool of white-collar workers.

Despite the 1930s being associated with economic depression, this was not the case in all areas and sectors as new industries emerged and demand for consumer products grew. Increased leisure because of shorter working hours, inspired the growth of gardening and of DIY as a pastime, creating new forms of masculinity for the suburban male. More time spent at home with children meant middle-class families now desired gardens for their children to play in and comfortable furnishings for their home. This did not always lead to harmonious relationships between neighbours. Percival W. Allcock, a heating and ventilation engineer who lived on the odd-numbered side of Sunnycroft Road, was annoyed by the Wagstaffs who lived next door when they played in their garden with a tennis trainer, perhaps a game similar to swingball. One Sunday in 1931, Mr Allcock peered over the garden fence, presumably to see what was causing a noise, and asked Mr Wagstaff to stop, which he did. The next Sunday Mr Wagstaff's little boy was playing with the ball on the tennis trainer. This time Mr Allcock got so annoyed he banged on the asbestos garage wall so hard he punched a hole through it. Instead of sorting out payment for repairs as neighbours between themselves, Mr Allcock was taken to the County Court by a claim for damages.[502] The conflict over the game in the garden may have arisen solely because of the noise of tennis rackets hitting a ball but the issue could have been exacerbated because it was

501 *Leicester Mercury*, 1 September 1939
502 *Leicester Evening Mail*, 6 October 1931

Life Without Servants *book cover, 1930.*

on a Sunday, a traditionally quiet time observed more strictly at the time than nowadays.

Keeping animals as pets rather than as working animals was another growing 20th-century lifestyle change. What to do when a beloved pet died was a problem solved for owners of a suburban garden. A garden was an ideal burial place for pets. As well as the usual dogs, cats, rabbits and cage birds, a more unusual pet lived with the McDonald family of Gowrie on Sunnycroft Road. Alexander Brookfield McDonald taught at Leicester College of Art and Technology and was a member of the Leicestershire Archaeological and Historical Society. His daughter had a pet monkey that died in January 1930 and was buried in the garden with a little stone over the grave. In his will Mr McDonald requested 'that respect be paid to one very small piece of land at Gowrie'. The will stated that when the property was sold to a new owner, that a similar request be made to those who acquired it, 'so that she who rests there may not be disturbed'.[503]

A suburban garden changed the way people saw nature. As wildlife adapted to the invasion of the countryside, gardens became a haven for hedgehogs, squirrels and what became defined as 'garden birds'. Suburban women, too, had a new role, the ideal of the stay-at-home housewife who kept her own home clean and tidy and cooked her family's meals herself without the aid of a servant, using gas or electric cookers, although some in the larger houses sometimes had a daily help. This suburban lifestyle represented a retreat into domesticity centred around the nuclear family, of a married couple and their children, rather than multi generational dwelling units.

503 *Leicester Evening Mail*, 14 May 1931

Dovelands School

Surprisingly, Dovelands School predates most of the Western Park houses. With the population of the West End growing, by the 1900s there was an urgent need for an additional school for the children of the community, a new public elementary school, for pupils aged five to 13. A two-acre site on Hinckley Road was identified in 1903 and initially rented for £8 a year, while a temporary school was set up on Fosse Road. The site was purchased in 1906 from the Mellor Estate for £1,409, plus £250 towards half the cost of a side road, that became Eastfield Road. When Hinckley Road Elementary School was first opened, the class size was limited to 60 by the Board of Education, or in spacial terms, ten square feet per scholar or nine square feet for younger children.

Initially, there were plans to build the school at an estimated cost of £17,000 with three departments: for 400 infants, 400 girls and 400 boys. A private architect, W.M. Cowdell of Grey Friars, was commissioned to design the school, for which plans were approved in October 1911.[504] The builder contracted was J. Bradford. The estimated costs rose to £18,500 but with provision reduced to just two departments. The school's capacity was reduced further, to 458 infants in what is now the main building, and costs cut to £6,000, losing a potential 319 school places in west Leicester. To build the intended, larger school was too costly and would have needed more and smaller classrooms, as well as a bigger boiler for heating and greater running costs. The changes meant that every child in the new school would have 50 cubic feet of airspace, more than in any other in the town.[505]

Hinckley Road School opened on 25 August 1913 with Mr J.S. Flint as the headmaster and his staff, who transferred from the temporary Fosse Road school. There were 442 children in the first intake, some drawn from Mantle Road, Shaftesbury and King Richard's Road Schools. In a change from earlier education methods, there were no monitors or child teachers, a number that had fallen from 155 in Leicester in 1903, to only 20 by 1912.[506] The school had electric light, efficient low-pressure water heating, a central hall and rooms that could accommodate 60 or 48 children. It had the latest design of desks with lift-up tops and a sand pit with buckets for building sandcastles. The toilets were in a separate outbuilding, with only washbasins in the indoor cloakroom. The building elevations were described as Georgian in character, of local red sand stone with purple-brown artificial stone dressings and a roof of hand-made tiles.

At the time of its opening the local newspaper headlines dubbed the new school 'the House in the Fields', because of its almost rural setting.[507] It was surrounded on

504 Elaine Allen: *The Story of Dovelands School*, 1903–78, p.2
505 *Leicester Mercury*, 20 December 1911
506 *Leicester Chronicle and Leicestershire Mercury*, 2 November, 1912
507 *Leicester chronicle and Leicestershire Mercury*, 30 August 1913

three sides by fields and there were gardens by the road. On the other side of Hinckley Road were allotments, those opposite containing pigsties. The houses on the town side only reached as far as Gimson Road at the time the school opened. Hinckley Road itself was only asphalted as far up as Kirby Road until 1922, when the road was metalled and a curb provided. Eastfield Road, next to the school, was made up in 1925. Next to the school on the west side, where the garage is now, there remained a field, later used for sports, and to the north was a 3,000-square-yard garden area, used to grow vegetables between 1917 and 1923, when it became a flower garden once more. Thirty boys over the age of 12, worked in the garden in relays as part of their education. The sale of produce enabled a Singer sewing machine to be bought for the older girls in 1919. Former boy pupils could pay rent of a shilling a year to use the garden.

During World War One, despite their young age, pupils made their contribution to the war effort. They collected food and clothes for Belgian refugees in Leicester and for the Leicester Frith Home for soldiers suffering from neurasthenia. To raise money for wounded soldiers, they held a rummage sale and made articles for the Mayor's 'Old English Faire'. Younger children brought money for wool, which was knitted into 1,303 helmets, scarves and body belts for soldiers abroad by the older girls in their free time.[508]

In 1954, Hinckley Road School was renamed Dovelands, a reminder of the ancient wood and brook nearby. Over the decades Dovelands has undergone changes to meet the needs of local children. Temporary mobile classrooms used in the 1970s and 1980s were replaced by extensions and enhancements to the building. As an 'all through' primary school it now caters for 550 local children aged from three to 11.

508 Allen, pp.3-4

7

POST-WAR DEVELOPMENTS

New Parks Estate

The major post-war development project, not just in the west of Leicester but in the whole of the city, was the New Parks Estate. The housing development in the area now named Western Park had been undertaken by private builders, creating many bespoke properties in the area to the north of Hinckley Road and houses built speculatively for sale to owner occupiers or to rent on the other side of the road. The next stage in the urbanisation of the district was to be for council-owned, social housing to be rented to local residents, in order to provide new homes for those living in overcrowded properties or for people displaced by the demolition of slums elsewhere in the city.

In May 1939, Leicester Housing Committee members decided to build 204 houses on what was referred to as the Freakes Estate. These new homes on Stephenson Drive and Swannington Road, built on Freak's or Freake's Ground, were to be the start of a housing scheme on a brand new estate. The initiative was proposed by Cllr J.L. Harrison at a council meeting, who also moved an amendment that the question of building be held over until a plan had been prepared for the area to be cleared and redeveloped around Wharf Street. 'Eventually there will be 24 acres cleared in the Wharf Street area.' The Council had promised that a plan for its redevelopment would be prepared before any further housing schemes were undertaken.[509]

The proposed scheme for New Parks included 60 bungalows, and the rest would be three-bedroom, non-parlour houses on 20 acres of land that adjoined the city side of the estate at John Freakes Avenue, the original name given to Stephenson Drive. House building on Freakes Ground, where there were allotments, had been proposed in 1919. Allotment holders protested and questioned whether the Council realised that the land that side of Fosse Road was mainly composed of household refuse which had been tipped there. From the lane leading from the former isolation hospital to the top end there was a depth of about 20 feet of ashes, by then covered up.[510]

Freak's or Freake's Ground was purchased by the Borough of Leicester in 1624 or 1625. As part of the deal, the Corporation agreed to pay an annual rent to Wyggeston's

509 *Leicester Daily Mercury*, 12 May 1939
510 *Leicester Daily Post*, 27 September 1919

Hospital for ever, although for ever seems to have ended in 1828. The first road for the new estate, John Freakes Avenue was laid out in 1934.[511] One of the first structures on the road was a police box. Soon, homes were built there and on Swannington Road, which were occupied by 1935. At the request of a number of people in the district, the Leicester Highways Committee agreed to change the name of John Freakes Avenue to Stephenson Drive.[512] Residents were tired of the jocularity of their friends who saw something in the old name that led them to talk of freaks.[513] Apparently, the name had made them a stock joke of pantomime dames, despite John Freakes having been a fine and respected old Leicester worthy.

As well as that obtained from Captain Aikman, described in Chapter 2, another large purchase of land in the 1930s was from the Westcotes Estate, owned by Cecil Harris. This transaction included the 178 acres of New Parks Farm and Western Park Dairy for £48,000. The Westcotes Estate had bought the 92 acres of the Western Park Dairy from John Harris Cooper in 1902, who also sold Manor Farm to Samuel Stone of Kirby Frith at this time. The Corporation obtained a government loan of £48,870 including the legal costs, to be repaid at £1,934 a year, an amount that would be merged into the costs of the homes built. Negotiations on the sale had begun by 1930, when a price of £120 an acre plus £4,500 for the buildings and timber had been offered.[514]

William Keay of surveyors and architects Pick, Everard and Keay was appointed to draw up plans, value the property, and to act on behalf of Westcotes Estate in the negotiations with Leicester Corporation. Keay advised Harris to sell the combined 280 acres of both farms of the estate and an area next to Western Park rented by Westfields Tennis Club as a whole but not to appear too anxious to sell.[515] Leicester City Corporation passed a resolution in April 1935, authorising the land to be acquired by compulsory purchase unless an agreement was reached, under Section 64 of the Housing Act 1925, although Cllr Swain thought that a halt should be called to council housing.[516] Harris's accountant advised him to delay until after 13 August 1935 and to obtain the best price, not allowing compulsory purchase to lower the price because of the previous voluntary sale. A concern was that compulsory purchase might mean the land would be valued as agricultural rather than prime building land owing to a surcharge that the Corporation might face.[517]

511 *Leicester Chronicle*, 8 September 1934
512 *Leicester Evening Mail*, 4 March 1939
513 *Leicester Daily Mercury*, 26 April 1939
514 Letter from William Keay to Cecil Harris, 14 March 1935, ROLLR DE9128/175
515 Letter Keay to Harris, 9 October 1935, ROLLR DE9128/175
516 Letter from H.A. Pritchard, Town Clerk, to Keay, 9 August 1935, ROLLR DE9128/175
517 Letter from Mr Goddard of Goddard, Fryer and Mellersh of London, accountants, to Harris, 31 July 1935, ROLLR DE9128/175

The sale of the Westcotes Estates lands to Leicester Corporation was completed in July 1936. Some of the land purchased provided an extension to Western Park and sites for schools, playing fields, allotments and open space were reserved. At the same time, 100 acres were bought from Captain Aikman, with 40 acres around New Parks House preserved for amenities. A planned 3,000 new homes were to rehouse displaced slum dwellers. The overall cost of the scheme was £81,627. An additional 15.5 acres between Sandhurst Road, Tetuan Road and the New Parks House estate were bought from the Paget Trustees for £6,350. Two 60-feet-wide town planning roads were proposed to cross this land.[518]

In a report on Municipal Housing published in 1939, the Council was able to announce, 'With regards to the future, the Council has acquired a large estate at New Parks, which it proposes to utilise for housing purposes. This estate will accommodate roughly 4,000 houses.' These would be in addition to those already built on and around Stephenson's Drive, renamed after the railway engineer. The beginnings of a road network were soon created under the provisions of the Housing Act of 1930, but they were left undeveloped due to the cessation of subsidies in 1932.[519] Concrete, a new innovation in road building, was used in their construction as the material was economical and the surface durable.

The outbreak of World War Two brought a halt to all redevelopment and municipal house building schemes. Any tenders were withdrawn. Fortunately the only houses in the course of construction in Leicester were 38 on George Street, off Belgrave Gate, and these were almost ready for families to move in. The Housing Committee decided to turn the land on the extensive New Parks Estate over to the County Agricultural Committee for the duration of the war.[520] However it was requisitioned by the Royal Army Ordnance Corps, which was expanding its storage depots as vehicles poured in from British factories or from Canada and the USA. Out of three depots in Leicester, one was the No.8 Armoured Fighting Vehicle Depot on what was to become the New Parks Estate. The newly constructed roads were used as hard standings on which to park tanks. The Royal Electrical and Mechanical Engineers No.2 Command Workshop that carried out repairs was also on site.[521]

Throughout 1943 and 1944, tanks and other military vehicles were delivered and stored ready for the invasion of Europe on D-Day and afterwards. Aerial photographs taken in April 1944, clearly show long lines of vehicles parked along the partly constructed road layout of New Parks.[522] After the invasion, battle-damaged,

518 Conveyancing document, ROLLR DE9128/176
519 *Civic Affairs – City of Leicester 1939–40*, City of Leicester Publicity and Development Programme, c.1939, p.45
520 *Leicester Mercury*, 15 September 1939
521 Holyoak, p.161
522 Cartwright, p.7

Convoy of Sherman Mk III tanks at Issues gate, No.8 Armoured Fighting Vehicle Dept. Swannington Road is in the background. By Capt. Lockeyear, 25 April 1944, Imperial War Museum, London.

sometimes blood-stained vehicles, were sent back for repair. They were collected from the railway station, where they arrived on flat-bed wagons, to be driven to New Parks.

Once the War Office had removed the last of the vehicles, a Crusader tank, from its armoured vehicle park in New Parks on 27 September 1945, work could proceed on Leicester's new flagship housing estate, under the leadership of the Leicester Reconstruction Committee responsible for post-war planning. This committee was set up by Cllr Charles Keene, with a brief to develop a post-war planning strategy.[523] New Parks was to be the first of three major new estates on the outskirts of the city, the others being Thurnby Lodge and Eyres Monsell.[524]

523 Richard Rodger and Rebecca Madgin: *Leicester – A Modern History*, Leicester, 2016, p.178

524 Ben Beazley: *Post War Leicester*, pp.15, and 36

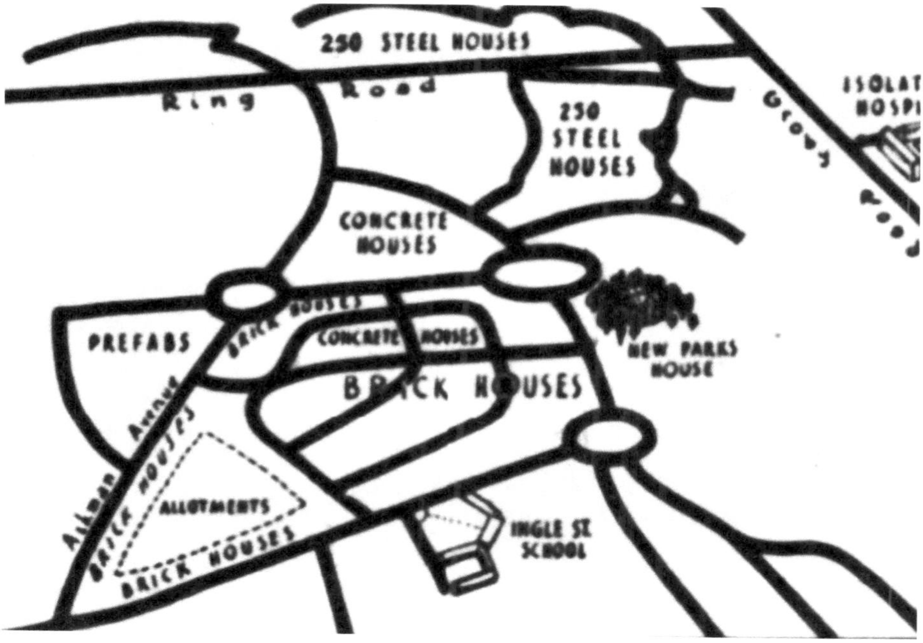

Plan of New Parks showing locations of different types of house construction, c.1946.

The task of digging out more new roads, drainage and service systems for the planned estate was done by German prisoners of war, working under armed guard who began the task by the summer of 1945.[525] As construction work got under way, the seven different contractors engaged in different sections of the planned estate began advertising for workers. As well as work for large numbers of building tradesmen and labourers, there were jobs for women. Canteens were opened by contractors J. Laing and Company on Aikman Avenue, and by Sir Lindsay Parkinson and Company on Glazebrook Square. They were advertising for cooks and canteen assistants in June 1946.[526]

With a shortage of workers, having a canteen would help attract men, many of whom may not have lived locally, to work for the company and help with their retention. Advertisements for sub-contractor joiners, people to work on the brickwork in manholes, to build party walls and wing walls appeared as the work progressed.[527] As well as experienced tradesmen, there were 17 building trainees from the Government Training Centre on Gipsy Lane, helping to build houses.[528] The trainees had spent four months learning at the Training Centre, followed by two months' work outside, what nowadays would be called work experience or placement, before going into

525 *Leicester Chronicle*, 16 June 1945
526 *Leicester Evening Mail*, 25 and 28 June 1946
527 *Leicester Evening Mail*, 22 November 1946
528 *Leicester Chronicle*, 29 June 1946

Brick houses in New Parks, 1949. (Records Office of Leicester, Leicestershire and Rutland)

employment as fully trained construction workers. Schemes like this were devised to combat the problems of labour shortages after the war, and to retrain returning servicemen.

Beginning in January 1946, by October 1949 a total of 2,748 houses, including 120 'Portal' houses or prefabs, had been built on a 90-acre site. At the opening of the first two brick-built houses, 59 and 61 Bateman Road, on 5 September 1946, Cllr May Goodwin was presented with a ceremonial key by builder Lewis Sherriff. The contractor Sir Lindsay Parkinson and Company celebrated completing a house a day, 162 houses in 162 days, in October 1947, when the key of the 162nd home, a steel-framed house with three bedrooms and two other rooms, was handed to Daisy Nichols by Cllr May Goodwin. All Parkinson's employees and their families were invited to a day of special events including sports and games, concluding with a dance in the evening.[529]

After World War Two, in the immediate post-war period there were fewer houses built for private sale as construction now focussed on social housing. No private houses were allowed to be built until March 1946. Building could be slow as there were shortages of materials and developers needed a licence before they could apply for planning permission. The homes built from then and in the 1950s had less decorative detail than those of the 1930s. With 14,012 Leicester people and families on the housing waiting list in 1951, building council homes at affordable rents remained the

529 *Leicester Evening Mail*, 2 October 1947

Steel houses in New Parks, 1949. (Records Office of Leicester, Leicestershire and Rutland)

priority into the next decade. Social changes meant that young couples wanted a home of their own rather than living with their parents or in-laws in multi-generational households or shared properties. Inner-city slums were no longer socially acceptable and the intention was to demolish these houses and end the abominable conditions in which some people were forced to live, as had been proposed before the War. However, the War had brought additional priorities which caused delays.

To encourage local authorities to build social housing, the post-war Labour Government, led by Prime Minister Clement Atlee, announced a programme of subsidies for council house building, with the aim of creating many thousands of three-bedroomed houses available for rent at ten shillings a week. The government provided a subsidy of £16 10s a year per house over 60 years while the council provided its own subsidy of £5 10s for the same period of time. The city architect J.S. Fyfe selected a design for steel houses by the British Iron and Steel Foundation. The steel design was chosen because of a shortage of bricks although the houses were more expensive to build. The first batch of 205 of them, consisting of an aluminium frame and four outer wall sections, costing £1,205 for a three-bedroom home and £1,493 for four bedrooms were built at the rate of four a day.[530] The first house was ready in October 1946 and this initial phase of development was completed the same month in the following year. Altogether 500 steel houses were erected.[531]

530 Beazley, p.36

531 David Nash and David Reeder (eds): *Leicester in the Twentieth Century,* Alan Sutton, Avon, 1993, p.21

Concrete houses in New Parks, 1949. (Records Office of Leicester, Leicestershire and Rutland)

By the end of 1948, there were contracts in place and under way for the construction of 2,450 houses, with 1,420 of them already occupied, and plans in the pipeline for another 250 brick-built houses. Another innovative building technique, applied in New Parks due to the urgent need to build houses quickly, was John Laing's 'Easiform' factory-assembled system with poured concrete walls.[532] In September 1948 approval was given for 150 houses on Battersbee Road, Heays Close, Overseal Road, New Parks Boulevard and Bonney Road. Then in January 1949, drainage was approved for 250 more Easiform houses on Bonney Road, Dillon Road, New Parks Boulevard, Chadwell Road, Kerrial Road, Frolesworth Road, Drayton Road and Bringhurst Road. Altogether, 600 of these concrete-walled Easiform homes were erected in New Parks.

As well as the more permanent structures, there were 120 American-designed prefabs on the Hinckley Road side of the estate, a further 141 near Groby Road and more on Aikman Avenue. Building costs for each one of these was £23 10s a year, to be repaid to the government.[533] Although these were only meant to be temporary homes, lasting for just ten years, many survived for decades before they were finally cleared and replaced by other facilities or permanent houses. The prefabs covering 4.47 hectares of land on Aikman Avenue were cleared away in 1977, to be replaced by

532 Nash and Reeder, p.21
533 Beazley, p.33

Design for Aikman Avenue Flats, 1949. (Image Leicestershire)

66 flats, 125 houses and a shop. When built, these homes became Mossgate, Withens Close and Wood End.

On the other side of Letchworth Road, off Aikman Avenue and St Oswald's Road, approval was given for 100 new homes in 1978. Development in this area, which included parts of Piper Way, continued from then until around 1992, with the creation of the Ridgeway with seven new houses adding to the mix of housing types in New Parks. Demonstrating the social changes in relation to private ownership of motor cars since the 1950s, these houses built for Leicester Housing Association, had space off the road to park two cars and dropped kerbs and ramps at street crossing points for wheelchair users and prams.[534]

Having so many three-bedroomed family homes in the new estate led the Housing Committee to worry that it was creating an unbalanced neighbourhood, one where everyone lived in a similar home and residents were all of a similar demographic and age distribution.[535] To ameliorate this, flats and bungalows for older people were added in to the New Parks housing mix. Based on Scandinavian designs from Copenhagen and Stockholm, plans for seven blocks of flats on Aikman Avenue were put in place in January 1950. The aim was to build 372 of them over a period of 18 months to two years at a cost of £544,710. Although they did not object to the principle of building these new homes, Labour councillors protested at the high construction cost

534 Leicester City Council Planning Applications Database
535 Nash and Reeder, p.149

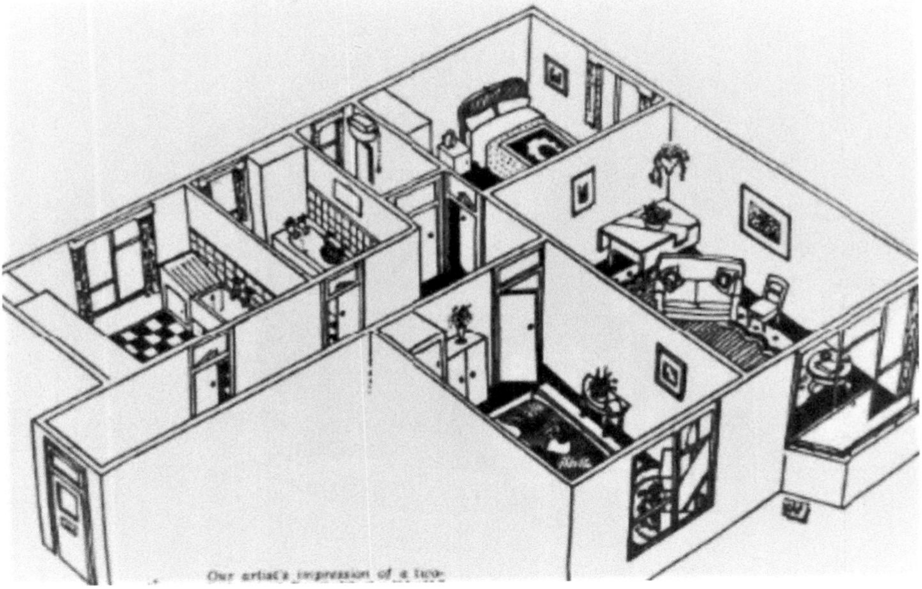

Interior layout of an Aikman Avenue flat.

of building flats compared with traditional houses. At the same time, the Labour Group of Leicester City Council made it clear that they were prepared to support any scheme to improve the city's housing position and so it was agreed that the next phase of development would be the Aikman Avenue flats.[536]

Work on the first of these blocks began in September 1950 and it was ready for tenants to move into in the middle of 1953. The rents for the flats were £2 12s a week for a three-bedroomed apartment, and £2 7s for two bedrooms.[537] The blocks were named, in alphabetical order, Auburn, Bentburn, Crayburn, Deansburn, Emburn, Fairburn and, finally, Gorseburn which was completed in 1956. Each flat was self-contained, sharing a communal laundry with electric washing machines, driers operated with a penny in the slot for an hour's drying time, and airing cupboards. The buildings were centrally heated from a single main boiler. Outside each front door was an automatic refuse chute, which carried waste down to be collected by a caretaker. Television and wireless could be accessed through a single shared aerial on the roof, a forward-looking innovation in the early 1950s, when most homes did not yet have a television set. The flats were originally built with flat roofs but in 1987 planning permission was granted to replace these with energy-saving pitched roofs, along with swivel windows and updated hot water and heating systems. Shared grounds provided outdoor space and each flat was said to have a fine view from the large lounge windows.[538]

536 *Leicester Mercury*, 3 January 1950
537 Beazley, p.37
538 *Leicester Chronicle*, 20 June 1953

Aikman Avenue, library and shops, taken in 2021.

Between 1946 and 1953, 25 per cent of all new houses in Leicester were in New Parks, a total of two-fifths of all new housing was eventually built there.[539] Excluding the flats, there were 3,000 houses on the estate, providing homes for around 12,000 residents. These people needed somewhere local to shop and so a modern shopping parade on Aikman Avenue was constructed, a splendid example of 1950s architecture which won a design award from the Royal Institute of British Architecture in 1959. The largest retailer in the central shopping parade was the Co-op. This led to objections from the Chamber of Trade and opposition councillors, about premises in the central shopping sites on new estates going to multiples or chains, rather than individual traders. The Chamber of Trade thought that shops ought to go to ex-servicemen.

Shops were in great demand from people hoping to run their own business: there were 250 applicants for 24 retail units on the subsidiary sites around the estate.[540] Apart from the Co-op, other shops, more like the traditional corner shop, were strategically situated, including a post office on Bonney Road, run for 37 years between 1951 and 1988 by Cliff and Irene Ford. Mobile shops also added to the mix of retail outlets. For efficiency in carrying out repairs and maintenance, a House Repair Depot was included in the development, one of four across the city.[541] Other community facilities were added: churches, community centres, libraries, a fire station, and later a leisure centre with swimming pool and manager's house, approved in May 1972.

In the early days of the estate there were no community or meeting facilities for residents. They had to meet in what was New Parks House. The first community

539 Nash and Reeder, p.22
540 *Leicester Chronicle*, 28 February 1948
541 *Leicester Mercury*, 15 March 1950

centre, on Aikman Avenue, was built of timber until it was relocated to a new brick built building on St Oswald Road, now the New Parks Hub. Parks Medical Centre on New Parks Boulevard received planning permission in 1981. A library was built on Elgin Avenue, to the rear of the Aikman Avenue shops, replaced by a new modern library incorporating other facilities in 2011.

Despite acute shortages of materials and labour, making it hard to meet house-building targets, by the end of the 1950s there were five times as many Council tenants across Leicester than there had been in the period 1946 to 1951.[542] Advertisements placed by contractors offering construction workers jobs building the estate appeared regularly throughout the building period. 'Bricklayers, labourers and scaffolders, good bonus, long job,' invited potential workers to apply to W. Deane Limited on site at Frolesworth Road.[543]

Another of the construction firms engaged in building New Parks was Sherriff and Company Limited, based on two sites used as depots. They were constantly advertising for staff throughout this period. 'Bricklayers and bricklayers' labourers wanted, generous bonus terms and two years' work guaranteed for good men,' was one advertisement inviting workers to apply in person to the site agents for New Parks Estate, based at Hamelin Road School or the company's Barkby Road works. Another, posted in the *Leicester Mercury* on the same day in July 1950, called for, 'Plasterers and labourers, at least one year's work to suitable men.' The job offered good bonus rates and candidates were asked to come to the Western Park School site on New Parks Estate.[544]

To finish off the new neighbourhood and create an attractive environment in which to live, the Corporation accepted a tender of £22,450 to clean up after the building works and to add finishing touches, including grass verges.[545] For the residents this was a contrast to the cobbled and paved terraced streets of the areas of the city from which they had moved away. Nationally, the Labour Government of 1945 built hundreds of thousands of homes, and in doing so transformed many people's lives by lifting them from overcrowded slums into comfortable homes with modern amenities.

For many families moving into their brand new homes, with their gardens and modern features, it was like a dream come true, despite the lack of local facilities to start with. Those moving from the poorer slum districts now had their own toilet and running water indoors for the first time, as well as the ultimate luxury of a bathroom and electricity. From the start, they began to organise themselves to create a community. A group of residents felt that in the building-up of an estate like New Parks, with people being shifted from their old homes in other parts of Leicester, that

542 Nash and Reeder, p.149
543 *Leicester Mercury*, 26 April 1950
544 *Leicester Mercury*, 31 July 1950
545 *Leicester Mercury*, 7 January 1950

Tom Murtha, outside his home on Bonney Road, Christmas 1955. (Courtesy of Tom Murtha)

a break-down in their social life would be inevitable, and so the Tenants' Association was formed in 1947 to create a feeling of community, and provided an example of good citizenship and public spiritedness.[546]

New Parks Tenants' Association acted as a pressure group and provided liaison with the Council. Its first honorary secretary was Mr H. Packer. The Association came into being when New Parks was 'an arid waste, with no shops, no proper school, no medical or health facilities, and no amenities for normal social intercourse'. Within a couple of years, it had between 800 and 900 members. Different groups met in each others' homes because of the shortage of local community facilities.

The Association had its own magazine, *The Voice*, edited by teacher Mr T.S. Foss. Through its pages, it led campaigns for a day nursery, public telephones, school meals, playgrounds, a resident doctor, gates and fences, a library, community centre, street lighting and new schools. After just two years in existence, it could proudly boast that every facility that exists or is in progress, had either been hastened or granted because of pressure by the Tenants' Association.[547]

The first bus service to New Parks, provided by Midland Red, began in November 1947 but tenants wanted more buses to come to the estate and the service to be extended to Kemp Road and New Parks Boulevard.[548] There was a problem of too

546 *Leicester Chronicle*, 3 December 1949
547 *Leicester Chronicle*, 3 December 1949
548 *Leicester Mercury*, 22 March 1950

Bateman Road street party, celebrating the coronation of Queen Elizabeth II, 1953. (Courtesy of Tom Murtha)

few buses caused by staff shortages. The problem of not enough public transport was an issue in the local elections to the Council in 1950. One Labour candidate in the local elections suggested that the bus operators should consider taking on older men. 'There are many men of 40 and over quite capable of doing a conductor's job', said Mr Haines, standing in De Montfort Ward. Staff shortages were eventually solved by Commonwealth immigration, including by people from the West Indies, the so-called Windrush Generation, who later, in 2018 disgracefully found their right to live and work in the UK compromised.

Problems with public transport were not entirely to do with shortages of drivers and conductors. As early as 1954, the lack of proper roads that created traffic problems in New Parks and Braunstone Frith was identified as a serious issue. The problem was that the roads were too narrow for buses to comfortably negotiate; some of the service roads were only ten feet wide. Local MP Barnett Janner raised the issue in Parliament as the problems were not caused by the Council, who no doubt got the blame, but by government regulations. When the Council applied for loans to build roads, national government never gave them enough to make them a suitable size.[549] Sacrificing some of the verges to create parking bays has helped

549 *Leicester Chronicle*, 3 April 1954

reduce these problems in the early 21st century when many more residents have cars.

Another problem was that bus fares were too expensive for working-class tenants on Saffron Lane, Braunstone and New Parks estates, who had to get into town each day, according to the view of Communist candidate for North Braunstone, David Shepherd.[550] For people who were used to living close to their place of work, reliance on public transport was problematic. New estates, like New Parks, were built away from the areas of employment around the city centre. Daily bus fares to town could be higher than expected and often cost more than any saving in rents to private landlords. This made living on the outer estates quite expensive. Sometimes employers would advertise directly to New Parks residents as a pool of potential workers seeking jobs within walking distance of their homes. For example Caprice Shoes on Fosse Road North caught the eyes of *Leicester Mercury* readers with, 'New Parks Area – Machinists, punchers and skivers wanted for ladies' fashion shoes. Good conditions and high earning capacity for experienced operators.'[551]

As well as issues to do with buses, the New Parks Tenants' Association was concerned about anti-social behaviour. At its meeting in September 1950, it sent a request to the Leicester Watch Committee to stamp out 'rowdyism', after a Bateman Road resident spoke of hooliganism by youths and girls. The resident complained that gangs of 15 to 35 gathered on the street, 'And the girls were worse than the chaps.' He claimed they were using the area as a dirt track, using foul language, and creating noise and disturbance up to 11.30pm, five nights out of seven. 'We have got to stop this before the estate is spoilt by hooligans,' was the plea.[552] In response, residents pressed for activities on the estate for young people. A letter to the *Leicester Chronicle* in November 1951 drew attention to what the writer described as 'loutish youth running wild, shouting and yelling all hours of the night and no respect for property'. The letter concluded that a boys' club would be the answer as the young people 'just needed discipline'.[553]

The New Parks Boys' Club opened soon afterwards in temporary premises. A special day for the young people, youth leaders and families was when *Coronation Street* star Philip Lowrie, who played Dennis Tanner in the soap opera, was guest of honour at the opening of a new home for the club on New Parks Boulevard on 21 August 1965. New Parks Boys' Club has been there ever since. It was extended to provide more facilities and space in 1971. One of the young people who benefited from its facilities was snooker legend Mark Selby. The club is now open to all young people, girls and boys. In June 2017, Nev Turner was awarded a British Empire Medal in recognition of many years of voluntary service to the Club and young people in the area.

---

550 *Leicester Mercury,* 3 January 1950
551 *Leicester Mercury*, 25 November 1950
552 *Leicester Mercury*, 28 September 1950
553 *Leicester Chronicle*, 3 November, 1951

Not all young people could or wanted to join the boys' club or other youth organisations. To meet the needs of teenagers, now recognised as a distinct social group, who were not members or were not in an existing youth club, a Pre-fab Youth Centre opened, organised by Mr W. Tibden, where they could meet with minimum supervision in an informal atmosphere. Here the teenagers could meet their friends, drink coffee or soft drinks or dance to pop music on the small dance floor. The Youth Centre was opened by the Lord Mayor, Harold Heard, in July 1962.[554] Harold Heard was well known locally as he owned several shops in the shopping parade on Hinckley Road.

As well as being a forum for tenants to air grievances and make suggestions for improvements, the Tenants' Association also formed the basis for more social activities. These were organised by the Association for different members of the family, including an annual New Parks Festival Week. One of the events that made up the Festival was the Tenants' Association baby show. In September 1950, the joint winners were infant twins, Michael and Christine Tracy of Bringhurst Road.[555] The following year, the baby show was won by little Rosemary Dyson of New Parks Boulevard.[556]

The New Parks Tenants' Association Drama Group formed with just ten members in 1950. Its first production was of Noël Coward's *Blithe Spirit,* which debuted at the original temporary community centre in New Parks House, before being performed again in the city centre at the YMCA Theatre.[557] Also in July 1950, there was a garden competition organised by the Tenants' Association: first prize for a flower garden was won by Mr P. Woolman of 109 Wykes Road and the winner of the prize for a vegetable garden was Mr Hemmings of 110 Aikman Avenue.[558] The entrants to the competition would have worked very hard to establish their gardens in the short time since they had moved in.

Despite the optimism of a new start in New Parks, the first residents were still struggling with the austerity of the post-war years, with its shortages and rationing. In the winter of 1950, there was a coke shortage in Leicester which led to power cuts. Priority for supplies was given to schools, hospitals, industry and, uniquely for a residential area, New Parks. This was because in the new houses, coke was the only fuel capable of being burned for space and boiler heating.[559] Power cuts for electricity were on a scheduled rota and New Parks, with electric lighting in the houses, had its first cut in early November 1950.[560]

Other buildings in New Parks, that helped it develop into a community, were three pubs, the Good Neighbours on Aikman Avenue, the Two Triangles on Kerrial Road and

554 *Leicester Chronicle*, 20 July 1962
555 *Leicester Mercury*, 25 September 1950
556 *Leicester Chronicle*, 25 August 1951
557 *Leicester Mercury*, 31 July 1950
558 *Leicester Mercury*, 17 July 1950
559 *Leicester Mercury*, 30 December 1950
560 *Leicester Mercury*, 6 November 1950

the Rocket on Stephenson Drive. Planning permission was granted to the brewery and licensed premises chain Ansell's to build a pub on the corner of Aikman Avenue and Kay Road in June 1954. The new pub was to be called The Everest in honour of the first ascent of that mountain the year before. An illuminated sign bearing this name received planning approval in July 1955. Ansell's, however, had a change of heart or perhaps the excitement about Tensing and Hillary conquest of the peak had died down, as in 1956, a new application was made to change the name on the sign to the Good Neighbours Inn. The Two Triangles was sold in 2009, demolished and ten houses built on the site for East Midlands Housing. The Rocket, owned by Everard's Brewery, was granted planning permission in 1956 and opened in 1958. It closed down in 2015 and was replaced by a One Stop supermarket and fish and chip shop. Another venue where local people could meet to socialise and enjoy entertainment was the New Parks Social Club, built in 1951 with the help of the volunteer labour of its members. The Club, affiliated to the network of working men's clubs, the CIU, was rebuilt on the same site in 1968, with a large concert hall that could seat up to 700 people.

New Parks is now a mature community, where some families have lived for several generations. Community organisations such as the New Parks Community Panel, led by a team of volunteers including Lindsay Peberdy, provide support and activities that improve the lives of many residents. The running of the New Parks Community Centre was taken over and renamed The Hub by the Team Troupers Dance Academy, led by Joanne Randall with a team of volunteers, as part of the city council's Transforming Neighbourhood Services initiative that aimed to protect local services from closure in the face of government cuts and austerity in the 2010s. Not only dance lessons, but many community activities take place there for children and adults, such as annual celebrations at Halloween, Easter and Christmas, a cafe and advice sessions.

With many residents having bought their council home under the 'right to buy' scheme New Parks is now a mixed neighbourhood of council and private tenants, and owner occupiers.

Braunstone Frith

On the opposite, south-west side of Glenfield Road which becomes Dominion Road, and to the west of New Parks Way, the estate extended into the area formerly part of Braunstone Frith Farm and Western Park Dairy. This area developed into Braunstone Frith, with its own distinct identity. After World War Two, the aerodrome at Braunstone Frith was acknowledged as being too close to houses and its license to operate was not renewed. Houses were built at Braunstone Frith and Western Park Golf Course relocated to what had been the grounds of Kirby Frith Hall and Farm.

The area nearest to Hinckley Road became the Scudamore Road industrial estate on the site of the former aerodrome.

Braunstone Frith shopping parade, taken in 2021.

In 1952 plans were approved for 350 Easiform houses around Cokayne Road. In it early days, there were few facilities for those who moved into the brand new houses at Braunstone Frith. Mobile shops brought grocery supplies for sale to the residents. In December 1954 planning permission was given for a temporary shed to be used as a waiting room for shoppers and a paved area on which the mobile shops could stand. The first of these was on Cokayne Road, with a second on Marwood Road. A temporary wooden-framed, asbestos clad shed used for selling newspapers was given approval in October 1955. These temporary facilities would remain until permanent retail premises were built. The shopping parade on Sharmon Crescent was built by the early 1960s. Braunstone Frith soon had its own pub, the Shoemaker's, for which planning permission was granted to Ansell's brewery in December 1955 and January 1956. The pub was enlarged in 1977 and in 1985.

A new school for infants and juniors, Braunstone Frith, opened there in 1956. Shortage of space to accommodate the growing numbers of young children in the area, meant that mobile classrooms were added to the school over the years, until it was extended and modernised to include a Children's Centre in 2007.

More social housing was built by the City Council along Tatlow Road and Liberty Road, right up to and crossing the border with Glenfield in the county, when plans for 175 houses and 210 flats, including those in Dupont Gardens, Cranstone Crescent, Ibbetson Avenue and Forbes Close, were approved by Leicestershire County Council in 1962. In September 1965, plans were approved by the City Council for 72 houses and garages around Liberty Road, including on Cuffling Drive and Close and Outwoods Close. The empty Braunstone Frith Farm buildings was demolished at this time.

Braunstone Frith Farm, shortly before demolition, and new houses on Outwoods Close, 1971. (Records Office of Leicester, Leicestershire and Rutland)

More new houses were built in the 1970s off Cuffling Drive and Tatlow Road on Rowanberry Avenue, Mulberry Avenue, and Yew Tree Drive, following approval granted in April 1973 for 205 two-story houses and 136 one-bedroomed flats, car parking and garages, to be built on what had been farmland. Play equipment was installed in the open space in the middle of Sharmon Crescent in 1975.[561] The parish of St Aidan extended to include the area in 1982.

The Braunstone Frith Neighbourhood Centre for local people to meet and socialise, was built within the shopping parade on Sharmon Crescent. An active Tenants' and Residents' Association (TARA) was created to liaise between people living in the locality and Leicester City Council. Following restructuring of community and neighbourhood services by the Council, volunteers from the TARA took over the running of the Neighbourhood Centre themselves. Activities run in the Centre

561 Leicester City Council Planning Department Database.

include regular coffee mornings and Bingo sessions led by volunteers Joe Carroll and Ray Gavriel White. During the Covid-19 pandemic in 2020, a much needed food bank was run from the Neighbourhood Centre to help support families with low incomes in the area, many of whom were suffering hardship as a result of the impact of the Covid-19 pandemic.

Kirby Frith

Plans to extend housing development between the golf course, Braunstone Frith and the Scudamore Road industrial estate were not realised until the 1990s. In October 1993 plans were approved for a residential development of houses on and off Ryder Road. Fifteen per cent of these homes were to be built according to Leicester City Council's Access Housing Provision to ensure accommodation for people with disabilities. Incorporated into the estate's layout was a Nature Reserve, open amenity space and children's play area, carefully calculated to give three square metres per child's bed space or 7.5 square metres for each family dwelling. Foundation Housing Association submitted plans in 1995 to build 123 houses on 7.2 acres around Ryder Road. Then in 1996 plans for 136 more homes, submitted by KCH Designs of Wolverhampton, were approved on the Cherry Hills Road side of the estate. Plans for the play area were also approved that year, as well as a development of 152 houses by Mason Richards Partnership of Wolverhampton. A scheme for a shopping area soon followed, submitted by Richard Gley and Partners of Loughborough, so the residents of Kirby Frith had local stores, including a Tesco Express and a hot food takeaway within walking distance.[562]

Churches and worship

The first permanent church for Christian worship to be built in New Parks was the Methodist church on New Parks Boulevard. The first turf for the church's foundations was turned over by the Lord Mayor, Alderman F.E. Oliver, in July 1950, on land bought from the Council for £1,700. This followed a procession of children to the site.[563] New Parks Methodist Church took nine months to build and was dedicated and officially opened with a service on 29 September 1951. Its first minister was Revd Gordon Taylor. Even before the church building was erected, the Methodists were active in the area. The New Parks Methodist Sisterhood, led by Pat Hopkin with support from women who worshipped at Trinity Methodist, met in the homes of its members and helped with a Sunday School from 1947. In January 1950 the Sisterhood gave 465 local children a tea in the temporary huts of Forest Lodge School.[564]

---

562 Leicester City Council Planning Department database.
563 *Leicester Mercury*, 29 July 1950
564 *Leicester Mercury*, 16 January 1957

The temporary St Aidan's Church, c.1955.

For Anglican worship, the temporary Church of St Aidan's first met, under the leadership of the priest in charge, Revd Donald McCloud, in the hall of New Parks House School or, as it was also known at the time, the White House School. This was the former New Parks House, once home to the Stokes and Aikman families, at that time the only space available for community activity until others were created. St Aidan's first Harvest Festival was held there in 1946 and the first Sunday School festival also took place there in June 1950. There were special hymns and two children, Michael Morris and Janet Hutchcroft, read the lessons.[565] Since 1904, New Parks had been incorporated into the parish of St Augustine but in 1946 St Aidan's became a separate parish.

The site of the permanent St Aidan's Church, between New Parks Boulevard and St Oswald's Road was acquired for the Church of England community in 1954. A new hall, designed by architect A.L. Sharpe, was dedicated as a place of worship at the beginning of April 1955.[566] That same year, the Bishop of Leicester heard from his counterpart in Coventry that renowned architect Sir Basil Spence had supplied low-cost designs for three parish churches in that city. The Leicester Bishop contacted Spence, informing him that he had a 'modest amount of money' put aside to be spent on building a church. As a result of this and some legacies, the Diocese was able to commission the firm of Sir Basil Spence and Partners to design and build a new church for St Aidan's. The first turf was cut after the Bishop blessed the site from the roof of the new flats on Aikman Avenue. The foundation stone was laid in 1958

565 *Leicester Mercury*, 26 June 1950
566 *Leicester Mercury*, 2 April 1955

St Aidan's Church, taken in 2021.

Advertisement for the Estate Bingo Club at St Aidan's, 1960s.

and the modern church building was completed and consecrated in July 1959, with Revd Harvey D. Rowe as its first vicar. Spence, who designed the new Coventry Cathedral, created a simple church with a cloister and bell tower, that could hold up to 350 people.

Like much of New Parks, St Aidan's made use of innovative building techniques: it is mainly made up of steel-framed components, in-filled with exposed brick, with ceilings and panels above the cloister windows which are faced with timber. The church furnishings, such as candle holders, lectern pews and hymn boards were also designed by Spence's firm. In the entrance porch is a ceramic mural depicting St Aidan, designed by William Gordon.[567] As well as a place to worship, like most faith facilities, St Aidan's provides secular social activities, for instance its hall was the venue for the Estate Bingo Club in the early 1960s.[568]

Residents of the Roman Catholic faith had their own place of worship from 1957, Mother of God Church, at the corner of New Parks Boulevard and Glenfield Road. Since 1947 there had been a Catholic mission established by Father Gilleran from St Peter's Church. The new building, designed by Manchester architects Reynolds and Scott at a cost of £32,400 when it opened in October 1957, could seat 400 worshippers. The coming of a new parish priest in 1964, Canon Bernard Allen, saw the building of a new presbytery and parish hall, which were completed in 1967. The east end of the church was also re-ordered at the time. The initial debt for building costs was paid off in 1975 when the church was redecorated, an altar crucifix installed and the church consecrated.

Mother of God Church has a dramatic interior, with a long nave defined by a series of tall parabolic arches. It is partly aisled on both sides, with squat stair towers with hipped roofs at the west end of each windowless aisle. The sanctuary is paved with marble, with marble communion rails and pulpit. There is also a baptistry

567 Notes on Sir Basil Spence, Canmore, National Record of the Historic Environment, https://canmore.org.uk/site/287590/leicester-new-parks-boulevard-st-aidans-church, accessed 4 April 2020

568 *Leicester Chronicle*, 26 May 1961

Mother of God Church, taken in 2021.

and a sacristy.[569] Mother of God Church is part of the Roman Catholic diocese of Nottingham and in the 21st century serves a diverse community, with masses in both English and the south-west Indian language, Malayalam, led by priest Father George Thomas Chelackal who succeeded Father Nellikulam.

The Salvation Army joined the other places of Christian worship fronting on to New Parks Way, when planning permission to build its hall was granted in May 1977. This has served as a community hall, cafe and charity shop. There is a Jehovah's Witnesses Kingdom Hall on New Parks Boulevard and a Church of Latter Day Saints on Glenfield Road, near the junction with Gimson Road.

A small community of the Islamic faith meets for prayers on Fridays in the Hub and hopes to one day have its own premises for worship.

Schools

Alongside building thousands of new houses, Leicester City Corporation also had to plan for the education of younger residents of the new estates. Devised in the wake of the 1944 Education Act, the city's Development Plan, published in 1946, included plans for new single-sex secondary modern schools, a few technical schools in existing intermediate schools, and for six existing and two newly designated grammar schools which were transferred to the local Education Committee and would no longer accept fee-paying pupils. This was an important change as before the War, in 1938, only 13 per cent of 13-year-old children were in education. Although segregated as single-sex

569 Taking Stock – Catholic churches of England and Wales, Leicester Mother of God, https://taking-stock.org.uk/building/leicester-mother-of-god/ accessed 4 April 2020

schools were the preference, because the need for school places was so urgent, by 1952 there were already two co-educational secondary schools in Leicester, where boys and girls were educated together.[570] These were Crown Hills and Wycliffe. Some of the young people from New Parks had to study at Wycliffe as there was no secondary school nearby until a couple of years later.

The corporation's building programme for 1949 was announced in August 1948, when plans were in motion for eight new primary schools in Leicester. Included in this scheme were Forest Lodge and New Parks House infants and junior schools.[571] There were also plans for four new secondary schools to be built on the original site of Western Park Golf Course. These were first devised before the war when plans were made for the new estate, but the schemes had been held up due to lack of approval from the Ministry of Education that controlled school building. The four anticipated schools were New Parks Girls and New Parks Boys, plus the grammar schools, Alderman Newton's Boys and Alderman Newton's Girls, which were to be relocated from the city centre and enlarged.[572] The Development Plan would locate all four schools side-by-side in a campus setting, but this project had to wait a little longer.

As more families moved in to their new homes in New Parks, the problem of insufficient places for infant and junior school age children remained which was not overcome until the completion of New Parks House School in 1952. The plans for primary schools to cater for the younger children who moved into New Parks began with the creation of New Parks House School on Pindar Road began on 31 March 1947. The school was set in 11.5 acres of the grounds of the former home of the Stokes and Aikman families. After the Aikman family had vacated the property a caretaker, Emmanuel Briggs (born 1869), a former railway employee, had lived in the building.[573] Briggs died in Hillcrest Hospital, the former workhouse, in 1948, so by then the house was empty.

The first 164 younger school-age children were admitted to New Parks House Infant School on 2 June 1947. Like many others at the time, the school began with classrooms in temporary huts while building work went on around them. By 1950 there were 634 children on roll.[574] Like Western Park Open Air School 20 or so years earlier, New Parks House was designed by James Osbert Thompson, surveyor to the Education Committee. The frame of the structure was made with steel, salvaged from the wartime ARP, with cavity walls faced with brick on the outside and breeze blocks inside. The construction project was executed by city architect, J.H. Lloyd Owen and

570 John Mander: *Leicester Schools 1944–1974*, Leicester City Council, 1980, p.39
571 Mander, p.45
572 Mander, p.133
573 1939 Register
574 Mander, p.45

built by contractors, J. Chapman and Sons of Welford Road. It took 18 months longer to build the school than at first envisaged and cost £23,000 more than the original estimate of £32,290, because of the price of the steel, rising labour and materials costs and abnormal site conditions. By 1950, the final cost was projected to reach £55,290, still judged to be value for money by the City Architect and Cllr Walter Oram, the Labour chairman of the Education Committee, despite accusations of inefficiency from the opposition.

New Parks Junior school opened on the same site a little later, in 1952, with 373 children aged between seven and 11 years old. The number on roll rose to a peak of 841 in 1957, but by 1963 the post-war bulge in pupil numbers had passed and the number of pupils was a comfortable 376.[575]

Another new school for younger children was under way from May 1949 on land between Charnor Road and New Parks Boulevard. Desperately needed classrooms were provided by an aluminium-framed, prefabricated construction, with brick built halls and administration blocks at a cost of £40,000. The aluminium components for the permanent classrooms, perhaps wartime surplus from aircraft construction, were delivered by huge lorries from the Bristol Aviation Company, a sight that excited the children watching from their temporary wooden classrooms. The school would provide education for both infant and junior school aged children and was named Forest Lodge after Leicester Forest and the nearby Bird's Nest lodge.

The first headteacher of the Forest Lodge infant section was Miss M.M.I. Newton and the junior school head was Mr H. Chesterton. Initially, before building work was completed, temporary accommodation was provided in pale blue-coloured wooden huts holding eight classes. These admitted nearly 100 children on 11 July 1949, followed by 131 to the junior school on 19 September 1949.[576] These huts had been discovered lying derelict beside the River Thames at Fulham in 1946 and were relocated to Forest Lodge where they were in use for just over a year. The rise in the birth rate following the war and many families moving to New Parks, resulted in a huge demand for school places. Despite its small beginnings, Forest Lodge Junior School had 1,066 children there in 1957, a record locally as it was the only Leicester school at the time to have more than a thousand pupils on roll. This number gradually declined as the demographic of the post-war baby boom bulge grew older and moved through the education system.

By the 21st century the post-war buildings of Forest Lodge were inadequate to meet the needs of New Parks children. The school was rebuilt between 2015 and 2016 as part of Leicester City Council's Building Schools for the Future programme, a legacy of the Labour Government before 2010. On 26 January 2017, to the delight of the children, the new Forest Lodge was officially reopened by Claudio Ranieri, the

575 Mander, p.45
576 Booklet, DMU Special Collections; Leicester Mercury, 16 January 1950

Claudio Ranieri at the official opening of the rebuilt Forest Lodge Primary School, 26 January 2017.

manager of Leicester City FC, the recent English Premier League-winning team. The Premier League trophy was brought along and children and guests were able to be photographed with it, sharing in the excitement of the local football team's success of only a few months before.

In the beginning of December 1950, Minister of Education George Tomlinson came to Leicester to officially open seven new schools on the same day, including Forest Lodge, New Parks House and also Braunstone Temporary School in Braunstone Park and Wycliffe Secondary School where some New Parks children were educated.[577]

Other primary schools serving the New Parks area are Parks Primary on New Parks Crescent, another school built on the land around New Parks House, and the later addition on an almost adjacent site, Stokes Wood Primary. Work on the Gillman Road Infants School or Parks Primary as it became known, began in January 1950. Unfortunately work was delayed by hooliganism and the theft of building equipment that held up the construction work. The firm working on the construction of the school was J.C. Chapman and Sons Limited whose seven huts on the site were vandalised and broken into.[578] Stokes Wood Primary School opened in 1972, originally in a temporary building on Blackett Avenue, for children who moved into the Stokes Drive Estate off Groby Road. Its name recalls the Stokes family who once owned the land and who built and lived in New Parks House. Both Parks Primary and Stokes Wood schools are close to Stokes Wood Park.

Following the Education Act of 1944, which raised the school leaving age to 15 from the academic year 1947 to 1948, and which provided a free secondary education

577 *Leicester Mercury*, 2 December 1950
578 *Leicester Mercury*, 23 February, 1950

to every young person for the first time, three new schools were built side-by-side on Greencoat Road, off Glenfield Road. Although the original intention had been to build four new secondary schools, only two secondary modern schools, one for girls and one for boys, were planned for New Parks at this stage, to accommodate 680 young people in each at a cost of £161,000. Nevertheless, the Minister of Education delayed giving his approval, despite the desperate need for school places for the increased numbers of pupils entering compulsory, free secondary education for the first time.[579]

There was also an additional plan to relocate two grammar schools. At the age of 11, children took the 11–plus examination during their last year in primary school. The minority, up to 20 per cent, who scored highest in the tests, could attend a grammar school that offered an education system that emulated that offered in public schools. At grammar school teenagers were expected to stay on and take GCE O level examinations at the age of 16, which replaced the School Certificate in 1951. Some could even stay on to take A-levels at the age of 18, all free of charge. This provided a route into university for a few or into better-paid office jobs. A small cohort who had narrowly missed passing the 11-plus exam, went to intermediate technical schools. The majority of children, about 67 per cent in Leicester, went to a secondary modern school, many of them leaving at the age of 15 to work in local factories. Another important educational change of the time was that married women were allowed to work as teachers for the first time. Previously only single women were employed who had to give up their profession if they married.

It was disappointing that the two proposed secondary modern schools for New Parks were still excluded from the Ministry of Education's list for building in 1951, even though plans for two buildings, both of which could accommodate 680 students at a cost of £161,000 each, had been in place for some time.[580] There was no information about when they might be given the go-ahead, despite the urgent need. In 1950 there were 1,843 senior children from New Parks and Dane Hills going to the nearest existing alternative schools, a figure projected to reach 2,175 by 1953 and 2,801 by 1955.[581] When approval was finally given, the Local Education Authority was constrained by agreements made years before, in 1939, which tied the Education Committee to the services of the architect they had appointed at the time. Based on the original conception of the estate development, New Parks Boys and Girls Schools were built 'back-to-front', with their fine or polite facades overlooking the playing fields and the service areas facing the road. As a result of the influence of the Ministry of Education, there was little accommodation in the buildings for practical education, just 'practical alcoves' in each classroom, something that would be expensive to rectify in the future.

579 *Leicester Mercury*, 2 September and 5 September 1950
580 *Leicester Mercury*, 2 September 1950
581 *Leicester Mercury*, 6 September 1950

Another missed opportunity was a proposal to organise education in New Parks on a comprehensive basis from the start. By the time the comprehensive idea was raised, it was too late as the headmaster and senior staff of the boys' school had already been appointed with the aim to establish and develop a secondary modern school for boys from what was expected to be a 'difficult' area. The Education Committee discussed a memorandum from the Director of Education in June 1954, accepting that the two New Parks Secondary Modern School buildings would not, in themselves, prove adequate as the basis for a comprehensive school.[582] A note in the Education Committee's Annual Report in 1955 said, 'Much thought has been given by the Committee to the organisation of secondary education on the New Parks Estate where conditions appeared favourable for a possible comprehensive school experiment. As a proposal on these lines did not command the co-operation and support essential for an experiment of its kind, the Committee abandoned the idea.'[583] New Parks' Boys and Girls' Schools finally opened as separate single-sex establishments in 1954. The schools merged in 1981 to become New Parks Secondary School before another change of name to New Parks Community College, which offered a wider range of subjects and adult education classes, until it finally closed in 1999.

Another idea that had to be abandoned was the proposed inclusion of Alderman Newton's Boys' School on the site. There had been discussions about making Alderman Newton's Girls' a comprehensive by merging with the other schools, but its governors were opposed to the idea.[584] Another plan to merge the selective girls' school with the Junior Art Department and Gateway Girls on Elbow Lane to create a specialist girls' technical school went ahead, despite protests from Gateway parents and staff. The new Alderman Newton's Girls' School building was ready to move into in 1959 and the schools relocated there, but the curriculum developed as a normal grammar school rather than as a technical school. There were 375 girls in the school when the new building, with facilities for science, art, music, a gym and playing fields, was officially opened by former Alderman Newton's Boys' scholar and acclaimed author C.P. Snow. The green uniform worn by the girls at Alderman Newton's gave the road beside it, Greencoat Road, its name. Unlike the inner-city schools, mostly erected as Board Schools before 1903, both Alderman Newton's Girls' and the two New Parks Secondary Modern schools were institutions blessed with playing fields and modern facilities.

In the early 1960s the Education Committee, led by Labour councillor Charles Keene, initiated further discussions on whether to convert the schools on the New Parks site to a comprehensive system, where young people of all abilities would be educated together, a system already in operation in the county of Leicestershire.

582 Mander, p.133
583 Mander, p.132
584 Mander, p.134

This proposal was defeated by the local opposition but a compromise was eventually reached, which was to extend the opportunity to take O level examinations as well as CSEs in secondary modern schools and to abolish the intermediate schools.[585]

In 1977 Alderman Newton Girls' school merged with Alderman Newton Boys' to become a non-selective comprehensive school, for students aged 11 to 18, serving a local catchment area like New Parks Community College next door. The school closed on 31 August 1999 with Mr D. Butler as the last headteacher.

After New Parks and Alderman Newton schools closed, a new school was created by the merger of them both with Wycliffe Community College, which had mainly served the Braunstone Estate. The new larger school was on the same site where Alderman Newton and New Parks had been and was named New College Leicester. It opened during the academic year of 1999/2000. In 2010 it became a co-educational Foundation School, run by a board of trustees which includes representatives of Leicester City Council, Wyggeston and Queen Elizabeth I College and the CfBT Education Trust. The school was partially rebuilt as part of the Building Schools for the Future scheme, work being completed in spring 2015. This was half funded in the conventional manner and half through the controversial Private Finance Initiative. New College Leicester accommodated around 1,050 students by 2020, mainly from the New Parks, Braunstone Frith, Western Park and Braunstone areas. It has specialist sports facilities, including a gymnastics centre, football pitches and a cycling circuit which opened in 2016. These facilities are open to the public to use when not in use by students.

Within Western Park, the former Civil Defence Depot, near the gates off Hinckley Road became King Richard III School, what was called an intermediate school. Technical schools were another innovation of the 1944 Education Act which introduced a so-called tripartite system of three types of secondary school, intended to offer an education leading to skilled work in engineering and technical professions. In Leicester, there were already a small number of what were designated as Intermediate schools and these were used to provide this sector of the system. Technical or Intermediate schools were selective but less elitist than the grammar schools, catering for about ten per cent of pupils who were assessed as border-line, just missing the level of mark needed to pass their 11–plus examination.[586]

The Civil Defence Depot in the park was extended by the addition of HORSA huts, made by the Ministry of works, which provided light, airy and warm teaching accommodation. HORSA was an acronym for the 'Hutting Operation for the Raising of the School-leaving Age'. These were made of concrete and timber with corrugated roofs, which arrived as flat packs. Pupils were no longer assessed for Intermediate schools from 1961 and such enrolment ceased. King Dick's, as it was known locally,

585 Nash and Reeder, p.141
586 Mander, p.58

remained on the Western Park site until 1966 when the buildings were handed over to the Parks Department and the school became based on Fullhurst Avenue.

Christ the King was the first new school to be built in the Roman Catholic Diocese of Nottingham. In December 1950, 500 people watched the Bishop of Nottingham, Dr Edward Ellis, lay the foundation stone for the building on the site of Ashleigh, the former Gimson residence on Glenfield Road. The lower floor of Ashleigh is incorporated into the school building and some original features remain inside. Construction costs for the school, which could accommodate 280 infant and junior pupils, came to £72,000 and were met by the Leicester Catholic Community, with the council funding the dining and medical inspection rooms, and the school's running costs. The first pupils joined the school in September 1951, with the official opening by the Bishop of Nottingham taking place in June 1952. Christ the King provides an education based on principles of the Roman Catholic Christian faith for primary school children from across west Leicester, not just the local catchment area. With high demand for school places, in 2015 the infants department of Christ the King relocated into the former Emiley Fortey School buildings further up Glenfield Road, vacated by West Gate School when its new building opened.

Leicester showed how progressive it was in the field of education for children with additional or special needs when a new school was built on land off Glenfield Road, next to Western Park. At that time special needs provision was the responsibility of the Health Committee but what was ground breaking about the project was that it was actually called a school rather than an 'occupation centre', a recognition that children with learning disabilities had the right to an education and could learn. The new school was named Emily Fortey, after Leicester's first female Labour councillor, elected in 1923 for St Margaret's Ward. A scientist, trained midwife and social worker, Emily Fortey had always been supportive of people with disabilities. Coincidentally, she was a Western Park resident, whose home was on Meadhurst Road. The Emily Fortey School was opened in early September 1956 by the Minister for Health, Robin Turton and show business performer, Dave Gorman, who was to appear in the Palace Theatre's pantomime.[587] The first intake of young people, aged between 11 and 18, were transferred from a centre on Fosse Road and for the first time could say they went to school and not to a centre, an important step towards parity of esteem and equality.

On the opposite side of Glenfield Road, another school for children with learning disabilities, also opened in 1956. This was Greenacres, for pupils aged four to 19. This school closed in 1995 and a new school for children with disabilities, Piper Way, opened in its place on the same site. Reorganisation in 2005 saw the merger of Piper Way and Emily Fortey schools to form West Gate, initially based on the existing sites on both sides of Glenfield Road. In 2014, a new building opened on the former Piper Way site for 185 students aged between four and 19, with a range of disabilities and

587 *Leicester Evening Mail*, 5 February 1957

learning difficulties. This left the former Emily Forte site vacant, with Christ the King Infants School moving in a year later.

Post-war private housing

The private developer Jelley's, now branded as Jelson, continued their building projects to develop privately owned suburban housing after the War's end. On 8 March 1949, planning permission was sought to build 30 houses on the south side of Glenfield Road (numbers 112 to 134), and on a new road. This new road was to be the cul-de-sac, Brampton Avenue. This scheme progressed slowly at first, perhaps because of the licensing issues for private housing developers and shortages of labour already mentioned. The plans were amended in July 1949 to include 17 semi-detached houses, two more homes than in the original application. The development was not completed immediately, as in January 1956 a new application was made for six pairs of semi-detached and three detached houses on Glenfield Road and Brampton Avenue. A visit to Brampton Avenue will show that the houses built in the 1950s are substantially different to those completed before the war. Three distinct styles illustrate the different stages of the development.

A gated gap and track was left between 134 and 136 Glenfield Road, to provide access to St Andrew's Methodist Church's tennis club to the rear of the properties, for which planning permission for the sports club pavilion, designed by local architect Charles W. Christian of Westcotes Drive, was granted by Blaby District Council in 1923, when it was still outside the city's boundaries. Further up Glenfield Road, permission was given to build a pair of semi-detached houses, on a plot of land to become 196 and 198 Glenfield Road in March 1961. This was not by one of the property development companies but by private individuals, the executors of the late J.W. Faulks. The application was altered the following year, and a detached bungalow was built instead of the pair of houses.[588]

Approval to extend Letchworth Road across Glenfield Road for more owner-occupied housing and to develop the land between Hilders Road and Aikman Avenue was granted to Jelson in 1950. Permission was given for 189 homes and six shops on what was to become Lindfield Road with the cul-de-sacs off it, Poynings, Lancing and Ditchling Avenues. The shops do not seem to have materialised. This was an extension of Jelley's pre-war Dane Hills Estate, which included the cul-de-sac Danehurst Close, and the semi-detached houses on the Woodville Road end of Glenfield Road, built in 1937 and completed by 1939.[589]

At the other end of Letchworth Road, in the 1960s, builders W.A. Blackburn began to develop a modern estate on land in what was once a market garden in the

588 Leicester City Council Planning Database
589 Leicester City Council Planning Database

former garden of the Gimson's house, Ashleigh. This had been offered for sale by auction in six lots in 1945, when a plan showed that there was a central pond and a new road envisaged around the perimeter of the plot. The stables and a few old cottages were still standing in 1972. Permission to build on the site was first sought in September 1964 by Brightside Investment Company Limited of London, in an outline application to erect houses, shops and a pub. This application was refused because the layout was judged to be unsatisfactory. The introduction of a large group of shops and a pub in an area primarily allocated for residential use was inconsistent with the City Development Plan.

The noise and additional traffic for such a development would have had an adverse effect on the quiet enjoyment of the neighbouring residents. Nevertheless, planning permission to erect 14 semi-detached houses, 70 terraced ones, eight flats, six shops and a supermarket in the area at the top of Nevanthon Road, on the continuation of Clarefield Road, was first given the go-ahead in November 1966, albeit with no pub. A year later permission to build 16 semi-detached properties, 19 terraced houses and some garages was granted. Plans were revised in January 1971, to include ten maisonettes, six additional terraced homes and ten shops.[590] Denis Close was the name given to the new enclave. At the same time, this development opened up Letchworth Road to through traffic, the end of which had so far been an unadopted cul-de-sac. The road was adopted by the Council in 1970 when the route became connected to Nevanthon Road and Clarefield Road. An unusual name, it is claimed that the name Nevanthon is a combination of the two names Neville and Anthony who were connected to the development. There is also a Neville Road close by. Surprisingly, the Letchworth Road pavements remained unadopted by the city council until September 2007.[591] Residents took out private insurance to cover themselves in case there was an accident outside their house, for which they could be liable.

The Co-operative Society Dairy off Glenfield Road between Gimson Road and Neville Road, which was built in the 1920s was replaced by modern detached houses in the 1990s. The demise of the dairy's tall chimney featured in a television programme when it was demolished in 1993 by celebrity steeplejack and mechanic, Fred Dibnah. Plans for 30 houses with garages on the site, built by Redrow Homes, were approved in April 1992.

On the north side of Glenfield Road, near to St Catherine's Convent, an area that contained a disused sand quarry was developed for housing built on the new cul-de-sacs, Ambrose Close and Vincent Close. The initial planning application for this was made by Maynard and Company of Derby, acting on behalf of the convent. Plans were submitted in January 1978 and approved in the following May. The plans were

590 Leicester City Council Planning Database
591 Letter to resident of Letchworth Road from Leicester City Council, dated 10 September 2007.

amended in November 1979, with the final approval for three additional houses with garages given on 1 May 1980. When the convent closed, the nuns moved into a house on the opposite side of Glenfield Road and St Catherine's, which had been run as a nursing home, was bought by Leicester Housing Association in 1997 and opened as Highpoint Conference Centre in 2002, with a 130-seat conference theatre, 12 meeting rooms, a restaurant, bar and en-suite bedrooms. Highpoint closed in 2012. It was converted to a care home in around 2012 which stood empty until it was bought by the Alexandra Care Group in 2014. After investment of £5m, the building reopened as Dane View Care Home in 2018, offering residential support and nursing care for people with dementia and younger people who have had serious head injuries.

There was further housing development to the west of Western Park in the triangle of land between the park, railway line and New Parks Way during the 1970s. This new estate was built by Percy Bilton (Homes) Limited of Ealing on land that had been the fields of Western Park Farm, whose farm house still stands on Park View. Planning permission for new housing was granted in stages from around 1970 for Park Rise, Park View, Green Walk, Shire Close and Ashlyns Close. Wessex Drive was the last section to be completed, with plans for the terraced houses there submitted in 1978. This was a mixed development of properties of different sizes, from large detached houses, through semi-detached, to small terraced homes and maisonettes, including some social housing. A new public house to serve the community was the Sportsman, named because of its proximity to the pitches on Western Park. This was given planning permission in 1975 with amended plans approved in 1977.[592] A row of shops with living accommodation above serves the needs of local residents.

The estate is completely different in character to the pre-war and immediate post-war housing. The front gardens are all open-plan, without the boundary walls and hedges along the frontages that emphasised the individual plots of the earlier period. It took a while for some people, familiar with the older style of housing, to get used to these modern housing designs; 'rabbit hutches' was a term often used in popular culture to describe them and the contemporary development off Nevanthon Road. However, these houses remained relatively low-density with wide roads, grass verges and private rear gardens. A proposal by a private developer to build six new modern town houses on an area of land known as the Green, between existing homes near the Sportsman was made in January 2021.

Scudamore Road Industrial Estate

It wasn't until 1960 that the former Braunstone aerodrome site was allocated for a new industrial estate, to relocate some of the industrial and business premises that would need to be compulsorily purchased and demolished as part of the redevelopment of

592 Leicester City Council Planning Database

Advertisement for Reid cameras, made by Reid and Sigrist, c.1950.

the city centre and creation of the new ring road. Already occupying premises on the site was Reid and Sigrist, who had operated there since before World War Two, manufacturing aeronautical instruments, servicing planes and running the Civilian Flying Training School at Desford Aerodrome. Production at Braunstone diversified when in 1945 the government gave Reid and Sigrist the contract to produce a high quality camera for military use. This camera, branded the Reid, was based on models of the German prestige brand Leica, the plans for which had been captured during the War. Production was simplified, for what would otherwise have been an unauthorised copy, when all German patents were abolished in 1947. The lens for these high-grade cameras were provided by Leicester firm Taylor Hobson. Decca Records took over Reid and Sigrist in 1954.

Another of the first firms to be based on the industrial estate was AEI who secured a 600,000 sq ft site between Hinckley Road and Scudamore Road. A futuristic satellite dish attached to the building was a fascinating and unusual site associated with space exploration, in the days before satellite television or mobile phones. A merger of AEI with GEC, English Electric and Marconi led by Lord Weinstock, formed the GEC Group. Rationalisation and a move into electronics led to the firm's expansion on the site.[593]

Fox's was an iconic brand founded in Leicester in 1880. The confectionery manufacturer, famous as the maker of Glacier Mints from 1918 and other sweets, moved from Oxford Street to Sunningdale Road on the new industrial estate in 1967. Fox's was taken over by the Rowntree Mackintosh Group in 1969 and later became part of the Big Bear Group. A scaling down of operations there and the closure of the site was announced in 2019, when production became concentrated in Pontefract and Blackpool. The Fox's factory was sold in late 2020 to Leicestershire metal-working firm ADS Laser Cutting, a business planning to expand.[594]

Charlie Clore of Sears' Holdings purchased a 45-acre site in 1962 and the massive British Shoe Corporation premises opened there in January 1964.[595] The head office of British Shoe was established on the site, alongside one of the biggest warehouses of its time. The blue double-decker buses carrying workers out to British Shoe were a familiar site in Leicester until the massive warehouse closed in 1998. The site was demolished by 2016.

Another long-established Leicester firm that relocated to a purpose-built factory on the industrial estate in 1975 was knitting machine manufacturer Stibbe Machinery, founded in 1888 by Gompert Stibbe. However, its move was unsuccessful as it coincided with a decline in the market for textile manufacturing equipment and because the company had not managed to sell its city centre premises before the

593 Nash and Reeder (eds), p.72
594 *Leicester Mercury*, 30 November 2020
595 Beazley, p.151

British Shoe Corporation. (Records Office of Leicester, Leicestershire and Rutland)

move.[596] Despite being winners of the Queen's Award for Industry in 1972, the firm went bankrupt and went into liquidation by 1976.

An established and popular organisation based on the industrial estate since the 1970s is the Woodside Animal Sanctuary, which operates as the local branch of the RSPCA. It has kennels, a cattery and enclosures for larger and small animals, mostly waiting to be re-homed. There is also a shop selling products for pets on the site.

The Scudamore Road area has attracted new investment at Braunstone Frith, on the former aerodrome site. Samworth Brothers Supply Chain established a massive new distribution centre for its food products there, open 24 hours a day, in 2017 on the former site of the British Shoe Corporation. Samworth has incongruously named this 155,000 sq ft, high-tech warehouse 'Oak Meadow'. This is a national hub with facilities for storing chilled and frozen food. The Central England Co-operative has also opened a huge food distribution hub on Scudamore Road, which employs around 300 workers. The building is 120,000 sq ft, the size of six Olympic swimming pools. In 2019 the new distribution centre delivered 30 million cases of products to over 200 Co-op stores.

The Local Plan for Leicester, under consultation in 2020, included a proposal for the expansion of the industrial estate on the other side of Scudamore Road, on to some of the land of the former Western Park Golf Course. A decision was awaited in 2021.

596 Nash and Reeder, p.75

POST SCRIPT

This book is an attempt to tell the story so far of an area that since 2015 has seen its different communities combined to form the Western ward of Leicester City Council. Although Western is a recent political and administrative construct brought about by boundary changes reflecting population changes, the book shows that what might be seen as distinct neighbourhoods actually share a history as part of Leicester Forest, the Frith and the enclosure of the New Park in the sixteenth century. The Braunstone Frith, Kirby Frith, New Parks and Western Park we see now are the product of centuries of change brought about by human activities and interaction with the landscape and environment which over the last millennium saw the transformation of the area from a park for hunting by landholding elites with some common rights for local villagers and townspeople governed by Forest Law, through the enclosure that created the New Park that evolved into pasture and arable farm land owned by a few individuals to the exclusion of the majority. Changes in the agrarian economy and urban population growth led to the breaking up of the country estates, the sale of the farms and their division into smaller parcels of land for the creation of Western Park as public open space for the people of the West End of Leicester, soon followed by the suburban housing developments of the twentieth century.

This process of change continues in the twenty-first century. *Park to Parks* is not the end of the story. New discoveries about the past continually add to our understanding of how the area developed and no doubt new knowledge will soon update this history. The process of change is continuous and soon new developments for housing, employment for new communities and succeeding generations will add to the evolving story.

SELECT BIBLIOGRAPHY

Secondary sources

Baldwin, David: Richard III, Amberley Publishing, Stroud, 2013

Banbury, Paul: The Leicester and Swannington Railway In a Nutshell, Leicestershire Industrial History Society, 2014

Barton Susan and Brodie, Allan (eds): Travel and Tourism in Britain, 1700–1914, Pickering Chatto, London, 2014

Barton, Susan: Healthy Living in the Alps: the origins of winter tourism in Switzerland, 1860–1914, Manchester University Press, 2008

Barton, Susan: Working-class organisations and popular tourism, 1840–1970, Manchester University Press, 2005

Bateson, M.: Records of the Borough of Leicester, II, xx, 60

Beazley, Ben: Post War Leicester, Alan Sutton Publishing, Avon, 2006

Cartwright, Terence C.: Bird's Eye Wartime Leicestershire 1939–1945, Wigston, 2002

Fielding Johnson, Mrs T.: Glimpses of Ancient Leicester, Leicester, 1891

Foard, Glen, Curry, Glen and Anna: Bosworth 1485: A Battlefield Rediscovered, Oxbow Books. Oxford, 2013

Fox, Levi and Russell, Percy: Leicester Forest, Edgar Backus, Leicester, 1948

Fox, Levi: Minister's Accounts of the Honor of Leicester (1322–1324), Leicester, 1938

Goodacre, John: The Transformation of a Peasant Economy, Townspeople and villagers in the Lutterworth Area, 1500–1700, Routledge, 2017

Greaves, R.W.: The Corporation of Leicester 1689–1836, Leicester University Press, 1970

Holyoak, Vincent: But For These Things, Matador, 2014

Jenkins, Jess: The Burning Question, The Struggle for Women's Suffrage in Leicestershire, Friends of the Records Office for Leicestershire, Leicester and Rutland, Occasional Papers 5, nd

Langley, Philippa and Jones, Michael: The Search for Richard III, The King's Grave, John Murray, London, 2013

Mander, John: Leicester Schools 1944–1974, Leicester City Council, 1980

Martin, John E.: Feudalism to Capitalism: Peasant and Landlord in English Agrarian Development, MacMillan, Basingstoke, 1983Medieval Leicestershire, Recent Research on the Medieval Archaeology of Leicestershire, Leicestershire Fieldworkers, Monograph No. 3, 2015

Nash, David and Reeder, David (eds): Leicester in the Twentieth Century, Alan Sutton, Avon, 1993

Nichols, John: Bibliotecca Topographica Britannia, Antiquities in Leicestershire, 1780–1790

Nichols, John: The History and Antiquities of Leicestershire, 1795–1811

Ramsay, David A.: The Surnames, Occupations and Early working practices within the Bradgate area of Leicestershire, 1296–1890, 2003

Reg Twigg: Survivor on the River Kwai, Penguin, 2013

Rodger, Richard and Madgin, Rebecca: Leicester – A Modern History, Leicester, 2016

Ruddy, Austin J.: To the Last Round, Leicester Mercury, 2007

Simmons, Jack: Leicester Past and Present, Vol. 2, Modern City, London, 1974

Smiles, Samuel: Life of George Stephenson, Railway Engineer, John Murray, 1858

Stretton, Clement Edwin: The History of the Midland Railway, 1901

Swenarton, M.: Homes Fit For Heroes, Routledge, 1981

Thawley, James: A Certain Hospital Forever: A recent history of Wyggeston's Hospital, Leicester, 1996

Thompson, James: History of Leicester, from the time of the Romans to the end of the Seventeenth Century, Leicester, 1849

Thrush, Andrew and Ferris, John P. (eds): Sir William Woodhouse (c1570–1639): The History of Parliament: the House of Commons 1604–1629, 2010

Tymms, Samuel: A Compendium of the Ancient and Present State of Derbyshire, Leicestershire, Lincolnshire, Northamptonshire, Nottinghamshire, Rutlandshire, Warwickshire, Cheshire, London, 1832

Ward, Colin and Hardy, Dennis: Goodnight Campers! The history of the British holiday camp, Mansell, London, 1986

Wiener, Martin: English Culture and the Decline of the Industrial Spirit: 1850–1980, Cambridge University Press, Cambridge, 1981

Wilshere, Jonathan E.O.: Old Kirby, Leicester, 1986

Articles in journals

Billson, Charles J., 'The Open Fields of Leicester', *Leicestershire Archaeological Society Transactions*, Vol. 14, 1926, pp.1-29

Clark, Richard: 'Archaeology in Leicestershire and Rutland 1999', *Leicestershire Archaeological Society Transactions*, Vol. 74, 2000, pp.223-259

Clinker, C.R., 'The Leicester and Swannington Railway', *Leicestershire Archaeological Society Transactions*, Vol. 30, 1954, pp. 59-114

Courtney, Paul: 'Saxon and Medieval Leicester: The Making of an Urban Landscape', *Leicestershire Archaeological and Historical Society, Transactions*, Vol. 72, 1998, pp. 110-145

Crompton, James: 'Leicestershire Lollards', *Leicestershire Archaeological Society Transactions*, Vol. 44, 11-44
Hulme, Tom: ''A Nation Depends on Its Children': School Buildings and Citizenship in England and Wales, 1900–1939', *Journal of British Studies*, 54, April 2015, pp.406-432,
McWhirr, Alan: 'The Roman Road from Leicester to Mancetter', *Leicestershire Archaeological and Historical Society, Transactions*, Vol. 42, 1966–67, pp. 1-5
Perry, P.J.: 'High Farming in Victorian Britain: Prospect and Retrospect', *Agricultural History*, Vol. 55, April 1981, pp.155-166
R. Best: 'The Future Urban Acreage', *Town and Country Planning*, 32, (1964)
Tura, Edward: "A Roman Occupation Site', *Western Park, Glenfield and Western Park District Archaeological and Historical Group*, 1983
Whitehead, J.W.R. and Carr, Christine M. M.: 'The Creators of England's Inter-war Suburbs', *Urban History*, 28, 2, Cambridge University Press, 2001, pp. 218-235
Wykes, David L: 'The reluctant businessman: John Coltman of St Nicholas Street, Leicester (1727–1808)', *Leicestershire Archaeological and Historical Society, Transactions*, Vol. 69, 1995, pp.71-85

Newspapers

The Advertiser
Bell's Weekly Messenger
Central Somerset Gazette
Cheltenham Looker On
The Field – the Country Gentleman's Newspaper
Derby Mercury
Grantham Journal
Kentish Gazette
Leicester Chronicle
Leicester Chronicle and Leicester Daily Mercury
Leicester Daily Post
Leicester Evening Mail
Leicester Guardian
Leicester Journal
Leicester Journal and Midland Counties Advertiser
Leicester Mercury
Leicester Weekly Post
Leicestershire Daily Mercury
Leicestershire Mercury
Northampton Daily Echo

Northampton Mercury
Nottingham Evening Post
Nottingham Journal
Pall Mall Gazette
Railway Times
Worcestershire Chronicle
Yorkshire Post

Primary sources

Records Office for Leicester, Leicestershire and Rutland (ROLLR) – various indentures, documents and images
The National Archives, Kew – wills and other documents
Title deeds, conveyancing documents, registers of title and photographs, loaned by the Western Park and New Parks Community
Wyggeston's Hospital, Minutes of Governors' meetings and Estates Committee meetings

Printed primary sources, online and other material

100 Years – a Celebration and History of the Leicestershire Aero Club 1909–2009
1939 Register for England and Wales
A plan of Leicester shewing the limits of the borough, boundaries of parishes and extra parochial liberties, made from actual survey in the year 1828, published by A. Cockshaw, Leicester
Annual Report of the Medical Officer for the year ended 31 December 1929, Leicester Education Committee Minutes, 1929–1930, ROLLR
Census for England and Wales, 1841 - 1911
Church of St Anne, https://historicengland.org.uk/listing/the-list/list-entry/1389695, accessed 14 August 2020
Civic Affairs – City of Leicester 1939–40, City of Leicester Publicity and Development Programme, c.1939
Elaine Allen: The Story of Dovelands School, 1903–78
Footpath Rambles Up-To-Date, Leicester Mercury, nd, c.1930
Fowler, Kenneth Allan: *Henry of Grosmont, First Duke of Lancaster, 1310–1362*, Thesis presented for the degree of PhD in the University of Leeds, 1961
Glenfield Tunnel and Glenfield Station, Leicestershire Industrial History Society, 2018
Grace's Guide to Industrial History (online)
Historic Environment Record for Leicester
Holidays at Home, Official Programme, leaflet, Leicester, 1943 and 1944
https://www2.le.ac.uk/services/ulas/discoveries/projects/iron-age/glenfield-cauldrons

Iris Whiles, WW2 People's War, contributed by CSV Action Desk, Leicester to BBC.co.uk, httpss://www.bbc.co.uk/history/ww2peopleswar/stories/57/a4373057.html, accessed 1 May 2020

Kelly's Directory of Leicester

Leicester Aeroclub History, https://web.archive.org/web/20070922201544/http://www.leicesterairport.com/, accessed 30 April 2020

Leicester City Council Planning Department database

Leicester School of Arts records, De Montfort University Special Collections

Ned Newitt: *Who's Who of Radical Leicester*

Notes on Sir Basil Spence, Canmore, National Record of the Historic Environment, https://canmore.org.uk/site/287590/leicester-new-parks-boulevard-st-aidans-church, accessed 4 April 2020

Records of the Borough of Leicester, Chamberlain's Accounts, 1622–1623

Star Chamber Proceedings, Part of the Evidence in a 16th Century Suit relating to Leicester and the Forest of Leicester, with an introduction and Notes by S.H. Skillington, Leicestershire Archaeological Society

Taking Stock – Catholic churches of England and Wales, Leicester Mother of God, https://taking-stock.org.uk/building/leicester-mother-of-god/ accessed 4 April 2020

The Billy Butlin Story, London, Robson Books, 1982

University of Leicester Archives

West Bridge Wharf and Station, The Story of the First Railway Headquarters in the Midlands, Leicester Industrial History Society, 2018

Work Projects Administration Bibliography of Air Raid Precautions and Civil Defence, Washington DC, 1942

Wright's Directory of Leicester

Wyggeston's Hospital, Minutes of Governors' meetings and Estates Committee meetings

* 9 7 8 1 7 8 0 9 1 6 1 9 4 *

BV - #0043 - 121223 - C0 - 234/156/12 - PB - 9781780916194 - Gloss Lamination